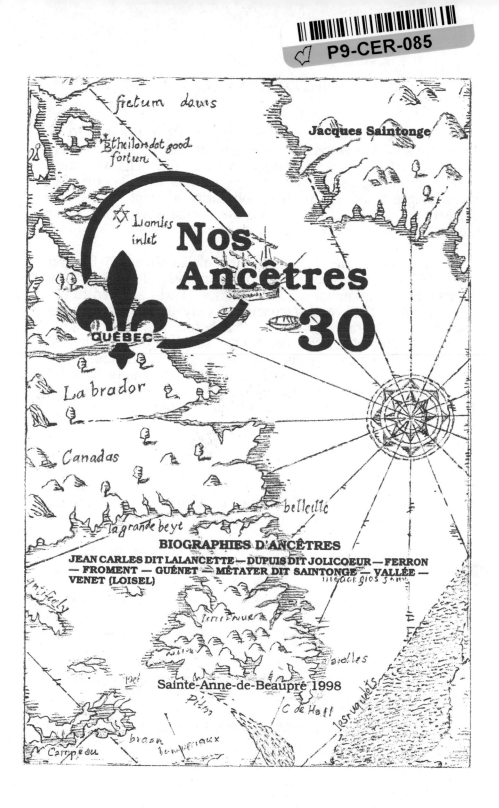

Jacques Saintonge

Nos Ancêtres

QUÉBEC

30

BIOGRAPHIES D'ANCÊTRES

JEAN CARLES DIT LALANCETTE — DUPUIS DIT JOLICOEUR — FERRON — FROMENT — GUÉNET — MÉTAYER DIT SAINTONGE — VALLÉE — VENET (LOISEL)

Sainte-Anne-de-Beaupré 1998

INTRODUCTION

After two years of silence, here at last is Volume 30 of the collection *"Nos Ancetres"* The death of Father Gérard Lebel, on 19 May 1996, created a difficult void to fill. His brimming enthusiasm, his great availability, his passion for his work and his willingness to remove from obscurity a great number of pioneers of New France finally led him to the gates of the other life, the one which he now enjoys for eternity.

Two days after his death, the mail delivered his last request for documents to the National Archives of Québec. In my capacity as co-author of the collection, I was allowed to examine them. This request concerned only the ancestor Pierre Guenet. I only recently learned that before his death, Father Lebel had already chosen the fifteen subjects of the planned Volume 30. The present volume is not the one that the founder of this collection wanted to publish, but I have willingly included the mason Pierre Guenet. Therefore, I dedicate his biography to the memory of Father Gérard and in memory of our great friendship.

The present work also pays homage to a few pioneers who lived in the eighteenth century.

First of all to Jean Carles dit Lalancette, who seems to me to be one of the most important surgeons of his era.

Also to Francois Dupuis dit Jolicoeur, **one of the** first residents of Maskinonge.

To Jean Ferron, father of twenty children, who worked for a few years at *les Forges Saint-Maurice*, before settling at Maskinonge, then at Yamachiche where he counts numerous descendants.

To Jacques Froment, soldier and one of the founders of Saint-Sulpice.

To Pierre Metayer dit Saintonge, tailor at Québec.

To René Venet, a modest worker in the Montréal region, the majority of whose descendants have, beginning in the third generation, adopted the surname of Loisel.

I have alotted a large portion of this book to our ancestor Jean Vallée, pioneer of the Ile d'Orléans, the intrusion of the scheming Jacques Charier into this family, and to Charles Vallée, Jean's son. This Charles settled st Sainte-Anne-de-la-Perade at the end of the seventeenth century and became the protaginist of a great family. One of these descendants, Msgr André Vallée, a priest of the *Société de missions etrangers*, is the current bishop of the diocese of Hearst, in Ontario.

Finally, I have included the biography of my own ancestor Jacques Payan dit Saintonge, the Admiral of Lake Champlain.

This 30th volume only comprises nine ancestral histories, however, each one is dealt with in detail not usually seen in this series.

Tom Laforest, the author of the English language version of this collection, entitled *"Our French Canadian Ancestors"*, has advised me that he will terminate his efforts with this Volume. Hopefully, another translator will come foreward to carry on his work.

Jacques Saintonge

OUR
FRENCH CANADIAN
ANCESTORS

Volume XXX

by

Thomas J. Laforest

OLDSMAR, FLORIDA

2000

ISBN: 0-914163-30-2
Printed in the United States of America

Library of Congress Catalog Card Number 83-81941

Laforest, Thomas John, 1917-
   Our French Canadian Ancestors
   Volume XXX, 250 pages, February 2000
   8 Chapters
   Bibliography
   Index of Names
   ISBN: 0-914163-00-0 (Series)

TABLE OF CONTENTS

"A défaut de savoir ou l'on va
on peut savoir d'ou l'on vient!"

THE PROVINCES OF FRANCE
UNDER THE OLD REGIME

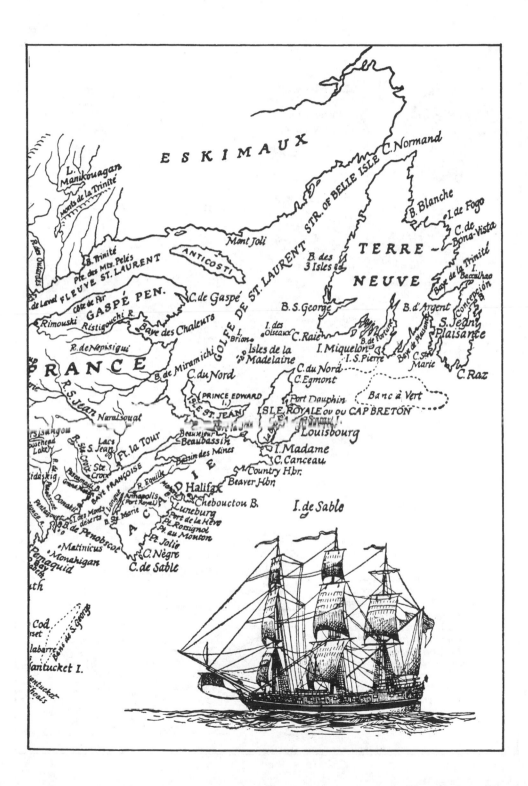

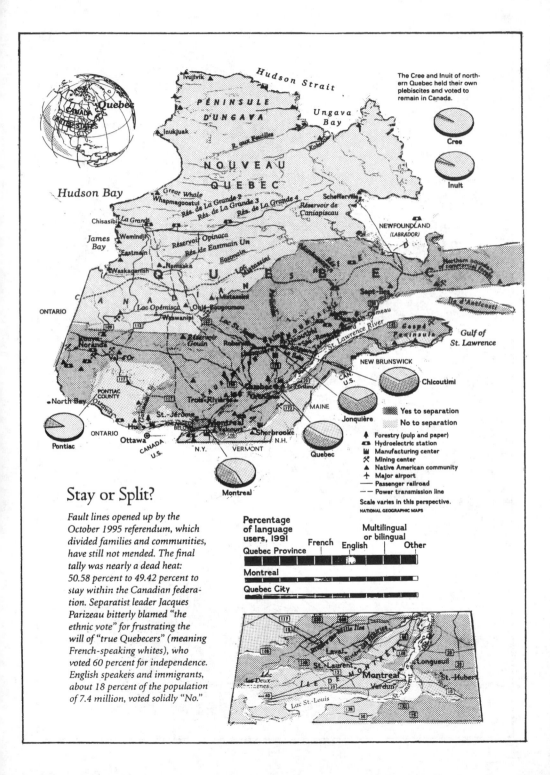

The Cree and Inuit of northern Quebec held their own plebiscites and voted to remain in Canada.

Cree

Inuit

Hudson Strait

PÉNINSULE D'UNGAVA

Ungava Bay

Ivujivik

Inukjuak

R. aux Feuilles

Koksoak

NOUVEAU QUEBEC

Hudson Bay

Great Whale
Whapmagoostui

Rés. de La Grande 2
Rés. de La Grande 3
Rés. de La Grande 4

Scheffervvlle

Réservoir de Caniapiscau

Chisasibi

La Grande

NEWFOUNDLAND (LABRADOR)

James Bay

Wemindji

Réservoir Opinaca

Rés. de Eastmain Un

Eastmain

Waskaganish

Nemaska

QUE   B   E   C

ONTARIO

CANADIAN

Lac Opémisca

Chibougamau

Île d'Anticosti

Waswanipi

Sept-Îles

Réservoir Gouin

St. Lawrence River

Gaspé Peninsula

Gulf of St. Lawrence

Rouyn

Val-d'Or

NEW BRUNSWICK

CAN. U.S.

Chicoutimi

North Bay

PONTIAC COUNTY

Trois-Rivières

St-Jérome

MAINE

Jonquière

Yes to separation

No to separation

Pontiac

ONTARIO

Ottawa

Hull

Montréal

Sherbrooke

N.H.

CANADA U.S.

N.Y.

VERMONT

Quebec

⬥ Forestry (pulp and paper)
⬣ Hydroelectric station
⬚ Manufacturing center
✗ Mining center
▲ Native American community
✈ Major airport
— Passenger railroad
-- Power transmission line

Scale varies in this perspective.
NATIONAL GEOGRAPHIC MAPS

Montreal

Stay or Split?

Fault lines opened up by the October 1995 referendum, which divided families and communities, have still not mended. The final tally was nearly a dead heat: 50.58 percent to 49.42 percent to stay within the Canadian federation. Separatist leader Jacques Parizeau bitterly blamed "the ethnic vote" for frustrating the will of "true Quebecers" (meaning French-speaking whites), who voted 60 percent for independence. English speakers and immigrants, about 18 percent of the population of 7.4 million, voted solidly "No."

Percentage of language users, 1991

French   English   Multilingual or bilingual   Other

Quebec Province

Montreal

Quebec City

Laval
St-Laurent
Longueuil
Montreal
Verdun
St-Hubert

Lac des Deux Montagnes

Lac St-Louis

CHAPTER 1

Quebec Today
by
Ian Darragh

eals of laughter filled the room. Louis Wauthier, our caller, was slipping his own risque variations into the *contredanse* we were performing at the folk evening in Chicoutimi, Québec. As in square dancing, in the *contredanse*, which originated in 18th-century France, you're supposed to unquestioningly obey the caller's commands. But Wauthier, who was wearing the brightly colored sash of the voyageurs--the early French explorers of Québec--was pushing the limits. We had started by forming into long, parallel lines. After swinging our partners and promenading up the middle, we completed a series of intricate figures at an increasingly frantic pace. Now Wauthier was ordering us to stand *dos é dos* (back-to-back), urging us to move closer until we were touching. After an initial gasp of surprise, everyone complied, and I found myself *derriere é derriere* with an attractive grandmother in a flowing dress out of the 1890s, with plumed feathers in her hat.

Suddenly my partner gave me a sharp push with her backside, sending me sprawling across the floor. She had understood the caller's command in French a split second before me and had obeyed all too enthusiastically. As the fiddle and accordion players led us on with their fast-paced jig, I picked myself up off the floor, moved down the line, and, with some relief, changed partners.

This was Chicoutimi's winter carnival, a yearly celebration of *Quebécois* culture, and although it was past ten o'clock, kids as young as six and grandmothers in their seventies were stepping and swinging with unflagging energy to dances such as *L'oiseau dans la cage* and *Le p'tit train de Jonquière*. At the beginning of the evening's festivities we had been divided into three teams. Each was given a family name common in the

1

region--Tremblay, Bouchard, or Simard--connecting us to the first French settlers in 1638. Between dances we had competed in log sawing and other contests, with much cheering and good-natured rivalry. As I looked around at the laughing, sweaty faces, I thought: This could only happen in Québec.

Largest of Canada's ten provinces, Québec is the only predominantly French-speaking political entity in North America aside from the islands of Saint-Pierre and Miquelon at the mouth of the Gulf of Saint-Lawrence--tiny vestiges of France's New World empire. In recent years the province has been the focus of the nation's worst unity crisis since its birth in 1867. In a referendum held in October 1995, Québecers voted by a mere one percentage point to stay within Canada, but a majority of French speakers--60 percent--voted for independence.

That the Canadian federation has survived this long has to do with various compromises made on behalf of Québec. The province retains its own distinct legal system and has been given special powers over immigration, enabling it to attract French-speaking newcomers. In the past 20 years, however, these compromises have worn thin, and constitutional amendments to patch things up have failed to win approval. Canada has come to resemble a bickering family, with one member periodically threatening to pack up and leave.

"We are on the edge of a precipice," Bernard Morin, an engineer from Jonquière told me. What he meant was that if Québec leaves the federation, the Atlantic provinces will have no land link to the rest of Canada. Prosperous British Columbia--with its thriving trade with the Pacific Rim--might also secede, and the entire nation could become unglued.

To federalists the prospect of another Québec referendum on independence is a sword of Damocles hanging over the province--and Canada--creating unbearable uncertainty that has stifled investment. But sovereigntists see referendums as the ultimate instrument of democracy. Lucien Bouchard, Québec's premier, has vowed to hold another referendum shortly after the next provincial election *"to ensure Québec enters the next millennium as a sovereign country."* If Québec leaves Canada, a growing number of Québecers, including aboriginal peoples who want to remain Canadian, say the province should be partitioned.

2

I wanted to find out why support for sovereignty has intensified among the Québecois, as French speaking Québecers are known. My search for answers began in the Saguenay, because this isolated valley surrounded by the ancient rocks of the Laurentian Mountains is the heartland of the separatist movement. Of the 300,000 people who live here, 98 percent are French speaking, and in the last two referendums, in 1980 and 1995, 70 percent of them voted for independence.

In Chicoutimi, the largest city, I stayed at the home of André and Ginette Bergeron. Both were born in the Saguenay, speak only French, and come from large families. André, a retired physical education teacher, has six brothers and six sisters. Ginette, who manages a day care in a nearby school, has two brothers and seven sisters. It was Ginette who took me to the *soirée folklorique* at the winter carnival.

"The people of the Saguenay know how to have fun," Ginette told me over one of her multicourse meals. We started with soup and crusty rolls, moved on to tourtière Lac Saint-Jean--a pie filled with beef, chicken, veal, pork, and potatoes--and ended with chocolate cake, all topped off with a plate of cheeses and grapes. Through it all Ginette never neglected my wine glass. *"We love music and celebrating,"* she said. *"At the carnival the dancing goes on till four in the morning."*

Every evening the Bergerons visit back and forth, and family members are greeted at the door with a bear hug and kisses on both cheeks. After a few days I grew used to the Bergerons' rapidly spoken French, sprinkled with local phrases and English words. I learned that *"jaser"* (like jaw in English) meant to chew the fat with *"la gang."* When I was offered a *caribou*, it was not a four-legged mammal but high-octane wine fortified with pure alcohol. *"C'est frette!"* (rather than the formal *"Il fait tres froid"*) meant it was so cold I'd better put on my long underwear.

"To me it's not just an issue of language," said Miville Larouche, Ginette's brother-in-law and a chemistry teacher, who dropped by one evening. The conversation, inevitably, had turned to the subject of independence.

"I have nothing against speaking English, or Chinese for that matter, because those are the languages of commerce. It's a question of preserving our culture. I have a strong feeling of belonging to Québec. I know we're a people. We're different. Inside me there is Latin blood. The French fact is there. You will speak with people here who will become very passionate."

During animated discussions around the kitchen table, I discovered that a focus of this passion is nationalism. *"It's a question of emotion, of a common project,"* said Miville, while André and Ginette nodded in agreement. *"We have everything we need to make a country: a common language and culture. We have the natural resources."* Indeed the Saguenay region itself is one of the largest producers of aluminum in the world, thanks to cheap hydroelectric power generated by Québec's swift-flowing rivers.

Miville thinks sovereignty makes economic sense.

"If we send all our taxes just to Québec, we could create a much better country," he said. *"Instead of having two ministries of industry, health, and so on, we would have just one. We would avoid the constant power struggle between public servants in Ottawa and Québec"*

In fact, studies show that Québec receives more (estimates range from two billion to four billion dollars U.S.) from Ottawa than it pays in taxes.

To see the Saguenay first hand, I asked André's brother-in-law, Bernard Morin, a licensed pilot, to take me on a flight. After circling the rugged mountains north of Chicoutimi, we flew east along the sheer cliffs of the Saguenay River. Every time I see those cliffs, gouged by glaciers some 10,000 years ago, they take my breath away. My grandmother was born at Tadoussac at the mouth of the Saguenay, and I've always had a special affection for this river, which to me is the most majestic in Canada. For now, I thought, it still is in Canada.

4

We skimmed over the pretty village of Sainte-Rose-du-Nord, nestled into a cleft in the granite. Just offshore was a suburb of fishing huts laid out in neat rows on the ice. Snowmobile tracks crisscrossed the snow like a gigantic spiderweb. Circling back, we passed over *La Baie*, where a plume of steam rose from one of the Saguenay's two pulp mills. A freighter, docked at Alcan Aluminium Ltd.'s deepwater port, was bringing in processed bauxite from Jamaica to feed Alcan's smelters.

Unlike most members of his wife's family, Bernard, who works for the federal government promoting industrial development, voted "No" to sovereignty. *"I really don't know why, with this high rate of unemployment, we have the self-confidence to say we can go it alone,"* he told me over dinner at his house. Automation is making the aluminum industry more efficient, but it's also putting people out of work. In 1996 the Saguenay's unemployment rate spiked to 15 percent. *"It's crazy,"* he said. *"You can't isolate yourself. All the world's economies are tied together now."*

When I spoke to students at the University of Québec at Chicoutimi, I found no such lack of confidence. Out of a class of 30, only one spoke in favor of federalism, despite the dire warnings from economists about the cost of independence: a devalued Canadian dollar, higher interest rates, a crushing public debt, the flight of foreign investment. The students dismissed these arguments. *"We're not afraid of taking our future into our own hands,"* one of them declared.

My trip to the Saguenay was the first time I'd ever sat down face-to-face with sovereign-tists and asked them why they wanted to break up the country. In the end it seemed to come down to a gut feeling. Ghislain Bouchard, a Saguenay playwright and neighbor of the Bergerons, put it this way:

> *"It's not a collective hysteria. More and more we Québecois want to control our own destiny. There's a terrible moment when inside yourself you realize that the Canadian flag, and all it represents, doesn't mean anything any more."*

I kept in touch with my new friends in the Saguenay and was saddened to learn that André Bergeron died of cancer last spring. I will remember his hospitality and our long talks about Québec's future.

In sharp contrast to the people of the Saguenay, 58 percent of Montréalers voted against independence in 1995. The morning I drove into my hometown--and that of nearly half Québec's people--the city seemed like a faded beauty queen looking back wistfully on her glory days of Expo 67, when she hosted a magical world's fair. Back then Montréal was not only Canada's largest metropolis but also its financial capital, a distinction since surrendered to Toronto.

"Look at all the boarded up shops and restaurants downtown," said Sid Stevens, a Montréaler born and bred. *"We've never seen this before. You start wondering, how much worse can it get?"* As manager of one of the city's largest food banks, Stevens has his finger on the city's pulse at street level. We went for a walk along Saint-Laurent Boulevard in search of a smoked meat sandwich at the Main deli and counted more than a dozen empty storefronts in two blocks. *"Montréal is the economic engine, the heartbeat of Québec,"* Stevens told me between bites of his sandwich. *"But now it's on life support."* He listed the main problems: one in five Montréalers out of work, 22 percent living below the poverty line--the highest rate of any city in Canada. The city's office vacancy rate has risen to 20 percent; companies are either not investing or simply packing up and moving out of the province. *"Food banks are Montréal's fastest growing industry,"* Stevens said. *"We now feed about 150,000 a year."* That's a tenfold increase in a decade.

For many Montréalers--including my parents, brother and sister, and four cousins--the solution has been to leave. More than 325,000 people have moved out since 1971; often it is the younger generation of English-speaking Québecers, those unencumbered by houses and children, who are voting with their feet. Peter Bean, a recent graduate in law from McGill University in Montréal, and his wife, Glenna Smith, are typical. They have fled to Ottawa, a two-hour drive west on the Ontario side of the Ottawa River.

Although they were born in Québec and will always consider Montréal home, Peter and Glenna said they feel like second-class citizens in their own province, that the government in Québec City doesn't consider them *"true Quebecois."* Peter has taken a job with one of Ottawa's largest law firms. Glenna, convinced she wouldn't get promoted at the Montréal bank where she worked because she doesn't have a French name, has found a new job in Ottawa with scope for advancement. *"Our generation is leaving,"* she said, *"because we see more opportunities outside Québec."*

Québec's language laws are an irritant, requiring French on outdoor signs and in the workplace and mandating French-language versions of software, websites, and films. The complex regulations are enforced by bureaucrats known in the English community as *"tongue troopers."* Their vigilance has led to some absurd situations: During Passover in 1996, stores in Montréal were ordered to take kosher products off their shelves because they were labeled in Hebrew and English but not French. The affair was quickly dubbed *"matzohgate."*

Québecers like Peter and Glenna are tired of the unending political debates. *"It's not a referendum; it's a never-endum!"* Peter said. *"They're going to keep doing it till they get the answer they want."*

Since the 1995 referendum, it has become clear just how close Canada came to splitting apart. Jacques Parizeau, a hard-line sovereigntist, was premier of Québec during the referendum campaign. Last May he revealed in a memoir that he had received secret assurances that the French government would quickly recognize a sovereign Québec and would influence other francophone nations to follow suit. Parizeau's strategy was to initiate a wave of international recognition so that Québec's independence would become a *fait accompli*. The province's minister of finance had quietly set aside a reserve of 27 billion dollars to buy Québec bonds in case they were dumped by panicky investors. A week before the referendum, a letter was sent to Québec-born soldiers in the Canadian Army urging them to transfer their loyalties to a new Québec army in the event of a *"Yes"* vote, and embassies in Canada were asked to recognize Québec's right to self-determination.

7

Now the debate has shifted to setting the practical ground rules for independence: What majority would be required in the next referendum? Would a unilateral declaration of independence violate the Canadian constitution? The federal government has referred that question to the Supreme Court of Canada. Lucien Bouchard says Québec's future is for its citizens alone to decide in a referendum and not by a *"foreign"* court of law.

What if Québec was to ignore the constitution and the Supreme Court? Jean Chrètien, Prime Minister of Canada and a fellow Québecer, says that if a clear majority choose independence in a fair vote, he is not prepared to launch a civil war to preserve the nation.

Mark Kotler, an English-speaking businessman I met, wants Canada to stay whole. Kotler is a Montréaler, and he has no intention of leaving the city. If Québec separates, he intends to ensure that Montréal stays in Canada, either as a city-state or part of a new province. Kotler has formed Action Canada, one of about ten grassroots partitionist organizations that have sprung up across Québec in places where a majority voted to stay in Canada.

As we talked in his office in the printing plant he owns, faxes were coming in from prospective Action Canada members (membership now stands at 4,000). Partitionists like Kotler have persuaded some 35 municipalities, including the city of Saint-Laurent (population 72,000) on the Island of Montréal, to support their cause.

Kotler said that separation from Canada would not be as painless as some sovereigntists would like to believe. An independent Québec, he said, must relinquish areas of the province that are pro-Canada, principally the Island of Montréal, the Eastern Townships along the Vermont border, western Québec (including Pontiac County), and the homelands of the Cree and Inuit in the north.

"The government in Québec City should have its knuckles rapped. Appeasement never works where nationalism is concerned," Kotler said, suggesting that the federal government should take the initiative and clearly spell out the boundaries of an independent Québec.

8

"Drawing lines on a map will not be so simple," countered Daniel Latouche, a political scientist and former adviser to the Québec government. *"Partition is a straightforward appeal to violence,"* he warned, implying that it could lead Québec into Bosnia-style warring enclaves. *"How far would you go? Would you divide apartment buildings?"* He pointed out that his mother lives on the west end of the Island of Montréal, which voted overwhelmingly *"No"* in 1995. *"Would she end up living in a separate country?"*

To take stock of one of the disputed regions, I left Montréal and drove 11 hours north to the Cree village of *Ouje-Bougoumou,* which means *"the place where people gather."* A special assembly of the Grand Council of the Cree, their elected governing body, was being held to discuss the expansion of logging into the ancestral lands of the Cree, encompassing 144,000 square miles in the James Bay and Hudson Bay watersheds--an area about the size of Japan. This would be an opportunity to talk to Cree leaders, who planned to attend the assembly.

Just before entering Ouje-Bougoumou, a new village of 500 laid out in the shape of the head of an eagle, I stopped by the side of the road. High overhead were 24 power lines, part of a network carrying 10,000 megawatts of electricity from generating stations on the La Grande River to light up cities in southern Québec and the northeastern United States. Transmission towers marched across the valley floor as far as the distant ridge of mountains. Snow-covered openings in the boreal forest--clear-cuts--stood out like white scars. Elsewhere, row after row of young trees revealed the orderly signature of plantation forests on lands leased by timber companies. The landscape brought home to me the radical changes Québec's 12,000 Cree have faced in the past two decades.

And now there's the issue of separatism. *"Québec independence is the greatest threat to the Cree since the arrival of Europeans in North America,"* Matthew Coon Come, the Grand Chief of the Cree, told me. We were having lunch in Ouje-Bougoumou's wood-paneled restaurant, with a fine view overlooking Lake Opemisca.

Wiry and articulate, Coon Come is equally at home working his family's trapline near Lake Mistassini or making a presentation to legislators in a suit and tie. He has emerged as a forceful defender of Cree interests since his successful campaign to stop the damming of the Great Whale River, the second phase of the James Bay hydroelectric project.

Québec's native people have treaties with the federal government, which is obliged to fund housing, health services, and education on reserve lands. Given the Cree's difficulties in obtaining compensation from the province for lands flooded for hydro projects or logged for timber, Coon Come does not believe the government of an independent Québec would assume those treaty obligations. His people share that mistrust. The Cree held their own referendum in October 1995, and 96.3 percent voted to stay within Canada.

"We are not the ones who want to split up this country," Coon Come said. *"But if Québecers have the right to self-determination, certainly the Cree do too. We cannot simply be traded from one country to another as though we were cattle in a field."*

If Québec secedes, the Cree say the hydro installations will revert to the original owners of the land. Québec's position is that its territorial integrity is protected under international law and that the Cree gave up their aboriginal land rights in 1975 when, in exchange for 133 million dollars, they signed an agreement authorizing the James Bay project.

Like the Cree, the province's other aboriginal groups-- including the Inuit, Mohawk, and Montagnais--say that their ancestral lands, which encompass two-thirds of Québec, will not be transferred to a new republic without their consent.

When I returned to Montréal, spring was bursting out after one of the coldest Aprils on record. Awakening from hibernation, people thronged along Sainte-Catherine Street, stopping to smell the lilies, mums, and azaleas at outdoor stalls and poking into bookstores. Through a plate glass window I watched a baker, with deft twists, making a fresh batch of bagels. He placed the circles of dough on a long plank and slid them into a wood-fired oven for that famed Montréal taste of real wood smoke. One restaurant had opened on the corner of Atwater, but amid the empty storefronts and vacant lots the once elegant Seville and York theaters were still boarded up and plastered with posters. On a wall of the York someone had spray painted *"Anglos go home,"* which someone else had edited to *"Anglos are home."*

In 1945 Hugh MacLennan, a Montréal novelist, attributed the gulf between the French and English in Québec to *"two solitudes"*--language and religion. Today politics, suspicion, and racism are the deeper solitudes: francophone federalists against francophone sovereigntists as much as English against French; Anglo and French Québecers against aboriginal peoples; and Montréal, with its large immigrant population, against the homogeneous outlying regions.

Most anglophones who could not, or would not, speak French left after the first Parti Québecois government was elected in 1976--an exodus of 200,000 in four years. The majority who remain, like Mark Kotler, speak French in business dealings and ensure that their children are bilingual. They have accepted French as the working language and that some measures are needed to protect it. The stereotype of the English boss who refuses even to say *"Bonjour"* is dead.

Nor are the old religious prejudices a major consideration any more. While the silver spires of cathedrals still grace cities and towns, religion, as André Bergeron's family illustrates, has lost its central place in Québec culture. André's parents were devout Catholics. He and his wife stopped going to church shortly after their marriage, and their three children have abandoned Catholicism.

While Premier Lucien Bouchard declares that the Québecois are *"un peuple"* and that Canada is made up of two nations and two founding peoples, native leaders like Matthew Coon Come insist that aboriginal peoples were also founders of Québec and Canada. And Jews such as Mark Kotler respond that Québec society is made up of not one or two but many peoples.

Yet Québecers--whatever their origin--seem attached to the province for many of the same reasons. *"Québec has a joie de vivre that no other place has,"* Mark Kotler told me, echoing Ginette Bergeron of Chicoutimi.

11

"There's more street life here. People in Québec know how to party. They're not straitlaced. If you go down to Saint-Denis Street in Montréal on any night in the summer when the festivals are on, you will see a friendship between the French and English you would not believe. I just wouldn't want to live anywhere else."

Kotler's remark made me wish more Québecers would wander down to Saint-Denis Street on a summer evening. But looming on the horizon is yet another divisive vote on Québec's future. I recalled the words of Bernard Morin of Jonquière: *"The red warning lamp for Canada went on with the last referendum, and it will flash as long as we continue with the politics of fear and confrontation."*

LEGENDS

Symbol of independence, the *fleur-de-lis* is proudly displayed on faces, flags, and T-shirts in Montréal on Saint Jean-Baptiste Day among French-speaking Québecois who want to secede from Canada. Chanting *"Don't mess with my vote,"* Québecers loyal to Canada demand an inquiry into voting irregularities during the 1995 referendum on Québec's future. Fraud charges were made in four electoral districts. Traumatized by how close Québec came to seceding, English-speaking Québecers are becoming more outspoken about protecting their rights.

A relic of British pomp and pageantry, the marching band of the Royal 22nd Regiment performs during a flag-lowering ceremony at the Citadel in Québec City, with the Château Frontenac Hotel as a backdrop. Founded in 1914 by French Canadians, the Royal 22nd has served overseas in both World Wars, in Korea, and in United Nations' peacekeeping. Most members are French-speaking Québecers, and if the province breaks away, they will face a dilemma: Resign, join a new army, or exit Québec as an intact Canadian unit? Québec is the *"cash cow"* of Canada, many Québecois think, convinced that they pay more taxes to Ottawa, the national capital, than they receive in benefits. Yet even Québec government studies show that the province receives a net cash flow of at least two billion

12

dollars U.S. from Ottawa, while other studies reckon it to be much higher. Québec's dairy farmers are themselves guaranteed a 47 percent national market share for processed milk. Despite such subsidies, support for independence remains strong in rural French-speaking areas. Fault lines opened up by the October 1995 referendum, which divided families and communities, have still not mended. The final tally was nearly a dead heat: 50.58 percent to 49.42 percent to stay within the Canadian federation.

Separatist leader Jacques Parizeau bitterly blamed *"the ethnic vote"* for frustrating the will of *"true Québecers"* (meaning French-speaking whites), who voted 60 percent for independence. English speakers and immigrants, about 18 percent of the population of 7.4 million, voted solidly *"No."* The young business crowd unwinds at a club atop one of Montréal's highest skyscrapers. *"This city is politically stressed out,"* says club manager Robert Ryan. *"But whether you speak English or French doesn't matter up here."* Derelict buildings, empty lots, and *"For Sale"* signs disfigure parts of Montréal, once Canada's financial capital. Soup kitchens feed 24,000 every day, and 22 percent of Montréalers live below the poverty line, the highest rate in Canada.

"Everybody's on standby," laments one businessman. *"The city's dead, and it's all because of this instability." "It's heartbreaking to leave family and friends,"*

said Elaine Perzow, taping up a box while movers load her possessions into a waiting truck. Tired of Québec's endless separatist debates, Perzow and her husband sold their house in Montréal and moved their family to British Columbia.

Demographics favor independence, since many who oppose it--as well as newcomers such as a family of Chilean refugees--eventually head down Highway 401 to Toronto and points west in search of brighter economic prospects.

"We will have our own country. You can count on my determination." Lucien Bouchard, Québec's premier, rallied separatists to their cause just before the referendum. A lawyer from the isolated Saguenay district, Bouchard draws much of his support from rural areas, such as the Ile d'Orléans on the Saint Lawrence River near Québec City. A roadside shrine in the vil-

13

lage of Grondines on the Saint Lawrence River is a legacy of a
time when Québec was solidly Roman Catholic. All that has
changed in the space of a generation, and now 19 percent of
couples live in common-law relationships, while 44 percent of
children are born out of wedlock. *"So powerful was the Catholic
Church in Québec that its collapse has left a deep void,"* observes
Lysiane Gagnon, a columnist with Montréal's La Presse.
Nationalism, she believes, has become the new religion of many
Québecois. In northern Québec, where cousins cool off in Lake
Opemisca, Cree communities voted to remain in Canada. For
transportation giant *Bombardier*, whose wall of snowmobiles
waits shipment from its Valcourt plant, separation might affect
free trade with the U.S. and require renegotiation of the NAFTA
treaty, warns CEO Laurent Beaudoin. A war of words erupted on
the walls and airwaves of Montréal before the last referendum,
but there was a remarkable lack of violence. To win the next
vote--expected within two years--separatists will have to gain the
trust of the city's large immigrant population.

END NOTES

1)   This Chapter, is a reprint of the November 1997 issue of National Geographic, for which permission was granted to copy. The author, Ian Darragh, a native of Montréal, was editor of *Canadian Geographic* magazine from 1989 to 1995. This is his first story for National Geographic.

2)   The frontis, a pictograph entitled *"Stay or Split?"* is also a reprint from the same article, for which permission was obtained to use.

14A TIMES ■ FRIDAY, MARCH 10, 2000   * * * *

THE CANADA REPORT

Separatists' fire about to flicker out

Washington Post

MONTREAL — After 40 years of bitter debate over whether to leave Canada — through two divisive referendums, the election of four separatist governments and two failed attempts at reforming the Canadian constitution — Quebecers have finally reached a consensus.

They have decided to move on to something else.

That seems to be the way the independence movement will end in this French-speaking province — not with a bang but with a whimper. For too many Quebecers, the secession debate has become sterile, the choices it offers unacceptable, the question itself largely irrelevant.

Recent polls show that support for sovereignty is at its lowest point in a generation. The ruling Parti Quebecois is considering whether to renege on its promise to hold another referendum on secession while a committee has been charged with coming up with a new rationale for its independence project.

In Ottawa, Canadian Prime Minister Jean Chretien is preparing to push through legislation that, under the guise of constitutional clarity, would make it more difficult for Quebec to secede even if a majority of voters were to support it. An expected backlash against the initiative in Quebec never materialized.

The sense that a turning point has been reached is almost palpable among separatists and federalists alike.

"The movement is a little bit stalled," said Michel Venne, the political editor of *Le Devoir*, Quebec's only pro-independence daily. "Even a lot of organizers and militants are asking themselves publicly whether it is possible to win. That's quite a change."

A poll published this week by the Leger & Leger organization found that two-thirds of Quebecers do not want another referendum in the next three years — with half of all voters saying they do not ever want one.

The preferred option remains an overhaul of the Canadian constitution to give more power to the provincial government and recognize Quebec's unique status within the Canadian confederation. But that idea has been rejected twice by English-speaking Canada.

Jean Carles dit Lalancette

CHAPTER 2

Jean Carles dit Lalancette

fter the war of the Conquest, English officers tried every means to be sympathetic to the ruling class of the vanquished country: the seigneurs, gentlemen and merchants-businessmen, men of law, notaries and physician-surgeons. Among the thirty members who made up this last brotherhood in the beginning of the 1760's, there was a certain *Jean Carles dit Lalancette*, a young man originally from *Miradoux*, in *Gascogne*. When and under what circumstances did Jean Carles come to New France? We don't know with certainty.

In 1982, a young French woman, Geneviève Menguy-Berthelot, presented to the University of Nantes, a doctoral thesis on the state of medicine, titled *"3778 Chirgurgiens navigans de Bordeaux au XVIII siecle"*. This thesis presented a file of names of these surgeons among whom is found a *Jean Carles dit le Moissac*, hired on 16 September 1754 as a doctor for the sailing ship *"Le Sagittaire"*. This ship left Bordeaux for Saint-Dominique on 23 September.

Less than two years later, a Jean Charles, also from Moissac, left Bordeaux on 5 April 1756 on board the ship *"L'Aimable Jeanne"*, which also was bound for Saint-Dominque. Were Jean Carles and Jean Charles the same person? It's very possible. According to Geneviève Menguy-Berthelot, of the 1214 surgeons who passed the Admiralty of Bordeaux examination between 1717 and 1792 and whose origin is known to us, 853 came from Guyenne, Gascogne and Bearn, and 122 from Languedoc (note 1506, p. 590). In the eighteenth century, Miradoux was not very populous, but Moissac already was a city with a Senechaussee and a famous Abbay, the Abbot of which shared with the king the title of local seigneur. And the town and the city were almost neighbors.

ORIGIN OF THE NAME

Tradition insists that all contemporary French people descend from Charlemagne. The last name of Carles, according to Albert Dauzat, (1) is a southern or Normand-Picard form of Charles. Probably evoking the memory of Charles the First, or Charlemagne, the most famous of the Kings of France, who reigned from 747 to 814. An advertisement for the Château de Carles, a house of wines located at Fronsac, in the Haute-Garonne, recalls that in 769 Charlemagne, completing the conquest of Aquitaine, established a fortified camp there. The Carles name borne by the present château goes back to the fifteenth and sixteenth centuries.

MIRADOUX

Jean Carles, son of Jean, an innkeeper, and Françoise Bignon (or Avignon), was born at Miradoux on 18 November 1734. He was brought to the church the next day to be baptized. His godfather and godmother were Jean Ricaut and Jeanne Malouat.

Today Miradoux is the head town in a canton of nine communities with a total population of three to four thousand inhabitants. During Jean Carles's time, this town was part of Gascogne, an ancient province located between the Pyrenees, the Garonne river and the Atlantic. After the Revolution, this community is foud the neighborhood of Flamarens and Saint-Meme, a few kilometers south of the town of Agen.

An ancient fortification founded in 1252, Miradoux developed around a church which dates from the same era and now is classified as an historic monument. This building in the Roman style is noteworthy for its absence of a belltower and the reproduction, on the front, of scallop shells, also known as *Coquilles Saint-Jacques*. A few narrow streets and half-timber houses are also very old. The inn of the parents of our ancestor Carles burned in 1955, but there still remains a wall which is used now as a fence. Within an area of a few kilometers are the Châteaux of Flamarens, Fieux and Gramont. Quite nearby flow the Anroue, Gers and Arrats rivers. Le Gers is covered with streams which flow from south to north. This region experiences early, often harsh winters; the summers are very warm with frequent storms. (2)

THE FRENCH FAMILY

Jean Carles, father of our Canadian ancestor of the same name, married Françoise Bignon or Avignon about 1729. His inn served as a resting place for the pilgrims who, coming from all of Europe, were ready to cross the pass in the Pyrenees to reach Saint-Jacques-de-Compostelle in Spain. The pilgrims were easily identified by the famous scallop shell which they wore as a sign of recognition.

Jean and Françoise had at least six children: Catherine, born on the first of September 1730 and died on the first of December 1759, at the age of 29; Jean, our Canadian ancestor, born in 1734; Marie, born on 28 December 1735; Martin, born on 20 January 1739, who immigrated to Wurtemberg, in southern Germany; Jean dit Mathieu, born on 12 May 1740, who took over from his father as innkeeper and married Marguerite Barbazan, at Miradoux, on 19 July 1758; finally, Jean-Baptiste, born on 4 December 1741. The innkeeper Jean Carles died on 2 October 1763 and was buried the following day in the church at Miradoux. He was 70 years old. (3)

JEAN CARLES COMES OUT OF THE SHADOWS

Did Jean Carles participate in the War of the Conquest? Probably. Was he present at Carillon, Saint-Frededic, Chouaguen or Fort Frontenac? Perhaps we will never know. In his capacity as surgeon, he had to dress the wounds of the injured soldiers, comfort the anguished, bury the dead. For us who live two and a half centuries after this drama, we discover him only on 24 December 1760 at Chambly, when he and his future wife, Marie-Anne Poirier, acted as godfather and godmother of Jean, a nephew of Marie-Anne, son of Guillaume Cassan and Josette Poirier. A few days later, on 9 January 1761, Jean and Marie-

Anne appeared at the home of the notary Antoine Grise, at Chambly, to draw up their marriage contract.

Jean said he was 26 years old and born to the marriage of Jean Carles and Françoise Davignon, his father and mother from the parish of Miradoux, jurisdiction of Auch (Gascogne). Jean stipulated for himself and in his own name. François Poirier acted in the name of Marie-Anne, his 22 year old daughter from his marriage to the late Madeleine Demers. Also present were François, Antoine, Joseph, Marie, Madeleine and Catherine Poirier, brothers and sisters of the bride. This family was not of Acadian origin, as we may have been lead to believe. Marie-Anne was the great-granddaughter of Jean Poirier dit Lajeunesse, a soldier in the Chambly Company, who arrived with the Carignan Regiment in 1665.

The bride and groom would have community property, according to the *coutume de Paris*. François Poirier promised them, as an advance of the inheritance, an arpent of frontal land by seventeen deep, in the shape of a triangle, bordering on the front, the small *Rivières de Montréal*, and in the rear, the land of Jacques Massé and Antoine Grise dit Villefranche; on one side, to the same Villefranche, on the other side, to a messire Carpentier. (4) This tip of land, valued by an appraisal at 400 livres, had no buildings on it. Poirier also made a gift of a milk cow, a thin pig and a sheep. For his part, the groom brought to the community a value of one thousand livres in furnishings and real estate. Jean Carles, some members of the Poirier family and messire Carpentier signed at the bottom of the act with the notary.

The marriage was celebrated on 12 January at the church of Saint-Joseph de Chambly, after the publication of the three banns during the parish mass on three consecutive Sundays. In this act, appears the surname of Lalancette, attributed to Jean Carles, a surname characteristic of surgeons, but also of a few soldiers. (5) The Récollet Charles-Claude Carpentier received the mutual consent of Jean and Marie-Anne and blessed their union. Their first two children were born at Chambly: Luc, whose baptismal act has not been found, was born at the end of 1761 or the beginning of 1762; Marie-Joseph dite Marie born on 23 May 1763 and baptized the next day by Father Carpentier. The godfather and godmother were Joseph and Marie-Joseph Demers, maternal uncle and aunt of the infant.

THE DEFINITIVE ESTABLISHMENT

Jean Carles and his family moved to Rivière-du-Loup about 1764. Our ancestor lived there until his death, in other words, for more than 35 years. On 23 February 1765, the notary Louis Pillard went to his home to make a private agreement dated the first of November 1764 and drawn up by the Récollet Felix de Berey, pastor of Saint-Joseph de Chambly. This act mentions the acknowledgment of a debt of one thousand livres contracted by the notary Antoine Grisé concerning Jean Carles. The debtor promised to repay everything to the creditor in five annual payments of 200 livres, the first due in February 1764. On 10 May 1765, an act by the notary Pierre Mézières reveals that the said debt was passed from the hands of the notary Grisé to those of Jacques Ginier dit Laviolette, who acknowledged receipt on the preceding 12 March.

Two days earlier, Marie-Anne Poirier had brought her third child, Magdelaine, into the world. She was held the same day at the baptismal font of the *"old church which is completely at the other end of the parish"*. (6) Her godfather and godmother were Louis Arsenault and Magdelaine Carly, wife of Ambroise Lavergne. The little girl only lived for two months; she was laid to rest on 9 May. The surgeon Jean Carles was held in high esteem in the parish. On several occasions he was asked to serve as witness to marriages and burials.

CONCESSION OF THE URSULINES

On 24 and 29 March 1766, in two acts in the records of Pillard, Jean Carles acquired on each occasion, a piece of land called *L'Ange-Gardien*, which Alexis Dubord dit Latourette offered to cede to him. This land had been ceded to the latter on 2 November 1762 by the Ursuline nuns of Trois-Rivières. (7) In a first act, Carles stated that he was charged with giving notice to these ladies and to assume the debts accepted by his predecessor. In the second, this is what he did: He made an appointment with the nuns and went to their parlor. They were represented by the mother-superior, Françoise Guillemin de Saint-Antoine, by her

21

assistant, Ursule Baby dite Thérèse de Jesus, and by trustee Marguerite Cavelier de Sainte-Ursule, and a few other discreet women.

The land called L'Ange-Gardien, we learn, was bordered on one side by that of the heirs of one Poitiers dit Saint-Gemme, on the other side by that of the representatives of Trottier Valcourt. This land was granted to Jean with appurtenances; a prairie which opened onto the lake (Saint-Pierre) and annexed to the said land, with rights to the commons. Carles was committed to bring to the nuns, on the first of February of each year, 30 minots of wheat *"good, dry, genuine and marketable, notwithstanding all damages"*. He had to farm the land as a good habitant would do and would be held to fence it and dig ditches, build a house and barn, and maintain everything in good condition without removing anything that had been done previously.

On 31 March 1767, Marie-Anne Poirier gave birth to her second son and last child. François was baptized the next day by the curate Médard Petrimoulx. His godfather and godmother were François Guillot and Marie Ratau, his wife. The record was signed by Guillot and Petrimoulx.

A FEW DIFFICULTIES

Like the majority of his contemporaries, Jean Carles experienced some difficulties with his creditors and his debtors. In spite of his two occupations as farmer and surgeon, he does not seem to be rolling in wealth. Two examples have been reported to us.

In 1771, the notary Barthèlemy Faribault (senior) was called to draw up a contract reached between Jean Leroux dit Provençal, a merchant from Sorel, and Jean Carles, surgeon from Rivière-du-Loup. This item recounts that on 11 March of the said year, Provençal had obtained from a judge of the Court of common pleas for the district of Sorel, a judgment ordering Carles to pay the plaintiff 158 livres and 10 sols in principal, as well as 10 chelins and 64 sous for expenses according to a receipt dated the first of September 1771. After this order, Provençal had Carles arrested and made him a prisoner. Having offered to give an account, Carles then promised to deliver to the home of Joseph Lupien, at Maskinonge, one hundred minots

22

"in both wheat and peas for which they will give satisfaction to each other according to the price which the said grain will be worth the next March, plus 50 minots of wheat or peas per year beginning in February 1772 until the claims of the said Sr Leroux are completely paid off".

If Jean Carles was barely able to pay off his debts, his clients sometimes had trouble paying him for his services. After his death in 1784, Louis-Joseph Godefroy de Tonnancour, seigneur of la Pointe-du-Lac, left a series of unpaid accounts which figure in the inventory which was drawn up by the notary Alexandre Dumas, from Québec, on 27 July 1785. Among these accounts, we discover that he owed 121 livres and 8 sols to Jean Carles, probably for extraordinary care in medical services.

OTHER CONCESSIONS

During his active business life, Jean Carles obtained other parcels of land, probably to allow him to practice his two professions of surgeon and farmer while living near his clients. On 29 July 1773, before the notary Benoit Lerol de Yamachiche, Augustin Arnois (Harnois), his wife Marguerite Lemaitre, and their donors Claude-Philibert Bergeron and his wife Louise Cousteau admitted having ceded to Jean and his wife, by means of the annual land rent, in perpetuity and non-redeemable, a lot located on the large rivière du Loup, in the seigneurie of the Ursulines of Trois-Rivières. This land was bordered on one side by the chemin du Roy which leads to Maskinonge, on the front by the chemin de Ceinture, on the other side the fence which surrounded it. It was established that the tenants could not sell or lease this lot without the express permission of the landlords. Each year they had to pay six livres or chelins of the province, the first payment due on the next Saint Martins Day. Jean Carles was also committed to be a barber and to shave and the said Bergeron, to care for him and his wife Louise Cousteau, to pull their teeth if there is need, and do all this for free, during their whole life. We must understand that at that time the profession of surgeon was not, in the mind of the clients, still completely dissociated from that of barber.

On 24 June 1775, Jean Carles went again to the parlor of the Ursulines of Trois-Rivières to receive another concession which he knew very well because he had already possessed it for two years. Those present were the mother-superior Marguerite Le Cavelier de Sainte-Ursule, her assistant Ursule Baby dite Thérèse de Jesus, the trustee Françoise Guillemin de Saint-Antoine, Geneviève Godefroy de Tonnancour de Sainte-Hélène, Marie-Madeleine Lapalme de Saint-Henry and other discreet and professed nuns, who leased by way of cens and rents, profits of lots and ventes, saisines and amendes when they are due, to Jean Carles, surgeon living at Rivière-du-Loup, a portion of land with 84 arpents in area, adjoining on one side the land of Pierre St-Hive, on the other side François Guillot, on the northwest side to the named Parent and on the southeast side the continuation of Jean-Baptiste Bergeron. This land was charged with eleven livres or chelins of the province in land rent payable on Saint-Martins Day, 11 November of each year, plus two sols for the cens. According to the agreement, the nuns allowed a year for the concessionaire to build a habitable house there (act by J.B.Badeau).

Three years later, on 12 August 1778, again before the notary Badeau, the Ursulines showed themselves generous to the surgeon of their seigneurie. This time, they gave him, by way of cens and rents, a 50 arpent plot bordering land which already belonged to him, and which was located behind the land of Jean-Baptiste Bergeron and Jean-Baptiste de Saint-Louis. The said field, of irregular shape, almost came to a point, at the property of Baptiste Lamy. Everything was designed to conform to the plan drawn up by the surveyor Pierre-Paul Arsenault and according to an official report dated 8 July. Located in the censive of the fief of Saint-Jean, the new concession was charged with five livres in ancient chelins. The nuns kept for themselves the right to take wood suitable for building or maintaining the church, the rectory, the manor or the mill, all without any compensation.

The following year, Jean Carles resold to his neighbor Pierre Saint-Yves the portion of land acquired from the Ursulines four years earlier. The contract was signed in the residence of Louis Saucier, at Rivière-du-Loup, on 12 November 1779. The said land bordered on one side the lands of the acquirer and Laurent Saint-Amant, on the other end that of the messieurs Davidson and Lee, who had acquired them from François Guillot. The other neighbors were named Morrisset to the northwest and on the southwest was the continuation of the property of Jean-Baptiste Bergeron, belonging at present to the said seller. The land sold included a small house, and some cords of wood and some square lumber which the seller kept for himself, *"and also the ability to take from there a pine tree which was cut"*. The sale was made for the cens, rents and other seigniorial duties, for 700 livres or old chelins of twenty sols each, paid in cash.

A part of the land obtained in 1778 would be sold nearly eight years later in a contract by Benoit Leroi on 12 January 1786. On that day, Jean Carles and his wife ceded to Eineman Pines (8) a 25 arpent field, being half of the original concession granted by the Ursulines in 1778. This field was surrounded by the lands belonging to Luc Carle, Baptiste Saint-Louis, Jean-Baptiste Bergeron, Antoine Lupien, Anselme Pellerin, Joseph Bellemare and Joseph Bouin dit Dufresne, everything according to the deed of concession and report by the late surveyor Arsenault. This sale was made for seigniorial rights and 350 livres, which Jean Carles admitted having already received.

AT THE SIEGE OF SAINT-JEAN

In the meantime, Jean Carles was recruited as soldier and surgeon to defend his adopted country against the invader from the south. In October 1774, the Congress of Philadelphia urged the Canadians to follow the Americans in the rebellion against England. Meeting with a refusal, the rebels of New England decided to invade Canada. In June 1775, two expeditionary corps set out for Québec by different routes. In September General Montgomery, at the head of 2,000 men began the siege of Fort Saint-Jean on the Richelieu river.

On 18 September, Montgomery's troops took the offensive. The engagement lasted about a half-hour. On the 22nd, an American deserter went to the fort and claimed that famine ravished the attackers. On the 26th, six Canadian volunteers from Yamachiche fled: one named "Carte" (was this Jean Carles?), Madore Desjardins, Adam Labranche, Joseph Hamelin, Joseph Chaine and one named Cécile.

On 2 October, the notary Antoine Foucher noted in his journal:

25

*"They reduced our rations today by half,
noticing that we have only had wine the first
two days, having lacked it suddenly, while
for several days we were thankfully given
some at 40 per bottle, but at present we can
have no more. We no longer suffer from
hunger, but we can not even sleep due to the
hardness of our bed, lying on wood and
having only blankets for our mattress".*

On 2 November, the Canadians capitulated. They were
evacuated first on twenty boats which awaited them at the edge of
the water. The English officers and soldiers were kept prisoners.
After a few days of detention, the majority of the Canadian
volunteers were returned to their homes in return for the promise
not to take up arms against the Americans while the conflict continued. The siege of Saint-Jean had lasted 45 days. (9)

On 3 July 1788, thus several years after the siege of
Saint-Jean, Lord Dorchester, who took up his post again as
governor-general of Canada after eight years of absence, remem-
bered the volunteers of Fort Saint-Jean. In order to reward them
for their services, he decided to grant them some land. A dozen
parishioners from Rivière-du-Loup are mentioned on this list of
concessionaires: Antoine Auger, Michel, François and Theodore
Lamirande, Pierre and Antoine Sicard, Pierre
Plante, Antoine Lesard, Antoine Dejarlay, Charles Auclair,
Augustin Houde and Jean Carles, surgeon, noted as coming from
Yamachiche. (10) The lands which the government offered them
were located on the edge of Lac Saint-François and the
Châteauguay river.

On 18 June 1788, in the house of the notary Jean-Baptiste
Deseve from Montréal, Joseph Laserte, Lieutenant of the militia
of Yamachiche, acting in the name of Joseph Adam, captain of
the local militia, Jean Carles, surgeon from Rivière-du-Loup,
Joseph Chene and Alexis Gelinas, from Yamachiche,

*"admitted having sold to François Delard,
merchant, half of the lands and concessions
which the said sellers hoped to have from the
government in appreciation for the good and
loyal services during the siege of Fort Saint-
Jean, the said concessions being promised to*

26

*them which they have said were to be taken
between Saint-Regis and Beauharnois and
which would go to them according to their
number and to use completely the said land
by each of them which the said Delard may
farm, clear, cut wood for use as the said
sellers will not take possession of it, everything to his profit".*

It was also agreed that the sellers would not take possession of their half before ten years and, as soon as they do, the
profits will be shared with the buyer. In August 1792, the Commission of lands reported that Joseph Laperle and other
petitioners, who have certificates in hand attesting to their rights
to obtain portions of land at Châteauguay, wanted to obtain deeds
of concession. On 24 January 1795, the notary Jean-Guillaume
Delisle, resident of Montréal, noted a transaction between the
merchants François Deslards and Alexandre Ellis concerning
several lands situated at Châteauguay. One of them, an area of
150 arpents, had been acquired in partnership with Jean Carles.
Ellis admitted that this acquisition had been made at his risk and
peril, knowing that the government had not yet issued the official
deeds.

A year later, on 12 May 1796, the agent John Richardson,
representing more than 70 petitioners, including Jean Carles, ad-
dressed Governor-General Dorchester, pleading with him to intervene so that the deeds of concession could be granted, because
the situation in which the said petitioners found themselves was
confusing, expensive for them and in some way harmful to the
province. Will Jean Carles live long enough to know the outcome of this affair?

MARIE AND LUC MARRY

Marie and Luc are the only two children of
Jean Carles and Marie-Anne Poirier who married and who gave
descendants to our Gascon ancestor. Marie had been the only
one to leave the paternal house after her marriage, because Luc
lived with his parents until their deaths.

On 11 January 1782, Joseph Laurent and Marie Carle appeared before the notary Benoit Leroi, living at Yamachiche, in order to commit to each other in bonds of matrimony. Joseph, son of Laurent Saint-Amant and Marie-Anne Brisard dit Saint-Germain, was 20 years old and a native of the parish of Saint-Antoine de la Rivière-du-Loup. We understand that the first name of his father had become his last name: he would pass it on to his descendants. Laurent Saint-Amant seems to be the only son of Antoine de Gerlais and Marie-Angélique Pelletier. This Antoine was the second son and sixth child of the ancestor Jean Jacques de Gerlais and Jeanne Trudel, who is counted among the first pioneers of Rivière-du-Loup. De Gerlais arrived in New France in 1665 with the company de La Fouille of the Carignan Regiment. On this 11 January 1782, Joseph Laurent was accompanied by his father and mother who stipulated for him, his brother Louis and Jean-Baptiste Perraut, a friend.

For her part, Marie Carle was said to be 18 years old and a native of Saint-Joseph de Chambly. Besides her father and mother, her witnesses were her brother Luc and his friend Charles Lamotte. The groom endowed his bride with 300 livres to be taken from the best part of his property. The said assets consisted of two-thirds of an arpent of frontage on the small rivière du Loup. This land belonged to the groom from an inheritance from his father and mother. One-third had been acquired from Agathe Laurent, their daughter and another third had been bought from Louis Laurent for 150 old chelins, payable on the next All-Saints Day. The marriage of Joseph and Marie would be celebrated on 28 January in the church of Saint-Antoine de la Rivière-du-Loup by the Récollet Dominique Petrimoulx.

Two years later, on 25 September 1784, it was Luc's turn, the eldest of the Carle family, to launch himself into the matrimonial adventure. Like his sister Marie, he first went to the notary Leroi to have him draw up his marriage contract with Marie-Josette Billy dit Saint-Louis, daughter of Amable and of Josette Lefebvre. The groom was 23 years old and the bride two years younger. Present were the father and mother of each spouse, Joseph Laurent and Marie Carle, Charles Paille, Jean-Baptiste Philibert, Pierre Ringuet and Prisque Trepagne. Among the signers, François Carle, youngest son of Jean and Marie-Anne Poirier, made his mark. It seems that this was the only known mention of François after his birth. We are unaware of what became of him later. The nuptial ceremony took place two weeks later, on 11 October, at Rivière-du-Loup. The act was signed by Jean-Baptiste Philibert, Charles Paille, Jean Carles and the pastor Dominique Petrimoulx.

WITNESS IN A MURDER TRIAL

On 6 March 1788, Jean Carles received a visit from the bailiff Jean-Baptiste Flamand who had received instructions from sheriff Gray, of Montréal, to deliver a subpoena ordering him to appear, at the same time as Antoine Lamontagne, another witness, before the King's Court on Saturday, 8 March 1788, at 10:00 o'clock in the morning. The two of them had to give their testimony in the case opposing the King against Paul Pauce, alias Kakioukabawy, an Indian accused of murdering Joseph Gervais. The subpoena signed by Isaac Ogden, prosecutor for the Crown, ordered that Carles and Lamontagne *"had to present themselves under punishment of penalties which they could be subject to"*. On this 8 March, Flamand admitted having received from Gray the amount of one livre, five chelins and eight deniers for having fulfilled his mission. (11)

DEATH OF OUR ANCESTOR

After more than forty years of life on Canadian soil, during which he had first fought on the battle fields and/or in the forts of New France, where he undoubtedly tended to the wounded and assisted the dying, performing the same duties fifteen years later at the siege of Saint-Jean; after having cared for hundreds of patients and dressed numerous wounds; after having toiled at clearing, plowing, seeding, harvesting and storing his hay and his grain, Jean Carles died at the age of 65 at the end of the eighteenth century. François Plessis-Belair (12) recorded the event in the parish registry of Rivière-du-Loup in the following terms:

> *"On the eighth of January one thousand eight hundred by us, priest/vicar of this parish, undersigned, buried in the cemetery of this parish the body of Jean Carle surgeon of this parish, who died yesterday at the age of seventy-five (sic) fortified with the last rites, husband of Marie Poirier. Present*

*were the sieur Augustin Sicard Derive under-
signed and Jean-Baptiste Rivard who stated
not to know how to write".*

MARIE-ANNE POIRIER

Marie-Anne Poirier barely survived the departure of her
husband into eternity.   On the following 22 January, in the
presence of the notary Antoine Gagnon and just as it had been
agreed to in the contract signed by Benoit Leroi on 29 July, she
returned to Augustin Harnois the lot located on the land of the
latter, which she and her husband had occupied for lifetime use
keeping nothing, except the old house built upon it which she will
have removed by the next April at the latest. This house probably was used as a *pied-a-terre* where Jean Carles could con-
veniently practice his profession of surgeon.

On this same 22 January, in another act drawn up by Antoine Gagnon, Marie-Anne Poirier offered Joseph Laurent acting
in the name of Marie Carle, his wife, to release the latter from
her support and her subsistence by means of a voluntary return of
all her rights and claims as heir to the late Jean Carles. Joseph
Laurent agreed to transfer her rights in favor of the widow in
both personal property and real estate. Marie-Anne could dispose
of it as she wished. Laurent hoped to express by this his kind-
ness to his mother-in-law and his willingness to be released from
all lifetime pension concerning her.

Marie⌐Anne Poirier would not see the end of the year
1800. As he had done for Jean Carles, the vicar François Belair
presided at her funeral and recorded the following act in the
registry of the parish.

> *"The nineteenth of December one thousand
> eight hundred by us priest/vicar of this
> parish undersigned, buried in the cemetery of
> this parish the body of Marie-Anne Poirier
> who died yesterday about the age of sixty-
> three and fortified by the last rites. Wife of
> the late Jean Carle surgeon of this parish.
> Present were Basile Racine and Jean Bap-
> tiste Rivard who has stated not to know how
> to write".*

Signed: F. Bélair vicar

An inventory of the estate left by Jean Carles seems never to have been made. Perhaps one could have been found, as was the case for the celebrated Michel Sarazin. (13)

A DEVOTED SON

On 8 January 1801, Antoine Gagnon intervened again to describe a sort of pact reached between the heirs of Jean Carles and Marie-Anne Poirier. Joseph Laurent and Marie Carle stated there:

"Considering the trouble, care, devotion and expense made and procured by the Sr Luc Carle their brother and brother-in-law to the late Sr Jean Carles and Marie-Anne Poirier their father and mother-in-law for a number of years and particularly in the different illnesses which they had had until the moment of their death he alone having furnished all the different little kindnesses which they needed on these occasions and also provided to have them buried decently after their death; considering that the few means that they had could not without his help have met all these needs, desiring thus that he be in some way compensated for all these attentions, difficulties and expenses towards the said deceased and that he remain peacefully owner of the few assets, even though of little consequence, which they have left after they died, have as a result voluntary cede and abandon purely and entirely from now on and for always in favor of the said Luc Carle here present and accepting cessionnaire for his heirs and assigns in the future of all their shares and claims to personal and real property generally anything which they could claim to repeat and report in the successions due from the said deceased Jean Carles and Marie-Anne Poirier their father and mother-in-law renouncing it entirely in

31

> *that he did not require them to contribute*
> *with him in the expenses that he could pay*
> *for them..."*

This declaration was made before the notary Gagnon in the presence of the witnesses John McBean and Abraham Boucher, who signed with Luc Carle and the notary.

LUC CARLE AND HIS FAMILY

Jean Carles and Marie-Anne Poirier had but four children, only two of whom had families. Luc and Marie-Joseph dite Marie, the two eldest, were born at Chambly, before their parents settled at Rivière-du-Loup. It is truly thanks to Luc that the Carles have continued on American soil. Marie is the proud ancestress of a great number of Laurents.

Luc Carle and Marie-Joseph Billy dit Saint-Louis were the parents of eleven children; nine sons and two daughters. All were born at Rivière-du-Loup and those who did marry were married in their native parish.

1. Louis, was born and baptized on 15 July 1785. he was married on 8 February 1813 (contract Charles Pratte, on 30 January), to Pelagie Gervais (Jean-Baptiste and Françoise Jouineau).

2. Luc, was born and baptized on 18 September 1786. He was married on 11 June 1811 (contract Antoine Gagnon, on the 4th), to Madeleine dit Saint-Louis (Joseph and Marguerite Bellemare). Inventory Pierre Bazin, 15 September 1823; Luc was named guardian of his three minor children: Jean-Baptiste, Emmanuel and Edouard. On 24 February 1829, he married Marguerite Paquin, widow of Julien Giguère. Luc died at Sainte-Ursule on 31 March and was buried on 2 April 1861.

3. François, was born on the 6th and baptized on 7 August 1788. On 21 May 1811 (contract Charles Pratte). François, speaking in the name of his father, was summoned to pay Michel Lefebvre 30 and 1/2 piastres (183 livres) which were owed following the sale of some land. François seems to have remained a bachelor.

4. Marie-Joseph, was born and baptized on 8 June 1791. She was married on 26 February 1810 (contract Antoine Gagnon, on the 19th), to Louis Bellemare (Joseph and Angélique Lambert).

5. Jean-Baptiste-Pierre, was born and baptized on 29 April 1793. He was married on 30 July 1827 (contract Pierre Bazin, on the 22nd), to Emilie Lupien (René and Victoire Lefebvre). he was buried at Sainte-Ursule on 24 December 1849.

6. Joseph, was born and baptized on 7 March 1795. He was married on 12 June 1820 (contract Pierre Bazin, on the 7th), to Marguerite Bergeron (François and Louise Lefebvre).

7. Emmanuel, was born on the 29th and baptized on 30 December 1796. He was married on 29 October 1821 (contract Pierre Bazin, on the 21st), to Madeleine Lemaitre-Duhaime (Alexis and Josephte Chevalier).

8. Jean-Baptiste, was born and baptized on 15 November 1798. He was married on 3 November 1818 (contract Pierre Bazin, on 20 October), to Esther Gervais (Jean-Baptiste and Françoise Jouineau).

9. Marie-Félicité, was born and baptized on 26 September 1800. She was married on 14 February 1820 (contract Pierre Bazin, on the 5th), to Louis Rivard (François and Geneviève Lafontaine).

10. Antoine, was born and baptized on 16 March 1803. He was married on 30 July 1832 (contract Joseph Bourret, on the 28th), to Marguerite Jalbert (Laurent and Angélique Bellemare).

11. Theodore, was born on the 15th and baptized on 16 January 1806. He was married on 3 October 1825 (contract Pierre Bazin on 14 September), to Marie-Narcisse Bergeron (François and Louise Lebrun).

From the notaries of his acquaintance, we know some of Luc Carle's activities.

a) From Antoine Gagnon, in an act dated 17 September 1801, we learn that Luc received from Louis Guy, seigneur of the fief of Grandpré, a piece of land with six arpents in frontage on which he was committed to clear, farm and build a home.

b) On 20 June 1814, Charles Pratte noted that when his sons Luc and Louis ceded to him, each on their own account, Luc did not yet own the land which had been bequeathed to him by his parents in his marriage contract.

c) On the following 19 July, the same notary noted that Luc bought from Jean-Baptiste Saint-Yves a plot of land with an area of four arpents, located in the fief of Saint-Antoine. He offered one hundred livres for it which he promised to pay on the next All-Saints day.

d) On 3 March 1819, we know from Antoine Gagnon that Luc contracted a loan of 300 livres from the sisters Catherine and Marie Sicard Derivé. He promised to repay this amount in a year. As a guarantee, he mortgaged his personal and real property present and to come.

e) On 7 June 1820, Pierre Bazin was summoned to explain an important decision by Luc Carle and his wife, to give all their property to their son Joseph who lived with them. These properties consisted of a piece of land with an area of about 53 arpents, located in the seigneurie of the Ursulines, all of it under cultivation, with house, barn, stable and other outbuildings. Jean Derosier, Pierre Saint-Yves, Theodore Bergeron, Alexis Desaulniers, François Paille and Joseph Pichette were their immediate neighbors. Joseph was committed to house, provide heat and feed, to support his parents, to care for them and to provide them with all their spiritual and temporal needs. After their deaths, he would be held to have them buried and to have 25 low masses said for each of them.

He must also keep his brothers Antoine and Theodore with him until they reach the age of majority. When they leave, he will give each of them a cow, two mother sheep and some chickens. To each of his sisters Josephte and Marie, he would give two chelins in place of the hereditary rights in the succession of their parents, since they had received other advantages when they married.

f) On 5 January 1821, the same notary informs us that Luc and Josephte also made a donation to their sons Pierre and Emmanuel of a piece of land with three arpents in frontage by 25 deep, located in the fief of Grandpré and opening on the small rivière du Loup. In addition, Pierre will receive a mare, a light carriage with its robe, a harness, a steer and a sheep. For his share, Emmanuel also will inherit a mare with its harness, a carriage robe and a black cow. This donation was made, it was specified, for the good services which they had rendered to the donors.

g) On the following 21 December, Pierre Bazin intervened again when Luc acquired from Eustache Branchaux a piece of land dependent on the fief of Grandpré. With an arpent and a half in frontage, this land ran along side the seigniorial boundary line of the Ursulines, ending at the boundary of Saint-Barthélemy and included half of the house and other buildings. The transaction was made for the amount of 1,600 livres which the seller admitted having received.

h) The same day, Luc exchanged the same land with André Vanasse for another of irregular shape located on the *chemin de la Carrière,* opening on the *chemin du Roy.* This land included a house, barn, dairy stable and other out buildings. In return, Luc agreed to pay the amount of 300 livres for which Vanasse gave a receipt immediately.

i) Finally, Luc took advantage of these transactions to borrow from Louis Lesieur-Desaulniers the amount of 3,000 livres *"for value received from a loan from the family, both this day and before this day".* The borrower was committed to repay 1000 livres per year, the last payment due on 20 December 1824. It seems that the debtor had some trouble in repaying because, on 26 February 1823, he had to sell his land on the chemin de la Carrière to his creditor and, on the same day, had to borrow from him another sum of 1100 livres payable in three payments, the last due on 26 February 1826. However, a rider informs us that on 27 March 1824, Luc had totally paid off his debt.

The poor state of his health undoubtedly made him apprehensive about his approaching demise, because a few months later, he was brought to his final resting place. On 18 August 1824, the pastor Jacques Lebourdais dit Lapierre (14) presided at his funeral. Luc had died two days before, at about the age of

60, according to the record. We can add at least two more years to his age. Sixteen years later, his wife went to join her husband in the here-after. Josephte Billy dit Saint-Louis died on 5 November 1840 and was buried two days later in the cemetery of Rivière-du-Loup. She was about 80 years old. Father Leandré Tourigny presided at her funeral. (15)

JOSEPH LAURENT AND HIS FAMILY

We wonder today how the genealogists of future generations are going to unravel the maze of compound last names which were given to the children in some families. We have invented nothing. Some of our ancestors knew the art of changing a surname, even a first name into a last name. This was the case with Gerlais who very early became Desjarlais. In the third generation, Laurent called himself Saint-Amand. This was the surname of his father and his grandfather. His children kept their father's first name and made it their last name. This was the beginning of the line of the Laurents who continue up to today. Joseph was the first of the Laurents. He was 20 years old when he married Marie-Joseph Carle in 1782. This couple had nine children, all born and baptized at Rivière-du-Loup. The dates which follow are those of the baptisms:

1. Jean, 4 May 1784; 2. Pierre, 15 August 1789; 3. Marie-Louise, 13 May 1792; 4. Julie, 22 April 1794; 5. Cyrille, 3 August 1796; 6. and 7; The twins Antoine and Albert, 15 January 1799; 8. Jacques-David, 13 February 1801; 9. Louis, 30 October 1805; buried the next day; Marie Carles died following this last birth, on 3 November at the age of 42 years and 5 months. She was laid to rest the next day.

Joseph remained a widower for only five months. On 3 April 1806, he and the notary Antoine Gagnon paid a visit to Jean-Baptiste Bergeron and Geneviève Brule; Joseph asked for the hand in marriage of their 35 year old daughter Josephte. He said he owned furnishings worth 495 livres and had a credit of 500 livres which Theodore Bergeron owed him, *"from the donation which his said father and mother made to him for his rights to their estate"*. It was agreed between the parties that the eight minor children of the groom from his first marriage to the late

36

Marie Carle would be fed, clothed and supported at the expense of the future community from only the income from their property

> *"and without reduction of their funds and to compensate the future bride for the trouble and care that she may give to raise these said children and to acknowledge her for the good advice that she will give to them in their behavior, the future groom gives hereby the present donation entre vivos a child's share in all the groom's property conforming to the decree of the second wedding followed in this country..."*

An act by the notary Pratte dated on 17 April 1810 informs us that Joseph Laurent and Josephte Bergeron received the 500 livres coming from the donation agreed to by Jean-Baptiste Bergeron and Geneviève Brule to their sons Louis and Theodore, the said amount taking place *"of all rights to the inheritance or legitimate to the succession of their father and mother"*.

Joseph Laurent and Josephte Bergeron were married on 21 April 1806 in the church of Rivière-du-Loup.

The union of Joseph and Josephte would add two more children to the Laurent family: Georges, baptized on 6 August 1808, and Marie-Josette baptized under the last name of Saint-Amant on 28 November 1811. The latter only lived for eight years. She was buried on 6 August 1820.

HELPFUL CHILD

By 1818, Joseph Laurent's situation had become precarious. On 7 December, he gathered his family in the presence of the notary Antoine Gagnon who drew up the report of this meeting. Present were Joseph, junior, Pierre and Louis Laurent, as well as Joseph Leblanc, the husband of Marie Laurent. Joseph, senior, explained that due to his great age his infirmities and his poverty, he was no longer able to work to support himself in his present existence. Everyone acknowledged the sad situation. Since there still remained six children in the home: Louise, Cyrille, Albert, Antoine, David and Julie, it was understood that each would contribute to provide for the support and subsistence of the elderly man, an amount of 33 livres per year for as long as he lived.

THE CANADIAN CARLES

According to Germain Lesage, (16) our ancestor Carles had been, in his time, one of the dominant figures of the parish of Rivière-du-Loup.

Several of his descendants were also famous in various fields:

A great-grandson, Louis Emmanuel (1832-1922), son of Luc and of Marguerite Paquin, was seigneur of the fief of Marie-Anne located to the northeast of the Maskinonge River; he was the first seigneur to occupy the seigniorial pew in the church of Sainte-Ursule;

Joseph Carle (1857-1933) was a very well known person at Saint-Boniface de Shawnigan. He was secretary-treasurer of the parish and the school committee, postmaster, justice of the peace and cantor of the church;

At Trois-Rivières, Leo Carle (1917-1984) was a remarkable musician. This former student of Ernest MacMillan led several instrumental ensembles and chorales, including *l'Orpheon* which made many tours of Québec, Ontario, New Brunswick and New England;

Gilles Carle (1925-1995) was a respected jurist and esteemed judge;

The film-maker Gilles Carle, the best known of all, was born at Maniwaki in 1929. He was by turns a painter, editor, publicist, literary critic and cinematographer, scriptwriter-producer and writer of several films.

Canada, particularly Québec, owes many of these people and probably many others to the surgeon Jean Carles.

38

FAMILY NAME VARIATIONS

As mentioned earlier in the paragraph entitled "Joseph Laurent and his family" Genealogists will have trouble sorting out the family name variations of these people. Some we know are:

Carles: Carle, Carm, Carme, Carte, Garle, Karle, Lalancette and Larocque;

Lalancette: Bonel, Bonelle, Breton, Carle, Carles, Claveau, Dubois, Fabre, Grace, Lacommande, Lebreton, Marion, Rauques, Scipion, Seguin and Vinzelle.

END NOTES

1) Albert Dauzat, <u>DENFPF</u>, tome 3, p. 2019, Paris, Librairie Larousse, 1969.

2) <u>Grand Guide des regions de France</u>, Encyclopaedia Leland, tome 8, page 2483. Other references provided by Marie-Maude Carle, who has visited the place.

3) <u>Source</u>: Marie-Maude Carle.

4) Charles-Claude Carpentier had been ordained a priest on 4 June 1746. He was the son of Claude Carpentier and of Geneviève Marchand. He had been the pastor of Chamblay from 1746 to 1763, then that of Longueuil (1763-1777), finally of Verchères (1777-1798), from where he died 2 November 1798.

5) La lancette was a small instrument used to draw blood.

6) Germain Lesage <u>Histoire de Louisville 1665-1960</u>, page 130.

7) In 1722 the Ursulines bought the fief of Rivière-du-Loup from the seigneur Michel Trottier dit Beaubien.

8) According to Germain Lesage, <u>Histoire de Louiseville</u>, page 114, this matter concerned Phineas Heinmann, Originally German and Jewish, "an outstanding person" who, with some other loyalist

soldiers under Frederick Adolphus von Riedel, had established the village of Rivière-du-Loup. Phineas opened a bookstore there. One of his children, Isaac, would becone a great store owner.

9)   Jacques Lacoursière, <u>Histoire populaire du Quebec- from its origins to 1791</u>, tome 1, Septentrion, 1995, pages 409 to 412.

10) Douglas Brynmer, *RAC*, 1891, Ottawa, 1892, page VIII.

11) <u>Correspondence du Secretaire civil et provincial du Bas-Canada</u>, serie "S", Vol.38, p.12308.

12) François Plessis-Bélair was the first vicar of Rivière-du-Loup. He was born in Montréal on 16 January 1770 from the union of François Plessis and of Josephte Baudry. Ordained a priest on 13 August 1797, he lived for 40 years at Rivière-du-Loup. He was also the pastor at Varennes, then at Sainte-Rose de Laval from where he died on 31 October 1830.

13) Arthur Vallée, <u>Michel Sarazin 1659-1735</u> (Québec, 1927, p.188).

14) Jacques Lebourdais, son of Joseph, merchant, and of Victoire Panet (sister of Msgr Panet), was born at l'Islet on 12 October 1783. He was ordained a priest at Québec on 22 February 1809. He was the pastor of Sainte-Geneviève-de-Batiscan before having arrived at Rivière-du-Loup, where he died on 23 September 1860,

15) Born at Bécancour in 1814, Leandre Tourigny was the first pastor of Saint-Maurice. He then carried out the same functions at Saint-Gregoire de Nicolet, where he died on 25 August 1873. In 1840 he was assigned as the replacement of the vicar Louis-Edouard Bois.

16) <u>Histoire de Louiseville</u>, p.103.

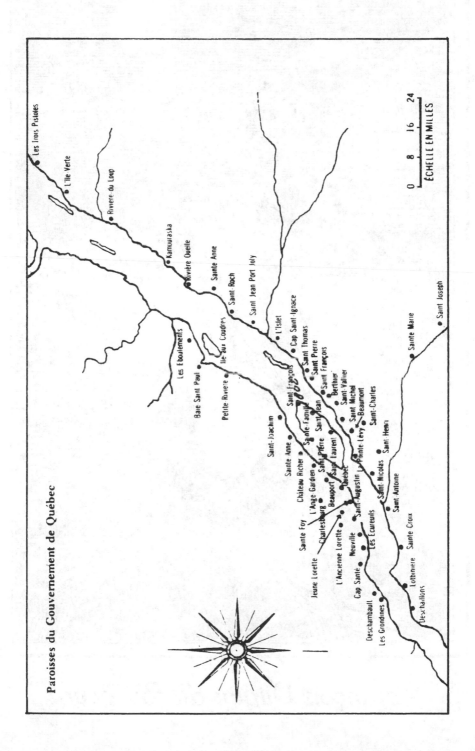

Paroisses du Gouvernement de Québec

ÉCHELLE EN MILLES

0   8   16   24

François Dupuis dit Jolicoeur

CHAPTER 3

François Dupuis dit Jolicoeur

upuis are numerous in Canada and in France. This last name was attributed for centuries to families owning or living near a well. Less widespread, the spelling of Dupuys has a different meaning: *le puy* meaning an elevation, a knoll, sometimes a domain or a place of origin.(1) According to Pierre Blanche, the Dupuis, Dupuy and Dupuys families from Paris, in the beginning, were molders, butchers, lawyers, prosecutors, makers of mirrors, notaries, captains and bourgeois. Those from Lyon were equerries, merchants, innkeepers and judges; those from Marseille were consuls, bourgeois and businessmen. Dauphine, Brittany, Perigord, Poitou, Hainaut, Picardie, Champagne and Lorraine counted noble families who bore this name. (2)

L'Aunis, l'Angoumois, Poitou, l'Anjou, l'Orleanais, Guyenne, Gascogne, Languedoc and the Ile-de-France were some of the French provinces which, in the seventeenth and eighteenth centuries, sent Dupuis and Dupuy people to New France. The latter often bore surnames such as Lamontagne, Lafontaine, Verdun, Montauban, Parisien, Beauregard, Saint-Pierre and Saint-Michel.

The best known of all is undoubtedly Paul Dupuis, who arrived in 1665 with the Maximy Company of the Carignan Regiment. Paul was a seigneur and towards the end of his life, occupied important posts as Lieutenant-General of the Provost of Québec. Jeanne Couillard, his wife, gave him a fine family of fourteen children. Jacques Dupuis dit La Garenne who, in 1684, was married at Trois-Rivières to Marie-Madeleine Prévost, never left the region. Neither did François Dupuis or Dupuy dit Jolicoeur. Their descendants are numerous in the region today.

At the time of his marriage celebrated at Champlain in 1698, François Dupuis dit Jolicoeur was a soldier in the company of La Groye. Charles-Henri d'Aloigny de la Groye, a navy guard at Rochefort, was promoted in 1683 to the rank of Lieutenant upon his arrival in Canada. Five years later, he was promoted to Captain by Governor Denonville, an appointment approved by Louis XIV in 1691. In 1695, La Groye would accompany Antoine de Crisafy during an expedition to rebuild Fort Frontenac. In September of the same year, Frontenac and Callière charged him with leading a detachment sent to Boucherville and to drive away the Indians who were pillaging the harvests there. (3) Did Jolicoeur accompany his captain on these missions? It is possible. History has kept the names of the officers, not those of the enlisted men who marched behind them. Fortunately for those of them who decided to remain here and found families, the pastors and the notaries have engraved their memory in their registries and in their notes, to the great joy of their descendants.

During the afternoon of 24 October 1698, the notary Daniel Normandin was summoned to Champlain, to the home of the colonist François Banliac, where several relatives and friends were gathered for the betrothal of Marguerite, the seventeen year old eldest daughter of the master of the house, and Marie-Angélique Pelletier. Marguerite, born at Rivière-du-Loup (Louiseville) on 17 April 1681 and baptized at Sorel on the following 12 July, was accompanied by her mother who would soon give birth to her seventh child (two others would follow) and several other people. François, the future groom, about twenty-five years old, said he was the son of the late François Dupuis and Philippe David, native of the town of Saint-Astier, in the diocese of Perigord.

The marriage contract indicates that the bride and groom would live in community property from the day of their wedding and that the dowry of the future head of the family would be 300 livres. Banliac and his wife promised to house their daughter and her husband in their house, and to feed them for a year. They would settle them later on land that they owned at Rivière-du-

44

Loup, would give them eight minots of wheat and four of peas. They would also provide them with a pair of oxen on the condition that they farm the land on which they settle.

On 10 and 13 June 1684 (contract Adhèmar). Banliac had indeed received from the seigneur Jean Le Chasseur lands with three arpents in frontage on the rivière du Loup, in the same neighborhood as those of Joachim Germano, with access rights to common land.

The wedding of François and Marguerite was presided over by the Sulpicien Louis Geoffroy (4) on 10 November 1698. The act indicates that the groom was an officer in a detachment of la Marine and that he was originally from the diocese of Perigueux. The witnesses mentioned were François Banliac, father of the bride, Philippe Montigny and Louis Clouet.

THIRTEEN BIRTHS

Between 1699 and 1720, a period of more than twenty years, Marguerite Banliac gave François Dupuis thirteen children.

1. Charles, born on the 30th and baptized at Champlain on 31 July 1699 by the pastor Louis Geoffroy, who noted that the male child had been baptized at home out of necessity. Godfather and godmother: François Banliac and Marie-Magdelaine Baudouin, residents of this parish.

2. Marguerite, a daughter about four days old, was baptized at Trois-Rivières on 28 February 1701 by the Récollet Elisée Crey. Godfather and godmother were Claude Crevier and Marie Banliac.

3. Marie-Josette, born about 1703.

4. Thérèse, born on 23 January at Maskinonge, *"conditionally baptized at home by a private individual"* and baptized at Trois-Rivières on 9 March 1705 by the Récollet Simeon Dupont. Godfather and godmother were Joseph Petit and Jeanne Petit dite Bruno.

5. Jean-François, born on 20 April 1707 at Maskinonge and baptized on 9 May by the Récollet Simeon Dupont. Godfather and godmother were Jean-François Lemire, resident of Maskinonge and Marie-Joseph Petit dite Bruno.

6. Marie-Catherine, born on the first of November at Maskinonge and baptized at La Visitation de Ile-Dupas on 28 December 1708 by Charles de La Gouladie, missionary priest. Godfather and godmother were Bastien Vanasse and Catherine Bellerive.

7. Marie-Anne, born at Maskinonge on 5 January 1711 and baptized on the 8th by the Récollet Simeon Dupont. Godfather and godmother were François Casabon and Marie-Anne Petit dite Bruno.

8. Exupère, born on 7 February 1713 at Maskinonge and baptized conditionally on the 20th of the same month by the Récollet Simeon Dupont. Godfather and godmother were Antoine Desjarlais dit Saint-Amant and Marie-Charlotte Mercereau, wife of Sieur Pombert. Exupère died on 22 July 1715 at Maskinonge, where she was buried the next day.

9. Gertrude-Michelle, baptized on 17 October 1714 by the Récollet Augustin Quintal. She was said to be originally from Maskinonge.

10. Brigitte, born at Maskinonge on 4 August 1716 and baptized on the 25th of the same month by the Récollet Cherubin Deniaux. Godfather and godmother were Jean-Baptiste Lupien and Marie-Anne Banliac.

11. Antoine, baptized at Maskinonge on 24 February 1718 by the Récollet Augustin Quintal (act at Saint-Antoine de Rivière-du-Loup). Godfather and godmother were Charles Dupuis, brother of the infant, and Geneviève Gateau.

12. Jean-Baptiste, born about 1719 (16 years old in 1735).

13. Ursule, born about 1720.

During all these years, the Dupuis family seems to have lived mainly at La Rivière Maskinonge, whose residents periodically received visits from the Récollet missionaries.

Brigitte, born in 1716, was the first to be mentioned as being baptized in the church of Maskinonge. The registries of this parish have numerous gaps. The baptismal act for Marie-Josette is lost, also those of Jean-Baptiste and Ursule.

AVEU ET DENOMBREMENT

In the census of the seigneurie of Maskinonge in July 1723, we read:

"François Dupuis, owner, 36 arpents of land in area, southwest side of the river, with house, barn, stable. Bordered on one side by Joseph Petit-Bruneau and on the other side by Jean-Baptiste Petit-Bruneau". (5)

In 1724, the notary Pierre Petit drew up in his turn the census of the seigneurie of Rivière-du-Loup, acquired the previous year from Michel Trottier by the Ursulines of Trois-Rivières. The third row of the parish located on the southwest side of the small Rivière du Loup counted four properties, including that of Jean (Jacques) Chretien, future husband of Marguerite Lamontagne (Banliac) and that of François Dupuis dit Jolicoeur, who lived at Maskinonge and who owned four arpents of frontage there, with no buildings, and only three arpents of cleared land. (6)

DEATH AND REMARRIAGE

This seems to be the last mention of François Dupuis during his life time. He must have died about 1726. His burial act is lost. Marguerite Banliac's mourning probably was of short duration. She must have known Jacques Chretien, her neighbor on the third row of the small Rivière du Loup. Son of our ancestor Vincent Chretien and Anne Leclerc, he was born on 14 August 1685 in the parish of Sainte-Famille on the Ile d'Orléans and was married in 1713 in a first marriage to Marie Beaudon, daughter of Jacques and of Marguerite Vcrieu. Settled first at Sainte-François on the island where the first three children were

47

born, this family moved to Rivière-du-Loup in 1718, and a few years later, to Trois-Rivières, where Marie Beaudon was buried on 15 May 1722, leaving behind five orphans.

In fact, on 13 August 1718 (contract Normandin), Jacques Chretien had bought from Pierre Delguel and his wife, Marie-Anne Lupien, a piece of land located on the small Rivière du Loup, consisting of five arpents in frontage on this river and extending as far as the seigneurie of the Ursulines of Trois-Rivières. There was a barn and a house built on an area of one arpent of land in the neighboring community. The price paid had been one thousand livres, a considerable amount, including 700 livres paid on the previous 26 March, the balance of 300 livres was to be repaid to the seller during the following three years.

On 10 February 1727, Jacques Chretien and Marguerite Banliac signed a marriage contract drawn up by Antoine Puyperoulx de LaFosse and they were married the same year at Rivière-du-Loup. This union was blessed by the Récollet Augustin Quintal, missionary fulfilling the duties of pastor in this parish, in the presence of Antoine Saint-Amant Dejarlais and a man named Decoteau. After the wedding, the Chretien family enlarged by the family of François Dupuis, settled at Trois-Rivières. Marguerite Banliac, who would soon be 46 years old, only gave two children to Jacques Chretien.

Sterile in this sense, yes, but her life would hence forth be fertile in another role, that of mid-wife, which she practiced at Trois-Rivières for many years.

An act by the notary Pierre Petit dated 15 September 1728 reveals that the Chretien family was now living in the fief of Tonnancour, a half-league above the city of Trois-Rivières. On that day, Jacques ceded to his neighbor Jean-Baptiste Dupont, who lived above Pointe-du-Lac, a half-arpent of frontal land, by twenty arpents in depth, across from the Saint Lawrence River. This transfer was made on the condition that the buyer dig and maintain a boundary ditch between the two concessions. This half-arpent was part of a piece of land with four arpents in frontage.

The other three and half arpents were sold on 9 May 1729 (same notary) to Jean Gendras for 300 livres: 200 livres paid on the next Saint-Michel's Day (29 September), the 100 other livres would be paid upon the return of six wooden chairs with straw seats.

It seems that the deed to the property of the land at Pointe-du-Lac had not been clearly established. At first it had been acquired by Antoine Therou, habitant of the Ile Jesus, on 18 February 1724 (act of Pierre Poulin). On 8 April 1730 (act by Petit), Chretien sold it again to Etienne Talon, habitant of Sainte-Anne-de-la-Perade, for 300 livres. On the following 8 August, Marthe Frichet, proxy for the said Therou, appeared at the office of Pierre Petit, affirming that an act drafted by the notary François Coron on the preceding 13 June, would have retroceded this land to Jacques Chretien. On the first of April 1731 (act by Petit), Jean Gendras resold it in his turn to Chretien. (7)

However it happened, the Chretien family was now settled at Trois-Rivières. On 24 April 1730 (act of Petit), Jacques bought from Jacques Larivée, shoemaker, and his wife Marie-Anne Pepin, a lot with 40 feet of frontage by 20 wide, located in the Lower Town, at the bottom of the hill. There was a house there surrounded by cedar stakes and covered with boards, as well as a stable also covered with boards. This sale had been made for 180 livres. The seller kept for himself the rights to the stable litter which was found on the lot, as well as a stone which would be used eventually in a chimney.

Two acts by Pierre Petit dated 26 March 1735 inform us that Jacques Chretien and Marguerite Banliac reached an agreement concerning the property which belonged to each of them. Following this, the husband and wife now lived with separation of property. First, Marguerite had the inventory of property drawn up in which she would keep for herself, an amount worth up to 198 livres. Second, a transaction reached between her and Jacques to resolve their dispute was taken into account. Jacques agreed to give to Marguerite the lot in Trois-Riviéres. She would be able to dispose of it *as property belonging to her*. In return, Marguerite promised to pay all the debts from the community property which existed between them and which were owed to some private individuals. She was also obliged to make her share of the fences on the common land, as her share of the desert and expenses occasioned by the construction of ferries which were used for crossing the channels. Finally, she would also assume the 30 livres in expenses required for the legal procedures of the separation.

After these events, Marguerite Banliac would live for more than twenty years. She was escorted to her final resting place at the very beginning of the year 1756. The Récollet Hippolyte Collet recorded in the registry of the parish of Trois-Rivières the following act titled

"Burial of the good wife Chretien".

"The year one thousand seven hundred fifty six on the 18th of January at nine o'clock in the morning in the cemetery of this parish was buried the body of Marguerite wife of Chretien seventy two years of age after having received all the sacraments of the church and practicing the duties of midwife for several years to the satisfaction of everyone".

On the following 27 January, the notary Pillard, at the request of Antoine Dupuis, his brothers and brothers-in-law, went to the house where Marguerite had died in order to take an inventory of her personal property and her liabilities. On 4 March, for lack of an agreement among the heirs, the notary Jean Le Proust acting as bailiff by virtue of an order from the lieutenant-general of Trois-Rivières on 16 February proceeded with the sale of the deceased's property. Then followed a list of the buyers and the items which they acquired.

Jacques Chretien would outlive his second wife by nine years. The old man returned to live at Rivière-du-Loup where a part of his family still resided. It was there that he surrendered his soul at the end of 1764. His mortal remains were buried on 18 December in the parish cemetery after a funeral presided over by the pastor Jean-Baptiste Petrimoulx.

WHAT THE CHILDREN BECAME

1. Charles, the eldest, was the first to leave the paternal home. On 28 December 1718 (act by Normandin) at the age of nineteen, he received a concession from seigneur Joseph Petit dit Bruneau, husband of Marie-Magdelaine Chesnay, daughter of Bertrand Chesnay de la Garenne. This land, with three arpents in frontage by forty deep was ceded by way of cens and seigniorial rents. It was located along the small Rivière du Loup and abutted the lands not ceded. The concessionaire would be able to pasture his animals there when he acquired some common land which was washed by the bay of Maskinonge.

Less than two years later, Charles said he was ready to take a wife. He didn't pay court to just anyone. Ursule Sicard, born at Saint-Pierre on the Ile d'Orléans on 17 September 1695, was the eldest daughter of the seigneur Jean Sicard de Carufel, from a noble family from Haut-Languedoc, who had arrived in this country in 1685 as a sergeant in a company detached from la Marine, commanded by François-Marie Renaud d'Avesne des Meloizes. Jean Sicard and his family first lived along the lower part of the Maskinonge river but, for some time, the seigneur had moved to his fief (present parish of Saint-Justin) in order to attract some censitaires. (8)

The wedding took place in the church of Rivière-du-Loup on 24 May 1720. After having obtained a dispensation from the three banns

> "granted by Monsieur de la Goudalie very worthy priest curate of la pointe aux Trembles de Montreal, grand vicar of Monseigneur Jean-Baptiste de la Crois de St Vallier our illustrious and reverend Bishop",

Charles, son of François Dupuis and Marguerite Banliac his father and mother of the parish of Saint-Joseph de Maskinonge, married damoisselle Ursule Sicard de Carufel, daughter of Jean Sicard, equerry Sieur de Carufel, officer in the troops of this country, and the dame Geneviève Ratté, her father and mother of the same parish. The celebrating priest was the Récollet Cherubin Deniaux who performed the duties of curate in this parish and in those of Saint-Antoine de la Rivière-du-Loup and Sainte-Anne d'Yamachiche. The witnesses were Pierre Gerbault dit Bellegarde and Antoine Dejarlais dit Saint-Amant. At least eight children were born to this union, five sons and three daughters.

In the census of the seigneurie of Maskinonge, dated in July 1723, it was written:

"François Dupuis junior, southwest side of the river owner of three arpents in depth...with house, barn and stable, 5 arpents of plowable land."

This obviously referred to Charles, not François junior, still too young to have achieved such an establishment.

At that time like today, male heads of family had to perform tasks, in addition to farming the land, in order to make ends meet. For Charles this was, at least for some time, traveling through the forest in order to collect bark used in the making of canoes. An act by notary Joseph Caron, dated 29 September 1745, reveals that the merchant Louis Lemaitre, from Trois-Rivières, and Charles Dupuis reached an agreement to put an end to the legal problems which confronted them. Charles admitted having already received from the merchant 18 livres in payment for some bark that he had not yet delivered. The latter demanded that he fulfill his commitment. Unable to do so in the time required, Dupuis was obligated, with the consent of Lemaitre, to deliver to him his entire harvest of bark for the next two years. To this transaction, Lemaitre would pay him an additional 5 livres for the chunks and the bark for the bottoms of the canoes.

On 18 December 1747 (act by Pillard), Charles accepted a concession from his sister-in-law Agathe Sicard, widow of Joseph Petit-Bruneau, principal seigneur of Maskinonge. Agathe acted as manager of the affairs of the seigneury by virtue of a mandate granted by the censitaires. This concession was made for the cens and seigniorial rents. It consisted of a piece of land with four arpents in frontage to a depth which extended as far as the seigneury of Rivière-du-Loup. The neighbors were Alexis Lacourse and Pierre Giraudeau. On 11 November 1749, this land was ceded to Giraudeau. Finally, on 4 September 1750 (act by Pillard), Charles made the most important transaction of his life. For 400 livres paid in cash, he bought from François Baril-Duchemy the mill of the seigneury of Maskinonge. He was not able to work it for a very long time, because he died unexpectedly and his body was buried in the cemetery of Maskinonge on 21 March 1754. The act by the pastor Louis-Michel Guay said he was 45 years old, but in fact he was ten years older.

After Charles had founded a home in 1720, seven years passed before his sisters and brothers committed themselves to marriage. And they did it in the chronological order of their births, or nearly so.

2, Marguerite, eldest of the daughters, left the single state about 1727. Her marriage act was lost, however, Jean-Baptiste Caille was the happy man chosen. He was born at Montréal on 25 January 1697, from the union of Jean Caille and Madeleine Galarneau. On 16 May 1725 (act by Petit), the seigneur Jean-Baptiste Jutras-Desrosiers granted him a piece of land with six arpents in frontage in the fief of Saint-Jean de Lusaudière, at Saint-François-du-Lac. It was there that he brought his young wife and where he raised his four sons and five daughters.

Marguerite was buried at Saint-François on 25 August 1747. Three years later, on 18 August 1750 (contract Pillard, 18 October), Jean-Baptiste was remarried, to Catherine Du Lignon who gave him five more children, three sons and two daughters. The head of the family was himself laid to rest at Saint-François on 3 September 1759.

3. It was at Cap-de-la-Madeleine on 18 November 1728 that Thérèse married Louis-François Tessier dit Laforest, born about 1700, son of Daniel Tessier and Marie Raimbault, from Saint-Martin in the city of Saint-Maxient, diocese of Poitiers, in Poitou (Deux-Sevres). Two sons were born to this marriage at Trois-Rivières. After the death of Thérèse, on an unknown date, Louis-François was remarried at Montréal on 12 August 1746, to Marie-Joseph Brisson, daughter of Sébastien and of Marie-Marguerite Rivière. On 4 November 1755, Marie-Joseph was married, in a second marriage, to Gabriel Bled, at Montréal.

4. As with Marguerite, Saint-François-du-Lac was also the village of Jean-François dit Destours. He was married in this parish on 28 July 1730, to Thérèse Marquet, born at Champlain on 10 July 1712, daughter of François dit Perigord and Louise Galarneau. Thérèse gave birth to thirteen children, six daughters and seven sons, the last two of whom were twins, born on 25

June 1753. Thérèse died following these difficult births and was laid to rest three days later. On 21 January 1754, in his parish, Jean-François was married a second time, to Marie-Joseph Leclair, born at Terrebonne on 19 March 1732, daughter of Pierre Leclair and Jeanne Bastien,. Marie-Joseph gave Jean-François six more children, three sons and three daughters. The name François Dupuy appears in the census of 1765; he owned 75 arpents of land at Saint-François-du-Lac. (9)

5. The existence of Marie-Josette is revealed to us by her marriage celebrated at Rivière-du-Loup on 14 August 1731, by the Récollet Salvien Boucher. Her husband was Louis Arcouet, son of the late Jean Arcouet and Isabelle Pepin, from Cap-de-la-Madeleine. The celebrating priest announced that a publication of the three bans was made not only in the parish of Saint -Antoine, but also in that of Cap-de-la-Madeleine, as attested to by a certificate issued by the pastor Jean-Auguste Mercier. The witnesses mentioned were Charles Pombert, Louis Desrives, Charles Banliac dit Lamontagne, guardian of the bride, Jacques-Vincent Chretien, her step-brother, and Pierre Lamirande. The married life of the Arcouet-Dupuis couple barely lasted more than a year. Louis was buried at Maskinonge on Monday, 24 November 1732, reported by the curate Salvien Boucher. I have not traced the presence of Marie-Josette after this date. Did she return to live at the home of Charles Banliac, her uncle and guardian?

6. Marie-Catherine was married at Trois-Rivières on 13 May 1732 to Guillaume Vacher dit Laserté, born in this place on 25 September 1693, son of the ancestor Jean-Guillaume Vacher and Marguerite Benoit. (10) The nuptial blessing was given to them by the Récollet priest Pierre-Baptiste Resche, in the presence of Pierre Papillon and Henri Luneau. Marie-Catherine brought two sons and three daughters into the world, but she prematurely left this same world on 2 August 1741, at the age of only 32. She was buried at Trois-Rivières the following day in the presence of the Récollets Nicolas-Albert Couturier and Clément Lefebvre, as well as a few local notables. Guillaume was remarried at Nicolet, on 11 January 1751, to Madeleine Saint-Aubin Lafrance, widow of François Malboeuf (contract Le Proust, same day) but had no other children.

7. Gertrude-Michelle entered into her marriage bonds at Trois-Rivières on the first of June 1733 (contract Petit, same day), to Pierre Blanchard dit Turenne, a soldier in the company de Montigny and son of Pierre Blanchard and the late Andrée Joffroy, from theparish of Notre-Dame de Poitiers. The Récollet Bernandin de Gannes de Falaise, born in Acadia in 1707, celebrated the marriage in the presence of Claude Le Proust and Jacques Chretien. Gertrude-Michelle was pregnant at that time. Marie, their first child, was baptized on 28 June. We later find this couple at Sorel, Chambly and Yamaska. Gertrude-Michelle and Pierre were the parents of a daughter and four sons. After Pierre's death, Gertrude-Michelle was remarried at Saint-François-du-Lac on 23 May 1757, to Jean-François Joyelle, born on 18 December 1722, son of François and of Marie-Catherine Rault. Jean-François and Gertrude-Michelle (Rigaud, 26 February 1758) made a mutual donation of all their property and real estate, in consideration of their good friendship and the reciprocal affection that they bore one another. This act reveals that they lived in the fief of Thiersant (Yamaska). (11)

8. For her part, Marie-Anne went to rejoin her sister Marguerite and her brother Jean-François at Saint-François-du-Lac. In 1734, it was there that she married Pierre Marquet dit Perigord, born at Québec on 3 November 1710, son of François Marquet and Louise Galarneau. At her wedding, celebrated on 16 November by the pastor Jean-Baptiste Dugast, (12) in the presence of François Bibeau and Jean-François Dupuy, she was called the daughter of the (late) François Dupuy and Marguerite Lamontagne, her father and mother from the parish of Saint-Antoine de la Rivière-du-Loup. Marie-Anne gave birth to four daughters, three sons and two anonymous.

9. Marie-Joseph, the eldest, was baptized at Saint-François-du-Lac; the following five children would be baptized at Trois-Rivières. From 1747 to 1750, the family was located at Baie-du-Febvre, then they returned to Saint-François-du-Lac. On 31 December 1759 (contract Pillard), Pierre and Marie-Anne sold their land at Saint-François to Joseph Niquet. On the following 22 February (contract Rigaud), Pierre, classified as a flour merchant at the mill of Saint-François and residing there, accepted from Gilles Badaillac a lease for a period of 29 years to work the said mill. Did he live long enough to be able to fulfill this commitment? This remains to be verified. By accepting this lease,

the Perigords were committed to providing shelter to Badaillac until his death and to have ten low Requiem masses said for him each year.

10. Ursule, probably the youngest of the Dupuis family, was married at Trois-Rivières on 12 January 1739. She chose for her husband Pierre DaSylva, born at Québec on 13 April 1715, son of Pierre dit Portugais and Marie-Jeanne Mingou. His grandfather Pierre, as indicated by his surname, was originally from Portugal, more precisely from Lisbon, the capital. The marriage was celebrated by the Récollet Clément Lefebvre, superior of the Trifluvien convent. Ursule and her brother Jean-Baptiste signed the registry. A marriage contract was drawn up by the notary Presse on the following 9 February. It was indicated there that Jacques Chretien and Marguerite Banliac stipulated for their daughter and step-daughter, while Pierre acted in his own name and as proxy for his trustee Pierre Savary. The sixteen children born to this union (four sons and twelve daughters) were born at Trois-Rivières. Pierre had, it seems, spent his life at the Forges of Saint-Maurice.

11. Jean-Baptiste, is another child whose baptismal act is lost. However, a transaction made in the presence of the notary Petit on the occasion of his death act imply that he was born in 1719. The said transaction was reached on 11 July 1735 between his step-father Jacques Chretien, living at Rivière-du-Loup, his mother Marguerite Banliac and the master edgetool maker André Corbin. On this occasion, the sixteen year old Jean-Baptiste, became an apprentice for a period of four years. Corbin was committed to feed the young man, and also to clothe him, provide him with lodging and support as a servant and apprentice. Upon the end of his apprenticeship, Corbin promised to clothe him *"from head to foot"* to give him hats, shoes, stockings, linens, cloak, jacket and breeches of serge. (13)

Having barely finished his commitment, Jean-Baptiste said he would be pleased to take a wife without delay. He did so at Saint-Michel des Forges on 25 October 1739 (act at Trois-Rivières). His chosen one was Catherine Constancineau, born at Pointe-aux-Trembles de Québec (Neuville), on 25 September 1723, daughter of Jean-François, carpenter at les Forges Saint-Maurice, and the late Marie-Louise Matté. The celebrating priest was the Récollet Augustin Quintal, missionary at les Forges and vicar at Trois-Rivières. Jean-Baptiste and his sister Ursule placed

56

their signatures at the bottom of the act with Frère Quintal and Pierre Bouvet. The couple only had their marriage contract drawn up two years later. On 23 October 1741 (contract by Presse), the representatives of the two families gathered at the house of Jacques Chretien to celebrate the event. Another act by the notary Presse, dated 17 May 1743, reveals that Jean-Baptiste had been injured and had to be hospitalized at the Hôtel-Dieu of Trois-Rivières administered by the Ursulines. Unable to pay for food and medicines provided by the nuns since 30 December, Jean-Baptiste, who usually lived at the Forges, offered to reimburse his hostesses by ceding them the share which came to him from a piece of land received from an inheritance from his parents, a quarter-arpent located at Maskinonge. The Ursulines accepted this offer.

Jean-Baptiste and his family left the Forges and later settled at Nicolet. On 4 July 1755 (act by Pillard), they received a piece of land ceded by the seigneur Cresse. This land was sold on 2 March 1759 (act by Le Proust), to Gabriel Cotteret for 200 livres paid in cash. This land had three arpents in frontage facing the small *"channel"* of the ile La Fourche. Jean-Baptiste and Catherine were parents of sixteen children: three sons and thirteen daughters. Their married life lasted nearly 47 years. Catherine was buried at Nicolet on 28 May 1786. Five months later, on 6 November, Jean-Baptiste was married at Nicolet to Geneviève-Françoise Laspron dite Desfosses, widow of François Saint-Laurent. The celebrating priest was Louis-Marie Brassard, a priest born at Québec in 1726 and died at Nicolet in 1800. It was he who, in 1784, had a stone church erected on land bought by the parish in 1770. Jean-Baptiste also died in 1800, on 11 February. The next day, his body was buried in the parish cemetery of Nicolet. He was 79 years old, according to the act.

12. On 9 May 1740, it was the 23 year old Brigitte's turn to take a husband. He was the 25 year old soldier, Elie Manseau dit Lajoie, son of Pierre Manseau and Madeleine Heliot, of the parish of Saint-Seurin de Bordeaux, in Guyenne (Gironde). The Récollet Nicolas-Albert Couturier blessed their union in the presence of René Truillier, Guillaume Laserté, demoiselle Magdelaine Duplessis and Marguerite Banliac. On the day of their wedding, Brigitte and Elie baptized a little girl named Magdelaine-Elizabeth *"whom they had from their natural marriage, who had been legitimized according to the prescribed*

forms". The godfather and godmother were René Truillier and Marie-Magdelaine Duplessis. On 14 August 1739 (act by Presse), Elie had acquired from Jean-Baptiste Jutras a lot with 31 feet in frontage by one hundred deep in the Lower Town of Trois-Rivières, undoubtedly with the intention of settling there.

The Manseau-Dupuis couple had twelve children, six sons and six daughters, whose descendants are still found in the region of Trois-Rivières. Elie worked as a laborer at the Forges of Saint-Maurice.

13. Antoine was the last to take a wife. On 10 September 1741, at Trois-Rivières, he joined his destiny to that of Marie-Ursule Alary, born at Saint-Augustin on 23 February 1717, daughter of Pierre dit le Grandalary and Marie-Joseph Lemay. Once again, the Récollet Clément Lefebvre, superior of the monastery of Trois-Rivières, blessed this union to which fourteen children were born, nine sons and five daughters, Antoine also worked at the Forges of Saint-Maurice before settling at Pointe-du-Lac, in the fief of Tonnancour, where he acquired from seigneur Joseph Godefroy, a piece of land with three arpents in frontage by twenty deep. Antoine was buried at Trois-Rivières on 11 September 1772. He had died at the Forges on the day before, about 60 years old, wrote the Récollet Isidore Marsolet who presided at his funeral. In reality, death surprised him in his 54th year. (14)

FAMILY NAME VARIATIONS

In addition to those variations listed in Chapter 1, the following permutations of Dupuis, Dupuy and Dupuys are also known: Anet, Beauregard, Caton, Chere, Couillard, De la Fosse, Destours, Duclos, Duell, Dunord, DePeux, Dupill, Dupray, Dupuyau, Dupee, Gervais, Gilbert, Goilard, Hilaire, Jolicoeur, Lagarenne, Laliberte, Lemarquis, Moyse, Parisien, Perou, Prudhomme, Raymond, St-Michel, St-Pierre, Terre, Thomas, Verdun, Well and Wells.

The surname Jolicoeur has the following known variations: Amand, Bernard, Bosslet, Bouchard, Boyer, Bruneau, Champoux, Coeur, Courage, Cou, Caseneuf, Chais, Chapmout,

Charier, Courtmanche, Contremine, Daveau, Deveau, Hart, Heart, Jolicard, Jolycoeur, LeParon, Martin, Monat, Monnard, Orley, Orly, Pilet, Poussard and Pronovost.

END NOTES

1)   Albert Dauzat, <u>DENFPF</u> Larousse-Selection, Vol.3, 1969, p.2074 & 2183.

2)   _____ . <u>Dictionnaire et armorial des noms de famille de France.</u> Nancy, 1974. p.71

3)   _____ . <u>DBC</u> II, PUL, 1969, p.15 & 16. Aloigny de La Groye had worked for 30 years in Canada. In the autumn of 1714, gravely ill, he decided to return to France. While sailing off the shores of Sable Island, the vessel transporting him was shipwrecked with the loss of all on board.

4)   _____ . <u>DBC</u> II, p.252 & 253. Louis Geoffroy arrived in New-France in 1985. He was a missionary in Acadia, then at Laprairie, Batiscan, Champlain, Countrecouer and Sorel. He died at Québec in 1705.

5)   Raymond Douville, <u>Correspondence</u>, 25 April 1955. Notes on François Dupuis dit Jolicoeur.

6)   Germain Lesage, <u>Histoire de Louiseville.</u> 1961. p.81 & 84.

7)   These acts of Pierre Poulin and François Coron are absent from the notarial records.

8)   _____ . <u>Nos Ancetres,</u> Volume 5, 1989, p. 148 & 155.

9)   _____ . *RAPQ* 1936-1937. p.96.

10)   _____ . <u>Nos Ancetres,</u> Volume 5, 1989, p.166 & 172.

11)   Pierre-François Thiersant, priest, was pastor of Batiscan, then missionary at Sainte-Anne-de-Beaupré. He rented his fief to Barthélemy Sicard-Marsille before returning to France.

12) Jean-Baptiste Dugast, born at Montréal in 1684, was ordained a priest by Msgr Saint-Vallier in 1714. He became pastor of Saint-François-du-Lac after his ordination up until 1761. He died in 1763.

13) Made from linen threads.

14) Isadore Marsolet had been the last Récollet at Trois-Rivières. In 1779 this convent was requisitioned by the English, who converted it into a hospital, then into a Palace of Justice, then into a prison. In 1821 the catholics tried in vain to recover it but Governor Dallhouse refused. In 1823 the Anglicans took possession of the convent and the church thanks to the intervention of King George IV of England.

OTHER SOURCES

Georges Panneton & Antonio Magnan, <u>Le diocese de Trois-Rivières.</u> Le Bien Public, 1962, passim.

J.B.A. Allaire, <u>Dictionnaire biographic du clerge canadien-française.</u> Volume 1, *Les Anciens*.

Benjamin Sulte, <u>Les Forges Saint-Maurice</u>, Ducharme, 1920, passim.

<u>Dictionnaires genealogique</u>, Tanguay & Jette.

Feu de la St-Jean aux Trois-Rivières

Jean Ferron

CHAPTER 4

Jean Ferron

 erron as a last name appeared in New France for the first time in 1671. This was the name of a daughter of the king, Marguerite, married that year at Québec to our ancestor Guillaume Bertrand, who settled at *Pointe-aux-Trembles de Québec* (Neuville). A certain Jean Feron dit Sancerre, originally from Poitou, arrived with the troops of *la Marine* at the end of the seventeenth century. He was a corporal in the company commanded by Captain Louis de Laporte de Louvigny. In 1689, Frontenac sent de Louvigny on a mission at the head of a contingent of 170 men, among whom, was *Jean Feron*. In 1692, the latter was at Montréal where he married Marie Poutre; four years later, he was remarried, to Elisabeth Patenaude. Several children were born, but the male descendants are rather rare; they do not seem to have been perpetuated beyond the third generation. It was quite otherwise for Jean Ferron, a Maurician who, by his very large family, planted some deep and indestructible roots on Canadian soil, beginning with the second generation.

THE FERRONS PRESENT DURING THE CRUSADES

In the beginning the French Ferrons were blacksmiths, ironworkers and/or iron merchants. (1) According to the Count de Puymegé, they were present during the Crusades. (2) Guillaume de Ferron, of the Knights Templar, was cited in a charter of Duke Conan IV in 1160. Another, Guillaume, commanded a company of thirty horsemen in 1371.

By the end of the fourteenth century, three family branches had evolved. That of Olivier, who joined with his brothers in 1379 into the ranks of the Breton seigneurs for the protection of the ducal rights. This Olivier was the father of Louis, whose son Olivier was the founder of the extinct branch of Quengo. That of Alain, founder of the branch which ratified the treaty of Guerande in 1381, and who fought with the Constable de Clisson. This Alain was also the founder of the branches du Chesne, de la Vairie and de l'Echapt.

A General de Ferron published a genealogy of his family in 1911. Noble families bore coats of arms with mottos. That of *La Ferronnays* (the Ferrons) was Latin: *"Hoc ferro vinces"* (by this iron you triumph); that of Chesne was *"Sans tache"* (without pockets). The origin of the Normand Ferrons was almost as old as that of the Bretons. It was from Normandie that Jean Ferron came to us in the middle of the eighteenth century; he seems to be the ancestor of all the Ferrons in America.

AT THE FORGES OF SAINT-MAURICE

Jean Ferron was born about 1718 at Reffuveille, in the canton of *Juvigny-le-Tertre* (Manche). We know, from other sources, that his family was living at *la Chapelle-Urée*, a neighboring town of *Reffuveille*, at the time of his marriage celebrated in 1750. The road from *Avranches*, the principal city in this region, follows the line of the ridge of *l'Avranch*, in between the valleys of *la See* and *la Selune*. It slopes down towards the west, in the direction of Reffuveille and Avranches. Offshore is *Mont Saint-Michel*, in the heart of the bay of the same name. A few kilometers to the south is the town of *Biards*, from where each year, during the same era, a great number of young men departed for cod fishing on the banks of Newfoundland and in the Gulf of Saint-Lawrence. A goodly number of them settled in New France at the end of the French Régime.

Jean Ferron surely was aware of these expeditions by the Normand fishermen off the Canadian coast. But his arrival seems to have been motivated by quite another reason, that of going to work at the Forges of Saint-Maurice which were beginning to show promising results. Let's recall briefly the history of this enterprise.

In 1663, the seigneur Maurice Poulin, whose first name was later given to the river of Trois-Rivières, had taken steps to have himself ceded a vast territory along the river. At nearly the same time, Pierre Boucher, then governor of Trois-Rivières, made Louis XIV aware of the existence of the iron ore which could be extracted from the area around this town. In 1668, the intendant Talon asked minister Colbert to provide the colony with iron workshops. However, it **was** only in 1733 that a company was formed, and it received a gift from the king of 10,000 livres, for launching the industry.

In 1735, the company hired Pierre-François Olivier de Vezain to manage the ironworks. He joined with the master Jacques Simonet who brought some workers from France. The factory was finally up and running by 1738. However, it soon failed. During the following years, other specialized workers came to lend assistance to the Canadians. Let's mention Pierre-François Michelin, François Godard, Jean Daniel, François Marquet dit Perigord, Pierre Chaillot, Pierre Martin, Gabriel Desmaisons, Jean-Baptiste Delorme dit Deslauriers, Pierre Marchand, Joseph and Jean Aubry, Nicolas Champagne, Pierre Labonne, Élie Manseau dit Limousin and others. Several of them remained in country and founded families whose descendants are numerous in the Mauricie.

On 3 August 1749, the Swedish naturalist Peter Kalm paid a visit to Trois-Rivières. Early in the morning, he visited the iron works, returning before sunset. The very rich ore, he reported, was found in open drills the thickness of two fists. These small masses are like sponges filled with holes which contain ochre, a yellow, clayish soil diversely colored by the presence of the iron. The soft mineral lay on white sand or under a thin layer of humus. Manpower was still scarce, with the inhabitants of the area preferring to devote themselves to farming.

At the time of Peter Kalm's visit to the Ironworks of Saint-Maurice, Jean Ferron must have already been part of a group of workers busy smelting the iron. Less than a year later, he had saved enough money to allow himself to start a family.

On 6 July 1750, he was at Rivière-du-Loup (Louiseville) to take a wife. He was welcomed there by the young pastor Louis-Michel Guay who, (3) on that day, drew up both his marriage contract and the church record of marriage. (4)

These two documents indicate that Jean Ferrand (sic) was the son of René Ferrand and Julienne Breye, from the parish of Saint-Léonard *"dit Chapelle-Urèe"*, of the diocese of Avranches in lower Normandie (Manche). The intended wife was Marie-Isabelle Bibaut, daughter of Joseph and Marie Minaut, residents of Rivière-du-Loup. Baptized at Yamaska on 7 February 1735, Marie-Isabelle was the third of the couple's six daughters. They were the granddaughters of our ancestor François Bibaut and all were born at Yamaska. François had arrived from La Rochelle in 1656. He is considered to be a pioneer of Saint-François-du-Lac and Batiscan.

In the marriage record that he drew up, Louis-Michel Guay, a missionary priest from Saint-Antoine de la Rivière-du-Loup, noted that he had received permission from his bishop to receive Jean and Marie's mutual consent, and that he had also received a certificate issued *"from the reverend father of the Forges Saint-Maurice"*.   Among the people present at the ceremony, the celebrant mentioned Marie-Anne Minaut (Moreau), maternal grandmother of the bride (and daughter of our ancestor Jean Moreau dit La Grange).

The marriage contract noted that the spouses would live in community property and, for the good friendship that they bore each other and that they hoped with God's help, to continue until their death, they made each other an equal and reciprocal donation of all their property *"to do with use and dispose of by the survivor until the day of his or her death, after which the land would return to the legitimate heirs"*.

The historian Benjamin Sulte, in his work entitled *"Les Forges Saint-Maurice"* (5) twice mentioned ancestor Ferron who he said would remain at the iron works with his family until 1761, the year in which he decided to devote himself exclusively to farming the land in his domain at Yamachiche. We have, however, ascertained that this statement does not completely conform with what the parish registries report to us, nor the contract of concession of his land at Yamachiche.

The sixteen year old Marie-Isabelle Bibaut, gave birth on Thursday, the first of July 1751, to her first child, a boy named Jean-Baptiste who was baptized by the Récollet Salvien Boucher, the missionary at Saint-Michel des Forges. The godfather was Jacques Tacé (Tassé) and the godmother Marie Mino (Minaut).

66

The baby only lived for eight months; he was buried at the Forges on 2 March 1752. Another Récollet, Brother Hyacinthe Amiot, conducted the ceremony of the angels.

On the following 13 January, the same priest baptized François, born the day before. The godfather was François Chaput and the godmother, Marie Sarrasin.

AT RIVIÉRE-DU-LOUP (Louiseville)

Shortly after the birth of François, the Ferron family left Saint-Michel des Forges for Rivière-du-Loup. There, Marie Bibaut rejoined her family, from whom she had been separated for three or four years. The Bibaut and Minaut families had known each other at Yamaska where they had lived for several years before going to Rivière-du-Loup, where they had worked, beginning in 1740, in the fief of Saint-Jean, the Ursulines' property at Trois-Rivières.

Marie-Joseph Ferron, third child of Jean and Marie, was baptized at Saint-Antoine de la Rivière-du-Loup on 27 June 1755. She was buried there on the following 9 February, at the age of seven months and a few days. (6) Marie-Hélène was born and baptized on 11 March 1757; her godfather and godmother were Michel Saint-Louis and Françoise Bibaut, her mother's sister. Again a short life. On 27 November 1758, the Récollet Jean-Baptiste Petrimoulx noted the burial *"of the body of the child of Jean Ferron about eighteen months old"*. The last baptism registered at Rivière-Du-Loup was that of Claude, born and baptized on 18 June 1759. His godfather and godmother were Claude Minaut and Louise Genon. All through his life, this Claude would almost always be present at the various events of the members of his family.

In 1759 and 1760, New France experienced some tragic events which inevitably led to its defeat. Rivière-du-Loup witnessed the activities of the soldiers on the Saint-Lawrence, but the soldiers engaged in combat in more strategic places like Montréal and Québec.

"In order to meet the needs of the troops and to reduce the shortage of food", wrote Father Germain Lesage,(7) *"the farmers who were not conscripted into the militia had to apply themselves to their work. And we can believe that the authorities demanded a larger yield from a seigneurie where, according to Bougainville, the lands were good, fertile and were not difficult to clear. But it was the end of New France. The residents of Rivière-du-Loup were able to take part in the last act of the defeat.*

"On 11 and 12 August 1760, the forty-six vessels of the enemy fleet did manoeuvres on Lac Saint-Pierre before passing, almost without firing a shot, by the fortifications at Sorel. We soon learned that Montréal had capitulated. And beginning on 14 September, we saw British ships come on the lake carrying the chevalier's troops to Québec from Lévis which was irreparably conquered".

AT YAMACHICHE

In the meantime, the Ferron family had put down roots at Yamachiche where seigneur Louis Boucher de Grandpré had just granted a concession to Ancestor Jean, who was still living at Rivière-du-Loup. The contract was drawn up by the notary Louis Pillard (8) in his study at Trois-Rivières during the afternoon of 5 November 1759, in the presence of the witnesses Pierre Talusier, wigmaker, and Joseph Chevalier, gunsmith. The seigneur Boucher, captain in the troops of the Mississippi, was absent, but he was represented by his agent Jean-Baptiste Fafard dit Laframboise, bourgeois from Trois-Rivières. Jean Ferron did not have to pay anything right now in order to take possession of the said land, except that he was committed to pay the cens and seigneurial rents *"for land and non-redeemables"*.

The concession, 25 arpents deep, had three arpents in frontage on the Rivière-du-Loup. On the northeast side lived his immediate neighbor Guillaume Solo; to the northwest stretched the lands not ceded; at the end of the 25 arpents stood the primeval forest of full grown trees. Jean Ferron accepted this land *"for him his heirs and assigns in the future to use, make and dispose as all property";* he said he knew the property well because he had visited it and said he was content and satisfied with it. Each year, he had to pay the seigneur the amount of six livres and ten sols in seigneurial rent, the first payment had to be made on 11 November of the following year and continue his annual contribution into perpetuity.

Ferron was also committed to clear his land, cultivate it, build a habitable house, to have a home there, to give open land to his neighbors as required, to provide and maintain on his concession the roads deemed necessary for public use according to the regulations of the place and the roadways, and to take his grain to the seigneurial mill to be ground, as soon as the mill is built. The landlord kept for himself, finally, the right to cut the wood necessary for the construction of the church, the seigneurial manor house and the mill.

Now a colonist and farmer, Jean Ferron continued to fulfill his conjugal duty.

1. Marie-Julienne was born during the night of 20 to 21 February 1762. The godfather and godmother were Augustin Girardin and Marie Lesieur; the pastor Maxime Chef de Ville-dc-la-Garenne administered the sacrament to her. Marie-Julienne only lived for three years and three months. She was buried on 8 June 1765 under the name of Marie-Louise.

2. Meanwhile, on 16 September 1764, two children were baptized during the same ceremony, a boy and girl. The boy, Marie-Joseph Ferron whose godparents were Maurice Melanson and Marie-Joseph Gaudet. This Marie-Joseph also must have died in childhood.

3. The girl, Angélique would be more fortunate. She was brought to the church on 24 March 1766 to be baptized. (9) She lived long enough to be married twice.

4. Baptized on 25 November 1768, Michel had as his godfather and godmother Michel Lacourse and Marie Blaye. Another short life, it seems.

5.   Rosalie appeared on the first of March 1770. Her god-father and godmother were Charles Fortier and Marie-Anne Comeau. Rosalie was married three times before her death.

6.   Jean-Baptiste, the eleventh and last child of Jean Ferron and Marie Bibaut, was baptized on 29 January 1773. (10) He would be father of at least ten children.

The numerous gaps in the registries of Yamachiche leave us unaware of the destiny of the remaining progeny.

DEATH OF MARIE AND REMARRIAGE OF JEAN

Of the eleven children of Marie Bibaut, only five sur-vived: François, Claude, Angélique, Rosalie and Jean-Baptiste. After her death, Jean Ferron began the search for another mother for his children. Once again, his choice fell on a person twice as young as he, or nearly so, Marie-Charlotte Pépin, born at Char-lesbourg on 29 November 1751, had not yet been born at the time of the first marriage of the man who courted her.   This daughter of Pierre Pépin and Marie-Joseph Verret had moved with her family after the death of her mother in 1754. The mar-riage took place on 18 February 1776.   Three days earlier, ac-companied by the notary Benoit Leroi. Jean appeared at the home of his future father-in-law to formalize the terms of his second marriage. It was there that he revealed that he had been born at Reffuveille, diocese of Avranches, in Normandie.   He was 48 years old and his fiancee had the freshness of her 25 years. The future husband and wife promised to have their marriage celebrated in *"our Holy mother Church"* as soon as possible and stated that they would live in community property according to the *coutume de Paris*.   Marie-Charlotte agreed to take care of Jean's children and to raise them in the fear of God, and to assist them with her good advice and counsel.

This second marriage gave Jean Ferron the opportunity to contribute once again to the revenge of the cradle. Nine more children would come, each in his or her own turn,   to enliven the home with their murmurs or their whimpers. Five sons were followed by four daughters.

1.   Pierre, the eldest of the second marriage, was baptized at Yamachiche on 23 November 1776. He had for his godfather and godmother Pierre Pépin and Marguerite Grignier (Grenier).

2.   He was followed by Joseph-Charles, baptized at Yamachiche on 27 May 1778 whose godparents were Joseph Pépin and Louise Duvivier.

On 7 June 1779, a first marriage was celebrated among the children. François, the eldest son of the family, took a wife at Lanoraie. Her name was Victoire Janot, born in 1760, daughter of Jean-Baptiste and Elisabeth Desmarest. François then left his loved ones to settle at Saint-Sulpice. It was there that he and Victoire were buried a few days apart in 1827, he on 22 November, she eight days later.

3.   Augustin, the third son of Charlotte Pépin, born on 12 April 1780 and baptized the following day at Yamachiche, had as his godfather and his godmother his brother Claude and Suzanne Venner, wife of Pierre Grenier.

4.   Louis, Charlotte's fourth son, was born and baptized on 24 September 1782. His godparents were Augustin Gaudin and Josephte Heroux.

The next day, on the 25th, it was Claude's turn to prepare for his marriage. He had a meeting with the notary Benoit Leroi, whom he asked to draw up the terms of his commitment to the 15 year old Thérèse Noel, originally from Maskinonge. She was the daughter of François Noel and Agathe Tessier. Claude stated that he owned a piece of land which had been ceded to him by the honorable Conrad Gugy, Seigneur of Yamachiche. This land, which he said was not very developed, was placed into the community property that he was forming with Thérèse. The actual wedding was celebrated on 30 September at Yamachiche, where the two families were living, by the pastor Laurent Bertrand.   In her burial act recorded in the registry of Yamachiche on the first of October 1854, Thérèse was said to be 89 years old and the widow of Claude Ferron. She had died two days before. Claude had preceded her to the grave on 11 May 1837. He had died two days before.

71

5.   Jacques, the last son, was baptized on 14 May 1785. Jacques Blais and Marie Maheu, widow of François Gagnon, appeared at his baptism to act as godfather and godmother.

The four daughters were born afterwards:

6.   Marie, baptized at Rivière-du-Loup, on 30 June 1787; (11)

7.   Rosalie, born on the 21st and baptized at Yamachiche on 22 November 1789 (godfather and godmother, François Lamy and Rosalie Ferron, the infant's sister); this Rosalie was buried on 3 August 1791. We do not know the destiny of Jacques or Marie.

8.   Marie-Joseph dite Marie was born and baptized at Yamachiche on 30 July 1792; her godfather and godmother were her brother Jean and Marie-Louise Servan.

9.   As for Josephte dite Rose, she was the last to leave her mother, now a widow and remarried. We are unaware of awareof her birth date.

When Marie-Joseph was born in 1792, Jean Ferron began his 75th year. For more than 40 years, the cradle which had rocked his twenty children was barely empty. The time to retire finally came in the following year. The rest which Providence reserved for him was an eternal one. Death knocked on his door on 12 April 1793. Two days later, the parishioners of Yamachiche came to pay him a final and respectful homage. The pastor Thomas Kember (12) wrote the following note in the parish registry:

> *"The year one thousand seven hundred ninety-three on the fourteenth of April by me undersigned priest buried in the cemetery of this parish the body of Jean Baptiste Feront husband of Marie Pépin, died on the twelfth, fortified with the assistance of the Church about seventy-five years old, present Joseph Caron, Joseph Cheyer who did not know how to sign."*

Shortly before the death of their father, two other daughters had decided to leave home and take husbands.

1.	Angélique had succumbed to the charms of a fine German, Sébastien Welfert, son of Sébastien and of Catherine Kirinine. She was married at Rivière-du-Loup on 15 September 1788. In order to allow this marriage, a certificate of liberty had been issued by messire Augustin Hubert, curate at Québec. Born in 1753, Sébastien was laid to rest at Saint-Leon on 16 September 1817. Some eight years later, on 30 January 1826, in the same parish, Angélique was remarried, to Jean-Baptiste Jalbert. In a first marriage, he had married Marie-Rose Dubé, at Saint-Roche-des-Aulnaies, on 11 January 1779. Jean-Baptiste was buried at Saint-Leon on 14-October 1839, having died two days before at the respectable age of about 90, according to the act, an age somewhat inflated since he had been born in 1755. Angélique in her turn was buried in the same place on 19 June 1844. She had died the day before.

2.	For her part, Rosalie was married three times. The first time on 19 September 1792, to Joseph Colin dit Laliberte, a *coureur des bois*, son of Joseph and of Marie-Veronique Tessier. Some twenty years later, Joseph died accidentally during a journey to the West, as reported by the pastor Charles Ecuyer when on 2 June 1814, Rosalie was married a second time, to the Acadian Alexis Aucoin, widower of Marie-Anne Lemaitre-Auger. Colin drowned on 11 May 1813, in the Detroit River, according to a statement made by two eye witnesses in the presence of James Frank, justice of the peace at Soulanges. In a third marriage, on 11 April 1825 at Saint-Leon, Rosalie was married to Jean-Marie Ouellette, widower of Rose Martineau dite Saintonge. The marriage act drawn up by the priest Louis Delaunay indicated that the wife had been living at Saint-Leon for nearly eight months. It was in this same parish that Rosalie was buried on the first of April 1841. She died two days before at the age of 62, according to the record. In reality, she was eight years older.

After the death of Ancestor Jean, some six years passed before another son crossed the Rubicon of marriage. This time, it was Pierre, the eldest son of Marie-Charlottte, who took a wife. On 8 April 1799 at Yamachiche, he married Marie Stuart, daughter of Pierre, a farmer at Rivière-du-Loup, and of Marie Laricherrière. When her children were born, between 1799 and 1808, curiously, this Marie most often bore the last name of Normand.   Pierre died at Saint-Leon, on 15 December 1861 and was buried two days later, at the age of 86.   The burial act reveals that he was a widower.

On 13 January 1800, it was Jean-Baptiste's turn to take a wife.   Six days earlier, he had gone to Rivière-du-Loup to meet with the notary Antoine Gagnon who drew up his marriage contract with the 17 year old Marie Gauthier, daughter of Louis (absent) and of the late Marie Langevin, of Yamachiche.   Marie was assisted by her godfather Didace Rivard and Michel Lemay, her friend and benefactor, who stated he thought of the bride as his own daughter, since he was the one who had raised her.   The curate Thomas Kember presided at the wedding.   Jean-Baptiste died at Yamachiche on 29 June 1847 and was buried there on the first of July.   Marie Gauthier was married a second time on 16 February 1849, to Louis Boucher, widower of Angélique Blais.

Joseph-Charles, more often called Joseph, was the next son to meet with the notary Gagnon on 28 October 1804, at Rivière-du-Loup in order to have him settle the terms of his marriage contract with Catherine Grenier, daughter of Étienne and of Marguerite Lavigne.   His brothers Claude, Jean, Pierre, Augustin and Louis, and his sisters Rose and Marie were present at his wedding celebrated on 5 November and presided over by the curate Charles Ecuyer.   This family settled at Saint-Leon.   It was there that Joseph and Catherine were buried: he on 19 September 1845 (he had died two days before), she on 26 December 1857 (she had died two days earlier, at the age of 80).

REMARRIAGE OF MARIE-CHARLOTTE

Alone more and more, Marie-Charlotte decided to plunge into another matrimonial adventure.   In 1805, she agreed to share her life with Charles Crochetière.   On 18 November, they went to the notary Antoine Gagnon to set the terms of their engagement. Her man was the widower of Marianne Normandeau, the village blacksmith.   He agreed to take under his guardianship Marie and Rose Ferron, the two daughters who still lived with their mother. He was committed to feed, clothe and support them at the expense of the marriage he was forming with his future wife.   The wedding was celebrated a week later on 25 November in the church of Yamachiche in the presence of several friends and relatives.

And life continued. Marie-Joseph dite Marie, the youngest, did not delay in finding herself a husband. On 6 August 1807, the notary Charles Pratte went to her home to write her marriage contract to Joseph Blais, widower of Marie Valcour. The young girl, who had just celebrated her 15th birthday, was accompanied by her step-father Charles Crochetiére. Marie would receive a dowry of 300 livres *"or shellings of 20 coppes"* and a preciput of 150 livres secured by the future groom if he survives, or by the rings and jewelry of the future bride if she lives the longest. It was also understood that Marie Blais, daughter from Joseph's first marriage, would be raised, fed, supported and educated in the Catholic religion by the future wife until her age of majority. The wedding, presided by messire Charles Ecuyer, took place on 24 August at Yamachiche in the presence of members of the two families. Marie-Joseph died on the first of May 1821 and was buried at Rivière-du-Loup two days later. The burial act said she was about forty years old.

In 1808, Augustin decided to end his bachelor days. On 27 January, he went to the notary Pratte, at Rivière-du-Loup, in order to finalize his marriage contract with Elisabeth Deziel dite Labreche, daughter of Jean and of Angélique Lampron-Lacharité, from Maskinonge. It was in this parish that the marriage took place on the first of February. The pastor Ignace-Prudent Vinet-Souligny received the couple's mutual consent. Augustin kept an inn and canteen at Yamachiche. He died there on 27 May 1842 and was buried two days later.

In 1815, Louis went to find a wife at Saint-Sulpice, where, for more than 35 years, his brother François had lived. He chose a young widow, Louise Arbour, married in a first marriage to Claude Beaupré. The wedding took place on 30 October. François was present for the ceremony, as well as Antoine Ferron, his nephew. Messire Pierre-René Joyer (13) received their mutual consent. Louis was practicing the trade of cabinetmaker at that time. It was to Yamachiche that he brought his bride and it was there that he died on 21 November 1838 and where he was laid to rest the following day. He was 56 years old.

On 5 August 1826, Augustin Saint-Pierre, accompanied by notary Pierre Bazin, went to meet Josephte Ferron at her home, the last daughter of Marie-Charlotte Pépin to leave the maternal home. On that day of the betrothal, the clerk explained

75

the contract for the future marriage. The document reveals that Augustin's parents were dead. He had chosen his brother Charles as witness, while Josephte dite Rose selected her mother and her brother Augustin to fulfill the same role. The wedding was celebrated at Yamachiche on 14 August by the priest Sévère-Nicolas Dumoulin, in the presence of friends and relatives, including Antoine Bergeron, Louis Hébert, Jean Ferron and Pierre Saint-Pierre.

THE LAST KNELL

After the marriage of Josephte dite Rose, events hurried along. On 12 February 1829, the knell tolled in the belltower of the church of Yamachiche announcing the death, the day before, of Charles Crochetière, second husband of Marie-Charlotte Pépin.

Son of our ancestor Claude Croisetière, originally from Saint-Barthelemy de La Rochelle, and Marie-Jeanne Provost, Charles had been baptized at Québec on 18 January 1740. He was married successively, to Geneviève-Veronique Levasseur and Marie-Anne Normandeau before marrying Marie-Charlotte in 1805. He was 88 years old, not 94 as stated in his burial act.

Marie-Charlotte soon followed him to the grave. For her, the knell sounded again less than two years later and the presiding priest Louis-Onesime Desilets recorded in the parish registry the following act:

> "The tenth of November 1830 we undersigned priest have buried in the cemetery of this parish the body of Marie Pépin, wife of the late Charles Crochier (sic), day laborer during his lifetime, died the day before yesterday, at the age of eighty-four, present at the burial were Joseph Amel and François Allaire who stated not to know how to sign."

Poor Marie had also been aged by a few years, as often happened in that era. In fact, she only needed a few days to reach her 79th birthday. But it's of little importance. A few years more or less in the curriculum vitae of ordinary people does not usually change the important things about their family.

76

The preceding pages describe, perhaps imperfectly, the beginning of the family of Jean Ferron, the most important to bear this last name in America. Many descendants of this ancestor made their mark in different fields, notably in the arts, painting, literature, medicine, agriculture, law and religion. It all began at Yamachiche, where Jean and his family chose to live.

FAMILY NAME VARIATIONS

The only known variations of Ferron are Verron and Sanscerre.

END NOTES

1) Albert Dauzat, DENFPF. Larousse - Selection. Volume 3, 1969. p.2085.

2) M.L. d'Armagnac del Cer, Count de Puymége. "Les vieux noms de la France de l'Ouest et les familles d'origine française au-dela des mers" p.278 & 279.

3) Immediately after his ordination, on 20 September 1749, the Bishop of Québec, Msgr de Pontbriand, was assigned to be the pastor of Saint-Antoine de la Rivière-du-Loup and of Saint-Joseph de Maskinonge. He carried out these duties until 1757. Born at Lévis on 27 October 1722, Louis-Michel was the son of Michel Guay and of Marguerite Grenet. Later on he was appointed curé of Sainte-Anne-de-la-Pérade. He died there on 19 June 1785 after having been pastor of this parish for a quarter of a century.

4) Nine days later, this contract would be recorded in the records of d'Élie-François Rigaud at Maskinonge.

5) "Mélanges historiques", Volume 6, p.109 & 110.

6) The years 1755 and 1756 were never microfilmed from the registers of Rivière-du-Loup. These records are mentioned in the general indices of the same registries.

7) "Histoire de Louiseville 1665-1960", Louiseville 1961, p.98.

8)   Louis Pillard (1710-1767) was originally from Paris. He became the notary of the Royal Jurisdiction of Trois-Rivières for 30 years.

9 & 10)   Records mentioned by François Lesieur-Desaulniers in "Les vieilles famillies d'Yamachiche". Tome IV, p.35.

11)   From a record mentioned in the index of registers from this parish.

12)   Joseph Kember, the father of Thomas, was originally from Germany. Born at Québec in 1758 and ordained in 1781, Thomas was the pastor at Yamachiche from 1788 until 1802. He died on 19 January 1832.

13)   Born and ordained in France in 1764 and 1787, the Abbot René-Pierre Joyer was an exile from the French revolution. He had, among others, exercised his ministry at Ancienne-Lorette (1796-1798), Saint-Sulpice (1806-1815), Pointe-du-Lac (1817-1820), and at the Ursuline home in Trois-Rivières (1829-1831). He died at Montréal on 19 January 1841.

Ouverture des Forges St-Maurice – 15 octobre 1737

Jacques Froment

CHAPTER 5

Jacques Froment

rontenac returned to France in 1682, leaving the colony practically defenseless against the Iroquois. In his turn, his successor, Lefebvre de La Barre, stated that it was impossible for him to subdue the enemy with only the troops at his disposal. He was successful, however, in convincing Louis XIV that he needed to equip New France with a permanent army. On 7 November 1683, the new governor welcomed at Québec the first 150 soldiers of *la Marine*, who had just crossed the ocean on the frigate *"La Tempete"*. The voyage had been very difficult during which 19 recruits had died at sea. Thus began quite humbly the odyssey of the troops of la Marine in Canada. Several thousand troops would be sent from France during the following decades. They would soon be placed into 28 companies which would only be divided with the arrival of Montcalm and his battalions in 1756.

A great number of soldiers of la Marine never went back to the mother country. Lands had been promised to them and, after falling in love with the local girls, they decided to embrace a new career, that of colonist. Hard work awaited them, sometimes poverty, but they decided just the same that it was more advantageous to remain here, considering the uncertain fate that awaited them in France. About 1715, perhaps a little earlier, when the soldier Jacques Froment arrived among us, the situation had somewhat improved. It was no longer the Iroquois who presented the worst danger, but the English from New England who threatened to invade the French colony. And one of these paths of possible invasion was the Richelieu River.

"The Richelieu river, wrote the historian Jacques Lacoursiére, (1) *with the Saint-Lawrence river, comprises the principal path of invasion into the country. The burning of Fort Chambly by the Iroquois in 1702*

81

weakened the defensive system of this region...As a result, the leaders of the colony asked for 20,000 livres in funding to rebuild it in stone. The reconstruction of Fort Chambly stretched from 1709 to 1711."

At that era, in order to reduce the expenses of their stay and to support the army, many soldiers, always ready to intervene, found shelter with the families of the colonists.

"The soldier was quickly drawn to the life of the country, noted the historian Jean Leclerc.(2) He had a good relationship with the inhabitants. Since they were distant from each other due to the great size of their land, the inhabitants saw in the soldier a companion for work and for social life. Laborers being rare, the soldier was welcomed for his work on the land notably the harvest, the threshing, the cutting. The habitant gave him between 15 and 30 sols per day, which made an encouraging salary in relationship to the prevailing wage in the army. In the Canadian homes, the soldier often met his life's companion. The king encourages him to marry and settle in Canada. For this purpose, he gives him a piece of land which is still large in comparison to the parcels that he could obtain in France, the land also has varied resources: wood of all species, grain, fruit, large and small livestock, fishing and hunting, with exemption from the tax and the head tax, which augments his income, land which allows him to live comfortably provided that work and ingenuity are part of the effort. He allows him to draw his annual pay for the first year, to keep his military uniform...These few benefits and encouragements soon had a deciding effect."

A LEGITIMATE DAUGHTER

In 1715, Jacques Froment seems to have already stayed at Saint-Sulpice, perhaps with the family of his future bride, or in the neighborhood. The Richelieu River flowed a few kilometers from there, on the other side of the Saint-Laurent river.

Two years later, Jacques was ready to set up a home. He had gotten a head start, because he admitted being the father of a six-month old daughter, whom he now had to make legitimate. The marriage act drawn up by the Sulpicien Pierre Le Sueur recorded this early birth: (3)

> *"On the twentieth of October of the same year (1717) were married, after dispensing with three banns, Jacques Froment soldier son of Pierre Froment and Marie Cavalier of the parish of LaDouee diocese of Cahors, and Elisabeth Lescarbot daughter of Jean Lescarbot and Anne Baudouin, residents of St-Sulpice, in the presence of monsieur du Vivier captain and monsieur Louis du Vivier, Guillaume Lescarbot, Jean Lescarbot, witnesses. Also present were Marie-Charlotte six months old, legitimate daughter of the soldier Jacques Froment and Elisabeth Lescarbot who are recognized."*

The parish of "La Douee" mentioned in this act was none other than that of Douelle, located in the neighborhood of Cahors, a region in the Midi-Pyrenees, department of Lot, quite near the Spanish border.

> *"The sterile chalky causses, the numerous grottos, the picturesque "avens", form the major part of this territory. These regions, the quaintness of which attracts numerous tourists, only supports a sparse population for whom the main resource is the raising of sheep and the making of cheese. Narrow and deep valleys wind between the causses* (a type of chalky plateau). *At Douelle, we can still find the remains of buildings from the*

*thirteenth and fourteenth centuries and a
chateau from the Renaissance.   The community is located on a bend of the river Lot,
which gets its source in the mountains of
Goulet and empties into the Garonne."* (4)

The two messieurs Du Vivier who were witnesses to the
marriage at that time owned lands in the seigneurie of Saint-
Sulpice. Henri-Jules Le Fournier, Sieur Du Vivier (1666-1738)
had been a lieutenant, then a captain of a company in a detachment of the Marine. Son of Jacques Le Fournier, first exempt
(police officer) of the Prince de Conde guards, and of Marguerite
Le Carpentier, he had lived at Montréal for a few years at the
time of the marriage of Jacques Froment. His son Louis, born in
1695, was still a bachelor in 1717. (5)

Elisabeth Lescarbot, the wife of Jacques Froment, was the
third of fifteen children born to the union of Jean Lescarbot dit
Beauceron and Anne Baudouin. As his surname indicates, Jean
was originally from the Beauce, more precisely from Châteaudun
(Eure-et-Loir) and his wife was the daughter of Jean Baudouin
and Marie-Charlotte Chauvin, from the parish of Saint-Martin de
La Jarrie, near La Rochelle, in Aunis (Charente-Maritime).

CONCESSION FROM THE SULPECIENS

Settled in the seigneurie of Saint-Sulpice for at least two
or three years, it was normal that the Sulpicien seigneurs finally
ceded to Jacques Froment a piece of land in this place. The event
occurred on the first of September 1718, in a contract drafted by
Pierre Raimbault. During the afternoon on this day, in the study
of the notary, gathered for the occasion were François Vachon de
Belmont, priest from the Saint-Sulpice seminary in Paris, superior of the seminary of Ville-Marie and administrator of messire
François Leschassier, superior of the Saint-Sulpice seminary in
Paris, as well as messire François Citoys de Chaumeaux,
secretary and treasurer of the seminary of Ville-Marie, the seigneurs ceded by means of the cens, from then and for always, to
Jacques Froment, living on the Saint-Sulpice coast a dependency
of the island of Montréal, present and accepting, about six arpents in frontage by twenty deep, between the end of the homesteads of the named Jean-Baptiste Belair and (René) David, as far
as four arpents long, to begin at the stream and running towards

84

the Saint-Laurent River following the alignments which were given to him. Froment had to pay the seigneurs, each year, a half-minot of wheat *"good, clean, genuine and marketable"* for each twenty arpents of area, the first payment due on 11 November 1719, the said *"cens with profit, lots and vente, saisine and amendes when the matter is due according to the Coutume de Paris."*

The tenant was required to clear the said land, to build a home on it, to help clear the wilderness of his neighbors as they need it, to have his grain ground at the mill of the seigneurs, on penalty of having the said grain confiscated and with an arbitrary fine, and to pay the milling rights for the grain which he would have ground elsewhere. Froment had also to *"tolerate"* all the roads which the seigneurs would find appropriate to open, among others a large road *"suitable for the passage of carts"*. Finally, the seigneurs kept for themselves the right to take from the concession the wood which they would need for their buildings. The contract bore the signature of François Vachon de Belmont, François Citoys de Chaumeaux, witnesses Ignace Gamelin and Jean-Baptiste Hervieux, and that of the notary Raimbault.

TRANSACTION WITH THE LESCARBOTS

Some five years later, on 31 August 31 1723, while traveling to Saint-Sulpice, the notary Nicolas Senet stopped at the home of the widow of Jean Lescarbot, where Jacques Froment and his wife stated they had decided to sell jointly to Guillaume Lescarbot, Elisabeth's brother, a continuation of the concession located at Saint-Sulpice, consisting of three arpents in width by 40 deep, bordering on one side the concession of the late René David and on the other side the lands not ceded. This property, contiguous to that of the sellers, who said they had acquired it from the seigneurs of Montréal in a contract signed in the presence of Pierre Raimbault, was ceded to the buyer on the condition that he pay the cens and rents on 11 November of each year, and 50 livres, 20 of them payable on Easter and 30 on All Saint's Day of the following year. Guillaume thus committed himself to clear the same amount on the sellers' concession as he finds today: four arpents. The witnesses Gilles Marin and Henry Bellisle, master surgeon, signed the act with the notary Senet.

On 8 November 1728, the same clerk intervened for another transaction carried out between the members of the same family. This time, the parties appeared at the home of the notary Senet during the morning of the said day, in his study located in the town of Pointe-aux-Trembles. Jacques Froment and his wife agreed to sell to Pierre Lescarbot, another brother of Elisabeth, all their rights, claims, titles, reasons and actions which they could have and claim on the half of the concession located at Saint-Sulpice, which came to them through the death of the late Jean Lescarbot their father and the said part and portion of the said half of the concession located in the censive of messieurs the seigneurs of Montréal, charged with cens and rents, and seigniorial rights, according to the *Coutume de Paris*. The deal was concluded for 200 livres payable in silver or wheat at the price that it would be worth at the time of the delivery, namely 100 livres this year and 100 livres the following year. Two residents of Pointe-aux-Trembles, François Baudry and Jean Raynaud, signed the act with the notary.

Finally, on 5 March 1731, a last act recorded with the notary Senet and drafted in the hand of the Sulpicien Benoit Baret, (6) corrected an error which had been slipped into the contract written by the same notary on 31 August 1723. Guillaume Lescarbot and Jacques Froment stated that the continuation of land in question did not measure 40 arpents in depth, but instead 20, because this was all that remained of the said concession. This act informs us that Guillaume had settled on his lot and that he wanted, by this correction, to avoid any future lawsuit. On the same occasion, Froment said he was satisfied with the payment that he had received from his brother-in-law. Between Froment and the Lescarbots, there seems to exist good harmony and a peaceful fraternal agreement.

THE CHILDREN

1.   Let's recall that at the time of the marriage, on 20 October 1717, Marie-Charlotte, the eldest daughter was present and already six months old. She had been baptized at Saint-Sulpice on the preceding 14 April. On 8 January 1748, Marie-Charlotte was married at the age of 30, to Pierre Caderon, son of Pierre Caderon dit Saint-Pierre and of Marie-Madeleine Soulange, from Lavaltrie.

Marie-Charlotte had at least four children in this parish. Pierre died there on 26 February 1785 and was laid to rest the next day.   Marie-Charlotte soon followed him to the grave: she succumbed in her turn on 28 May 1787 and was buried two days later, at the age of 70.

2.   Marie-Rose was born and baptized on 8 August 1719.   On 4 June 1736, she joined her destiny to that of Jean Laurence, son of Nicolas and of Marie-Madeleine Magneron.   The children of this couple were born at Lavaltrie.   Joseph was buried at Repentigny on 27 December 1778; Marie-Rose died in her native land, the place of her burial on 4 September 1794.   She was 75 years old.

3.   Marie-Thérèse, born on the 13th and baptized on 14 June 1721.   Died on the 15th and buried on 16 August 1721, at the age of two months.

4.   Louise-Agathe, born and baptized on 8 September 1722, was married twice.   First, on 10 April 1741, to Gabriel Laporte, son of Paul and of Marguerite Matou dit Labrie;   she was remarried at Saint-Sulpice on 21 February 1746, to Jean-Baptiste Roberge,   son of Joseph and of Marie Lemelin,   from Saint-Laurent, Ile d'Orléans.   Jean Baptiste and Louise-Agathe died at Saint-Sulpice; he, on 25 September 1755 (33 years old); she, on 21 January 1770 (47 years old).

5.   Marie-Thérèse, baptized on 2 May 1724; buried on 2 June 1724 (one month old).

6.   Elisabeth, born and baptized on 3 September 1725; buried on 28 November 1727 (two years and two months old).

7.   Louis, born and baptized on 13 August 1728; died and buried on the first of September 1728 (two weeks old).

8.   François, born on the 16th and baptized on 17 September 1729.   Married at Lavaltrie on 30 June 1755, to Marie-Thecle Mandeville, daughter of Pierre and of Dorothée Pelletier-Antaya. This family lived at Lavaltrie, Repentigny and Saint-Sulpice, where François was buried on 2 November 1790.   Since he was the only son of Jacques to marry, all the Froments also descend from him.   He was a verger for several years.

9.   Joseph-Sulpice, born on 13 January 1732, died four days later.

We notice that five of the nine children died in the cradle. The others married and had children.   At the beginning of the twentieth century, Alcide and Léopold Froment counted among the pioneers of Morinville, in Alberta.   Their progeny is numerous.

THE CENSUS OF 1725

On 25 February 1725, messire Louis Normand, priest of the Saint-Sulpice seminary in Montréal, in the name of and as proxy of messire Lechasseur, superior of the Saint-Sulpice seminary of Paris, paid faith and homage for the seigneurie of Saint-Sulpice. He described the property of Jacques Froment in these terms:

> "At the end of the depth of the land of the said Belair, Jacques Froment also owns three arpents of frontal land by twenty arpents in depth, charged with thirty sols and one and a half minots of wheat for the cens and rents, he has a house, barn, stable and nine arpents of plowable land."

The Froments' immediate neighbors were Jean-Baptiste Belair, one named Deguire, the heirs of René David and Guillaume Lescarbot. (7)

DEATH OF JACQUES AND ELISABETH

Jacques Froment died at Saint-Sulpice, his adopted land, at the end of the spring of 1747. His burial record drafted by the Sulpicen Pierre Sartelon reads as follows:(8)

> "The year one thousand seven hundred forty-seven the eleventh day of June, I, missionary priest fulfilling the duties of priest in the parish of St-Sulpice, the undersigned buried in the cemetery with the usual ceremonies the body of Jacques Froment, the

*eighty-five years old husband of Elisabeth
Lescarbot and the son of the late Pierre Froment and Marie Cavalier his father and
mother of the parish of La Douel diocese of
Cahors in the presence of Louis Masse who
signed."*

Elisabeth Lescarbot survived him for some fifteen years.
Shortly before her death, she had time to initiate the sale of two
parcels of family land, according to contracts drawn up by Joseph
Daguilhe, notary residing at L'Assomption.

On 29 December 1761, she sold to her daughter Agathe,
widow of Jean-Baptiste Roberge, half of the land which she had
inherited from her late husband, an arpent and a half in frontage
by twenty deep. Located on the small coast of Saint-Sulpice, this
property comprised of half of a house and a barn in poor condition. On 3 February 1762, in the presence of the same notary,
she also sold to Pierre Guillebert dit Lefrançois, a resident of the
Saint-Sulpice coast, a strip 77 feet wide by the same depth of
twenty arpents.

Two months later, Elisabeth went to join her husband in
eternity. Another Sulpicien, Jean Matis, recorded her burial in
the following manner:

*"The fifth of April one thousand seven
hundred sixty two was buried in the cemetery
of this parish (Saint-Sulpice) the body of
Elisabeth Lescarbot about eighty years old,
who died the day before. Witnesses were
François Froment and Benoit Morin who
stated not to know how to sign."*

"Frumentum" or wheat was the staple food of the Roman
armies. The soldier Jacques Froment thus bore a predestined
name. The word *"froment"*, frequently used by poets, was introduced into French literature nearly a thousand years ago. Froment, is a celebrated principle and harmomious symbol in all the
countries of the world. Froment, spiritual and temporal food
which sustains the soul by the transsubstantiation of the bread of
the Eucharist, and it satisfies the body through the bread which
accompanies our daily meals.

FAMILY NAME VARIATIONS

The only known variation to Froment is Freeman.

END NOTES

1) <u>"Histoire populaire du Québec - des origines a 1791"</u>. tome 1, Septentrion, 1995 - Une rivière a surveiller, p. 204 and 205.

2) <u>"Le marquis de Denonville, gouverneur de la Nouvelle-France 1685-1689"</u>. Fides, 1976, p.97-98.

3) Founder of the city of Assomption, born in France in 1684 and died at Montréal in 1752. Arrived here in 1710. He was the first resident priest of Saint-Sulpice in 1715. This was at that time the only parish in the seigneurie by the same name.

4) Encyclopedie Leland, Vol.11, p.3469 & 3470; Vol. 6, p. 1735.

5) Cyprien Tanguay <u>"DGFC"</u>, Vol. 1, p.368; Vol. V, p. 289.

6) Messire Benoit Baret, arrived in Canada in 1718 and served at Notre-Dame de Montréal before he became the curé at Saint-Sulpice. He occupied this function from 1724 until his return to France in 1731.

7) <u>RAPQ</u> 1949-1951, p. 97.

8) Born in France in 1708, Pierre Sartelon had been ordained at the home of the Sulpiciens in 1734. Then he was successively pastor of Sainte-Anne-de-Bellevue (1735-1740), Saint-Sulpice (1740-1755), Longue-Point (1755), Saint-Laurent (1755-1758), Sainte-Anne-de-Bellevue (1758-1768), Pointe-Claire (1768-1781). He died at the Hotel-Dieu of Montréal on 4 November 1782.

9) Born in France in 1701, Jean Matis was ordained at the Sulpiciens in 1726. He was the pastor at Sainte-Anne-de-Bellevue (1728), Saint-Laurent (1730-1731), Again at Bellevue (1731-1734), Louisville with duties at Yamachiche (1734-1735), Saint-Laurent again (1735-1755), Saint-Sulpice (1757-1768). He died on 4 January 1769.

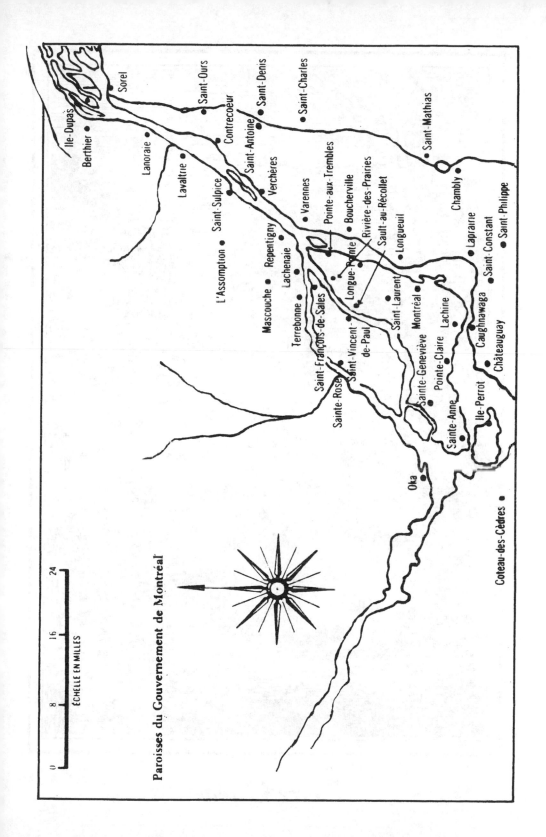

Paroisses du Gouvernement de Montréal

Pierre Guénet

CHAPTER 6

Pierre Guenet

 woman, and none other, was the first Guenet to tread the soil of America: Marie, born at Rouen on 28 October 1610, from the marriage of Roger Guenet, councilor at the parliament, and Anne Desloges. On 4 May 1639, with her Augustine nursing sister companions, Anne Le Cointre and Marie Forestier, she embarked at Dieppe on the flagship *Saint-Joseph* to undertake a crossing which was going to last more than three months. The first Ursulines, including Marie Guyart de l'Incarnation, travelled with them. The passengers debarked at Québec on the first of August and were welcomed by Governor Huault de Montmagny and an enthusiastic crowd. Upon their arrival, these brave women were subjected to a harsh ordeal. An epidemic of small pox was raging among the native people and soon the church, the governor's chapel and the Jesuit's house were prey to flames. Marie Guenet dite Saint-Ignace, first superior of her small convent at Québec, died of exhaustion on 5 November 1646, saying: *"My god, may Your will be done! I belong to You."* (1)

In 1664, the Sovereign Council of New France proceeded with settling the men sent by the king on board the ship *Le Noir de Hollande.* Among the first 50 arrivals, and the 250 who followed, was a merchant named Guenet or Quenet who could indeed have been the one with the first name of Jean, originally from Rouen, who was married at Montréal in 1675 to Etiennette Hurtubise, who gave him thirteen children. This Jean Guenet was controller of the king's farms in 1700. (2)

FROM PICARDY

Marie and Jean Guenet were originally from Normandy. The family of Pierre Guenet (sometimes called Ganet or Quenet) lived, according to them, in the neighboring province of Picardy, more precisely in the parish of Saint-Martin, diocese of Soissons. It was probably Saint-Martin-Rivière, whose patron Saint Martinus de Riveria, lived in the twelfth century. (3) This community, located nearly equal distance from Le Cateau to the north, and from Wassigny, to the south, was in the department of l'Aisne, quite near Cambrai. This town has a belfry, also called Saint-Martin, which dates from the twelfth century. Dotted by chalky plains and calcareous plateaus, this region is scored with a great number of waterways with canals which allow boats to pass unimpeded.

The first mention of Pierre Guenet in New France was his inscription in the registry of Sainte-Famille on the Ile d'Orléans on the occasion of his marriage celebrated on 19 May 1675. It states that he was the son of Jacques Guenet and Marie Saint-Los. The bride was Catherine Veuillot (a daughter of the king who arrived in 1667), baptized at Saint-Vivien de Rouen on 20 October 1642. Her parents were François Veuillot and Catherine Leblanc. Catherine had contracted a first marriage at Québec on 18 October 1667, to Jacques Dubois, buried at Saint-Laurent on the Ile d'Orléans, on 17 March 1675. She was already the mother of four children: François, born in 1668, two Clements born, one in 1670, the other in 1671, and Jeanne, born in 1673. At the time of her remarriage, Catherine was pregnant with Pierre, who was born on 7 October 1675. The first Clement probably died shortly after his birth. Pierre Guenet thus agreed to take care of the widow and her four children. In return, she welcomed her new husband into her home, where other Guenet children would be born.

Less than two years later, the first departure from the home occurred. François, *"8 or 9 years old"*, Catherine's eldest son, was *"leased and hired"* by Gilles Gautereau, resident of the island, for a period of five years. The indenture contract, drafted by notary Rageot on 24 January 1677, noted that the child would be taken in charge by his new master beginning on the first of February. Gautereau was obliged to feed him, support him and to treat him humanely. François would receive no salary, except for clothing.

FIRST CONCESSION

The following autumn, Pierre Guenet received his first piece of land. It was awarded to him on 19 October 1677 by François Chavigny, equerry, Seigneur of la Chevrotiére. The act drawn up by Romain Becquet reveals that the concession was made by way of cens and seigniorial rents. It concerned an area of 90 arpents located in the seigneurie of Chevrotière, three arpents in frontage on the Saint Lawrence river, by 30 arpents in depth, with hunting and fishing rights. The domain was located between the lands not ceded and a small stream. Guenet was committed to pay the seigneur each year 60 sols in silver and three live fat capons for the rents as well as three sols for the cens. He had to live on his concession and begin to work there within a year. Did he truly take possession of it? Nothing indicates this.

INSUFFICIENT LAND

On Monday, 7 March 1678, pleading that the inadequacy of the land that he occupied resulted in his inability to support his family, Pierre Guenet made a request at the Sovereign Council of New France, seeking permission to dispose of the entire said concession, or else he would be obliged to abandon it and go live elsewhere. The petitioner stated that he had been married three years earlier to Catherine Vieillot (sic), widow of Jacques Dubois and had the care of four children, three of whom he fed and supported, the fourth being supported by Gabriel Gosselin. For property Dubois only had a piece of land with three arpents of frontage located in the Demesnu fief, on which there were only eight arpents of abandoned land, a few buildings of little value and some standing trees. Guenet was therefore forced to relinquish this land because only half of it belonged to his wife and that it later would need to be divided among Dubois's children and his family.

In such circumstances, the petitioner stated, difficulties could be raised if all the land belonged to him *"for the work which had been made at the time of the death of the said Dubois was taken at its fair value with the half of the children of the said Dubois to be taken into consideration by him".*

This half could be paid by him and his wife when the Dubois children reach the age of 20 and that from now on,

"it be ordered that they live with him in order to compensate him by their work for the food and support that he gives them, and also the seigneur of the fief in which the said land is located, will sign a contract of concession, having only had in the past a note in his hand which had been burned in his cabin during the lifetime of the said Dubois".

Having heard the general administrator, the Council ordered that an appraisal of the land should be made by Gabriel Gosselin, Thomas Rousseau, Clément Ruel and Louis Sinadier, adoptive relatives of the minor children, as there are no relatives on the side of the deceased father. (4)

The intervention by Pierre Guenet to the Sovereign Council does not seem to have obtained the desired results. On 3 February 1680, in the presence of the notary Rageot, he stated he sold to Thomas Rousseau the half of the land which belonged to his wife, ajoinging on one side the property of François Noël, and on the other side, the half which belonged to the minor children of the late Jacques Dubois. The sale included a small log house covered with straw with appurtenances. A rider dated the following 12 August noted the consent of Catherine Veuillot to the said transaction.

AT THE "TROU SAINT-PATRICE"

Some fifteen months earlier, more precisely on 14 October 1678 (contract Becquet), Pierre Guenet, habitant of the county of Saint-Laurent, had accepted from Geneviève de Chavigny, sister of François de la Chevrotière and widow of Charles Amyot, Seigneur of Vincelot, a concession by way of cens and seigniorial rents, in her fief of Cap-Saint-Ignace. It concerned an area of 160 arpents of land covered with standing trees: four arpents in frontage by 40 deep, bordered on one side by Gilles Gaudreau and on the other by Jean Paulin. The tenant was committed to pay the seigneuresse eight livres in silver and four fat live capons for the seigniorial rents, and two sols for the cens for the entire concession, payable each year on Saint-Martin's Day in the winter beginning in 1679, promising to build and to work there as soon as possible. He will have the right to hunt and fish, but must not cut the oak wood suitable for building ships.

Once again, Pierre Guenet does not seem to have kept his commitment to the Chavignys. About 1679, he went instead to live much closer to his home, at a place called the *"trou Saint-Patrice"*, at Saint-Laurent. At that time, he settled on a piece of land abandoned by Pierre Doux or Ledoux dit Latreille. The acquisition contract for this land was only initialed seven years later by the notary Rageot. It was there that the Guenet family would be listed in the census of 1681. Pierre was said to be 32 years old, and Catherine 35. Living with them were Jeanne, 9; Pierre, 6; Thomas 4; Jacques, 3; and Marie, 6 months old. The first two were Dubois, the others were Guenets. (5)

THE MASON

It was while he was living at *"trou Saint-Patrice"* that Pierre Guenet took up his career as a tradesman. First, very briefly as a long sawyer, then, at least until the end of the seventeenth century, as a mason. On 8 November 1682 (contract Rageot), he was associated with Fabien Presseau to make 250 beams and 250 boards of pine and cedar for Alexis de Fleury, equerry, Sieur d'Eschambault. The delivery had to be made to the fief of the seigneur at the end of the next March. The workers would receive for their products 120 livres which the buyer would pay in the following fashion: 20 livres in merchandise, 60 in good solvent bills and 40 in silver.

Pierre Guenet began working as a mason in 1683. On 11 January he appeared at the home of the notary Rageot, where he promised to work for the architect Claude Baillif and the mason-surveyor Jean Le Rouge for all the masonry work which they will entrust to him for three consecutive months, even a fourth if it is needed. They advised him to find a man who will replace him when he does his harvest. According to the commitment, Guenet would occasionally act as laborer when his patrons decide it appropriate. He would be fed and receive a salary of 27 livres per month. But he must furnish his masonry tools.

On 12 July of the same year, probably deciding that it would be more convenient to have a *"pied-a-terre"* in Québec, Pierre acquired a plot of land located below the Sault-au-Matelot consisting of 26 feet in frontage to a depth to the bottom of the said street where a road is planned on which carts can travel. The neighboring plots were those of Michel Maillou and Jean Clouet. The transaction took place in the hall of the seminary in the presence of the notary Pierre Duquet and the priests Henry de Bernières, grand vicar of Msgr de Laval, pastor of Québec cathedral and superior of the seminary, Louis Ango dit Maizerets, assistant, and Germain Morin, administrator of the seminary. They admitted having sold the said land which had been given to the sellers by the bishop of Québec on 6 April 1680 and came from a donation made on 10 April 1666 by Guillemette Hébert, widow of Guillaume Couillard. Guenet paid 200 livres to acquire the plot, 10 livres per year for 20 years.

When his commitment with Baillif and Le Rouge was at an end, Pierre Guenet accepted on 17 August 1683 (contract Rageot), the offer that the mason Jean Poliquin, resident of the coast of Beaumont, made to him, ie, to work with him for the rest of the summer until All Saint's Day, as well as the summer and the autumn of 1684, for the sum of 40 sols per day and his food. He could even work that winter and two other winters without stopping.

In 1684, Guenet did not know unemployment. On 31 January (contract Rageot), he promised the master cabinetmaker Joseph Vandandaique of Québec to deliver 34 columns of wild cherry wood sawed and squared 7 feet long and 4 inches square, 6 planks 10 feet long, one foot wide and one inch thick *"franc sawed"*, and 10 cords of firewood. Everything would be brought at high tide to the delivery site. The deal was made for 8 sols for each column, 11 sols for each plank and 3 livres 7 sols per cord of wood. Everything would be paid at the time of delivery, half in silver and half in solvent bills.

98

At the beginning of 1684, on 27 January (contract Duquet), our ancestor resold to the stone cutter Joseph Maillou the plot at Sault-au-Matelot bought in 1683 from the priests de Bernières, Ango dit Maizerets and Morin for the same conditions and price that he had acquired it, probably deciding he no longer needed to keep it. Also no longer necessary was the land that he had worked for seven years at *"trou Saint-Patrice"*, at Saint-Laurent. This land, we recall, had never been acquired in a good and proper form. It had been occupied by Guenet and his family after its owner, Pierre Ledoux dit Latreille, had abandoned it.

On 15 October 1686 (contract Rageot), the latter, who was now living in the village of Saint-Bernard, went to Québec to state that he had sold to Pierre Guenet, resident of *"trou Saint-Patrice"*, on the island and in the county of Saint-Laurent, a piece of land and homestead consisting of three arpents in frontage on the river in the said place called *"trou Saint-Patrice"* and with a depth as far as the line which separates the island from end to end, adjoining on one side Michel Esnault dit Botte and on the other side René Le Merle. This land belonged to the seller by an acquisition from one named Ripoche (François) in a contract signed in the presence of Becquet (24 August 1677), and which the acquirer said he had possessed *"for about seven years by the seller relinquishing it to him without having signed a contract for it until today"*. This sale was made with the charges of the cens and seigniorial rents from the first day of the seven years and for the amount of 150 livres which the buyer said he had paid for the release of the seller, the sum of 138 livres to the merchant Charon by a note from the clergy of the seminary of Québec, and 12 livres in a note dated that day.

Four days later, on 19 October, before the same notary, Pierre Guenet stated having sold the same land to Pierre Leclerc, habitant of Saint-Pierre on the island. The said homestead included a cabin and a stable of logs, and a shed. The transaction was made for 250 livres tournois, including 150 paid in cash. The rest would be paid on Saint-Andre's Day (30 November), half in good notes and half in silver. It was also agreed that during the coming winter the seller would be able to cut 40 cords of firewood and to fell the wood required to build a house of boards 20 feet square, a fence and a roof of planks. Guenet finally obtained permission from the buyer to use this land until the following first of May. According to Léon Roy, Pierre Leclerc was still the owner of the land of *"trou Saint-Patrice"* at the time of the parish census of 25 May 1725. (6)

RETURN TO QUÉBEC

Towards the middle of the year 1687, Pierre Guenet and his family left the domain of *"trou Saint-Patrice"* and settled at Québec where our ancestor was able to practice his trade without having to continually move. On 7 June (contract Genaple), he bought from Lucien Boutteville, a merchant living on rue Sainte-Anne, in the Upper Town, a lot situated on Cap-aux-Diamants consisting of 20 feet in frontage, the depth of which stretched as far as the end of the coast. This land was the site of the new road recently opened which went to the bottom of the coast and joined the house of the mason François du Carreau. Boutteville had acquired this lot in 1680 from Antoine Dionne, a resident of the Ile d'Orléans.

The same day, in the presence of the same notary, Boutteville and Guenet concluded a deal for masonry work, namely an additional structure belonging to his residence. This carpentry would lie on a base 2 feet thick or more, the half-timber of which would be of stone, masonry and rough cast on the exterior and filled in the interior. Boutteville would provide all the necessary materials for this structure. Guenet had to begin to work there as soon as required and he would receive six livres for each toise of masonry, two toises of half-timber only counting as one. An amount of one hundred livres, the sale price for the lot bought the same day by the mason, would be deducted from the salary paid by the merchant. The extra would be paid in coin as soon as the work is finished.

On 20 July 1687, there was another contract, this time drafted by the notary Rageot. Pierre Guenet, at the same time as his 18 year old step-son François Dubois, joined with the master masons Guillaume Jourdain and Sylvain Duplais, in order to do with them some masonry work for the rest of the season, for a payment of 78 livres per month: 50 livres for him and 28 for the young man. The salaries would be paid half in silver and half in solvent notes. Guenet acknowledged having received an advance of 30 livres in merchandise.

Two other acts by the same notary, dated 22 June 1687 and 11 March 1688, reveal that Guenet had sold to Antoine Fortier, barge-master living at Saint-Paul (Saint-Laurent) on the Ile d'Orléans, and to the mason François du Carreau, two lots detached from the one acquired from the merchant Boutteville on 7 June 1687, for 50 and 25 livres respectively.

THE CHILDREN OF CATHERINE VEUILLOT--HER DEATH

The year 1688 was a crucial one for Pierre Guenet and his family. This was probably the last one in which Catherine Veuillot, his wife, was alive. The four surviving children from her marriage to Jacques Dubois were not yet married; they worked outside the home or still lived with their mother and their stepfather. All were born in the small log house covered with straw inherited from their father and all had been baptized at Sainte-Famille, the only church available on the Ile d'Orléans at that time.

Four children born to Pierre Guenet were added to the household, only two of whom reached adulthood. They were:

1. Jacques, born on 26 April and baptized at Sainte-Famille on 2 May 1677. On 25 November 1704 (contract La Cetiére, on the 23rd), he was married at Québec to Marguerite Boutin, widow of André Couteron and daughter of Jean and of Suzanne Rocheteau (1664-1730). Jacques worked mainly at the trade of baker. He was not in the census of 1716 at Québec. Marguerite had brought into the world eleven children during her first marriage.

2. Thomas, born on the 16th and baptized on 24 May 1679 at Sainte-Famille. Married at Beaumont on 10 February 1705, to Anne Maheu dit Paul (natural daughter of Jean-Paul Maheu and Catherine Bruneau). Thomas was a long sawyer. Buried at Saint-Charles on 17 September 1753. Three sons and ten daughters. Family of Beaumont.

3. Marie, born on 16 April and baptized on the first of May 1681 at Saint-Laurent. Died on the 25th and buried in the same place on 26 November 1687.

4. Michel, born on the 12th and baptized on 21 September 1683 at Saint-Laurent. Died on the 2nd and buried in the same parish on 3 November 1686.

On 26 November 1687, at the time of the burial of her daughter Marie at the age of six, Catherine Veuillot was still alive, as noted by the priest Francheville who drew up the burial act in the presence of Pierre Garand and Claude Salois. (7)

On 28 June 1689, a few months after his remarriage, Pierre Guenet was summoned explicitly by the bailiff Marandeau to appear before the tribunal of the Provost of Québec. The barge-master Pierre Feret, represented by his wife, claimed from him the seven livres and four sols that he owed him *"for leasing the house provided to him during the illness of his late wife"*. Guenet was absent and was not represented, but he was nevertheless directed to pay up and to also pay the legal fees. This document gives credit to the hypothesis that Catherine Veuillot died at the Hôtel-Dieu of Québec about the end of 1688. (8)

During the same era, Pierre Guenet contracted at the home of Genaple that which seems the most important deal of his career as mason. On 29 November 1688, he joined with Antoine Regnault to accept the offer by the architect Hilaire Bernard de la Rivière representing Msgr de Laval, to erect all the enclosing walls which the bishop wanted to have built around his episcopal palace. The masons would be required to provide their tools: pails, lines levels and trowels. For his part, the prelate was responsible for all the necessary materials, even water should it be lacking, by drawing it from the places where there usually is some. The work would begin "in the early spring" and had to be finished for All-Saints Day.

The walls would be two feet and three inches thick at their foundations,

> *"and 22 inches above of the recess which would be made at the pavement's step coming to 20 inches below the coping"*.

The deal was reached for 7 livres 10 sols for each toise of wall. Regnault and Guenet would be paid in silver as the work progressed. An advance of 40 livres was agreed to the workers.

102

A rider dated 18 July 1689 informs us that this contract had been annulled because of the disagreement between Guenet and Regnault which prevented the work from continuing. Messire Andrede Merlay, (9) grand vicar of Msgr de Laval, agreed to pay the masons for the work performed after the report of the survey made by the master mason Jean Le Rouge, dated on the 19th of this month. Had the illness and recent death of Catherine Veuillot forced Pierre Guenet to break this contract?

We know from the reports of the Provost of Québec that Pierre had some difficult moments in 1689. In the majority of the cases, he was sued for accounts not paid and, most of the time, he was not present. Each time, he was ordered to pay and to assume the costs of the court. On 12 July, among others, he was sued by René Robineau, chevalier, Seigneur of Becancour, Baron de Portneuf and Grand Voyer. The latter was represented by the notary François Genaple, while the merchant Pierre Pierre took on Guenet's defense. The proof established that Robineau had been asked to make an alignment and would have been upset to have been inconvenienced for *"a stone of four francs"*. Guenet was thus ordered to pay a fine of 20 sols for his behavior and his lack of respect.

On 27 January 1689, a few days before his remarriage, Pierre Guenet, now living at rue de Cul-de-Sac in Québec, went to the home of his favorite notary, Rageot, in order to borrow 109 livres and 10 sols in merchandise, meat, and silver, from the merchant Pierre DeRoy, living on rue Sous-le-Fort. The borrower was obliged to repay this amount at the end of May from all the work that he would be able to do or otherwise.

SECOND MARRIAGE

For a second time Pierre Guenet was ready to get married. This time to Elisabeth Pasquier, born on 10 May 1671 (thus, she was not yet 18 years old), eldest daughter of our ancestor Isaac Pasquier dit Lavallée and Elisabeth Meunier. (10) On 3 February 1689, in the presence of Vachon, notary for the bailiwick of the county of Saint-Laurent and the town of Fargy in Beauport, the future couple made a promise of marriage. Isaac Pasquier and his wife, residents of the parish of Saint-Paul, stipulated for their daughter, while Pierre Guenet, resident of the parish of Notre-Dame de Québec, acted in his own name in the presence of friends and relatives gathered for the occasion. Pierre and Elisabeth would have joint personal property and real estate according to the *coutume de Paris*. The parents of the bride *"give their daughter"* 100 livres in furnishings, money and an advance of inheritance. Pierre offered her a prefixed dowry of 300 livres. It was indicated that Jacques, 12, and Thomas, 10, children from Pierre's first marriage, would be fed and supported at the expense of the marriage until they had reached the age of 15.

The wedding ceremony took place in the chapel of Saint-Laurent with messire Francheville presiding, after the publication of three banns made on 30 January, 2 and 6 February in this parish, and two banns in the parish of Québec, with dispensation of the third bann with the consent of the bishop. The witnesses mentioned were Antoine Mondin, Jean Baillargeon, Nicolas and Antoine Godebout.

After the wedding, life continued, and our ancestor returned to his masonry work. On 24 June, he again took up the yoke with his colleague Antoine Regnault. On that day, they went to the notary Rageot to ratify a contract which had already been approved in a private agreement on the preceding 6 November with Pierre Paré representing Jean-François Bourdon, equerry, Sieur de Dombourg, to build the walls which would be indicated to them

> *"in the house and on the lot of the said Dombourg for him and his heirs through benefit of the inventory of the late Jacques Bourdon, equerry, Sieur d'Autray, his brother, namely all the foundations which they will make both in the courtyard and around the house on the side towards the crossroads of the street, and those which will be at the entrance of the said lot and the house of the widow of the late Mesny, master surgeon and to have the walls ready at the end of the month of July, for 26 livres per toise".*

The work would be paid for as they progress. In a rider dated on 13 July, Regnault and Guenet admitted having received 520 livres for 20 toises of walls.

The work which was done at the house of Jean-François Bourdon included several shutters which needed some repairs and improvements over the years. A report from the deliberations of the Sovereign Council, dated Monday, 13 August 1706, informs us that a great number of trades men took part in this construction after 1689. During the winter of 1705-1706, among other events, there was such an abundance of snow that the roof had been greatly damaged.

Did the Guenets stay on the Ile d'Orléans again during the winter of 1689-1690? Pierre, the first child of Elisabeth Pasquier was born at Saint⌐-Pierre on 10 January 1690. This is indicated in the baptismal act written by Jean-Henri Tremblay, young priest of French origin who was pastor of Saint-Pierre and Saint-Paul from 1689 to 1692. (11) The godfather was Pierre Leclerc, the same one who had bought in 1686, the land of *"trou Saint-Patrice"*. Elisabeth Pasquier was also able to stay at her parents' home in the beginning of 1690. Isaac Pasquier and Pierre Leclerc occupied lands almost neighboring one another during this time.

AT BEAUMONT

In 1691, the Guenet family crossed the river to settle at Beaumont. The seigneur Charles Couillard de Beaumont admitted having, on 11 November of the said year, ceded by a private document by means of cens and seigniorial rents, to Pierre Guenet a piece of land and homestead consisting of, according to the report of the survey made by Jean Le Rouge, on the date of 17 December 1694, three arpents, three perches and twelve feet wide by 40 deep, adjoining on the northeast the homestead of Michel Maillou and on the southwest that of François Chabot; on the front was the Saint-Lawrence, in the rear were the lands not ceded, with hunting and fishing rights (except hunting for partridge), the duty of paying each year at the seigniorial manor twenty sols and one live, fat capon for the rents, and three cens for the entire concession. Guenet must also bring to the seigneur one-eleventh of all the salmon that he would catch, build a home on the concession, to work there and to maintain it; he also had to give the seigneur the precedence for all the cord wood, to preserve all the oak wood suitable for building ships, and so forth.

The return to the land by Pierre and his family does not seem to have caused him to give up his trade as mason. On 25 April 1694, he brought his eldest son the 17 year old Jacques, to the notary Chambalon in order to lease his services as domestic servant to Étienne Landron, a merchant of Québec. The act indicated that our ancestor still kept his title of mason. His son's commitment would last for three years, beginning on the first of September. Jacques had to obey everything that his master ordered him to do honestly and legally. Landron was committed to feed him and to pay him his wages of 60 livres for the first year, 80 for the second and 100 for the third. He would also furnish him a pair of French shoes and pay the father a compensation of 10 livres.

On 27 April 1699, in the study of the notary Chambalon at Québec, Pierre Guenet relinquished his land at Beaumont to the benefit of the merchant Pierre Du Roy. There was a small log house there, a small shed covered in straw and other appurtenances. The act recalled that this land had been ceded about eight years earlier in a private document, accompanied by receipts for the cens and rents and by a note signed by the Sieur de Beaumont giving an order to the notary to draft a contract of concession in good and proper form to the seller. The sale to Du Roy was made with the duty of the cens and rents and for 280 livres, from which was deducted 121 livres, 16 sols and 8 deniers which the seller owed the buyer from a debt signed in the presence of Charles Rageot on 16 October 1696. Du Roy immediately paid 60 livres in silver and promised to pay the balance of 98 livres, 3 sols and 4 deniers to the seller or, if he was absent, to his wife Elisabeth Paquet. A rider dated on 3 May 1699 certified that the latter received from the buyer the said balance in merchandise and had given him the note of concession privately. On the following first of June, conforming to the wishes of the seigneur, Chambalon retroactively drew up the act of concession from Charles Couillard to Pierre Guenet so that Du Roy and his heirs would not suffer any possible subsequent disputes.

AT MONT-LOUIS

The sale of land at Beaumont for the Guenet family was the prelude to an adventure as brief as it was unfortunate. Yielding to the advances and the promises offered by Sieur Denis Riverin, (12) the Guenets embarked in the month of June for

106

Mont-Louis. *La Compagnie du Mont-Louis* had been formed in 1696, during a trip by Riverin to Paris. Upon his return, he began to recruit colonists and to distribute concessions to them. By 1699, more than 50 people were already settled there. Satisfied with this beginning of colonization, Riverin had a census made of his *"flock"*. We notice in it the presence of the entire Guenet family, composed at that time of eight members: Pierre, the father, 47; Isabelle, his wife, 28; their children: Isabelle, 10; Charles, 6; Pierre, 4; and Marie 2. Jacques and Thomas, the two sons of Pierre and Catherine Veuillot were also found there. Among the families in the census, we note those of Jean Gagnon and Jeanne Loignon, Pierre Morin and Françoise Chiasson, René Beaudin and Suzanne Vallée, Jean Hostain and Jeanne Tardif, as well as Jean Moreau and Marie-Anne Rodrigue. (13)

According to Andrea Poitras,(14) in order to be recruited

> *"the men had to show proof of ability, to practice at least two trades: fishing and farming, to also know masonry, carpentry, sawing, forging, and even medicine...Each adult was granted by the company a plot of land to farm of 21 arpents in depth by three arpents wide, bordering the Mont-Louis river, and a plot of 4,000 square feet in the village on which to build a house."*

In 1702, after some serious financial difficulties, the post was almost abandoned. Only three families were found there in 1706 and four in 1712.

On 27 September 1700, a dozen residents of Mont-Louis, among them Pierre Guenet and his son Jacques, told of their misadventure to the Sovereign Council which they asked to force Sieur Riverin to fulfill his promises. The official report drawn up by Bochart Champigny (15) on 30 September reveals that the petitioners, after commitments made by Riverin to induce them to settle at Mont-Louis,

> *"had sold their lands and homesteads that they had in the environs of this city (Québec), their livestock, except those that they had been able to bring to the said place*

107

called Mont-Louis and left all their customs
believing that they would be well settled....at
which place they had done some con-
siderable work on the homesteads ceded to
them..."

The petitioners recounted that during the previous summer they had been visited by an associate of Riverin, Sieur de Clermont, of whom they had requested some food and necessities, which he refused them. Seeing the impossibility of living in this place,

"they had been compelled to abandon their
settlements, wheat and other grain still on
the land, livestock and generally all that they
had there rather than die of starvation, and
nearly 60 people left to come to this city with
so little food that they had suffered much,
and that even the wife of one of them died
from distress during the journey about which
they brought their complaints to court upon
their arrival".

They asked finally that it be ordered that the said defendant be-held to return them at his expense to Mont-Louis with their families and that he compensate them for the losses and damages that the said abandonment caused them by the non-fulfillment of the promises that he made.

In his defense, Riverin recalled that his association had been constituted at Paris on 9 April 1696 with the aim of establishing a secondary fishing post on Gaspe Bay, and trade with the French and Indians in the area. Upon his return from France in 1698, he sent a barge loaded with food and provisions, with a missionary, a clerk, a surgeon and two families in order to start the settlement. In 1699, other families came. He ceded them homesteads and provided food for their entire subsistence for the first year, half for the second and a little for the third. These families had to pay for the merchandise in cod, planks, boards and lumber, masts, labor and other products from their lands. This was done until last July, when the ship *La Colombe* belonging to the Association arrived at Mont-Louis with the Sieur de Clermont who, far from bringing the 30 barrels of flour requested because of the shortage of wheat which plagued this country, would have overburdened the settlement by the presence of the Sieur de Clermont, four servants and twelve unnecessary engages which had placed the defendant in extreme difficulty. In agreement with the missionary Raffeix, he then ordered the Sieur de Clermont to send to Québec the twelve engages and the four servants to relieve the settlement and to prevent the inevitable abandonment by the inhabitants who could not all survive. Which the Sieur de Clermont had refused to do. Consequently, claimed Riverin, he should not be held responsible for the abandonment by the plaintiffs, because what happened was the mistake of his associates.

After hearing the parties, the Council ordered that Sieur Riverin give an account to the plaintiffs of the terms and commitments that he had made with them and that he send them back to Mont-Louis because they stated they wanted to return there. He must for this purpose provide boats, food and other necessary items as he is obliged. He must also provide complete subsistence for those that he sent to Mont-Louis during the last spring for the rest of the current year and *"half food"* for the next year. Finally, the defendant must assume the damages to the plaintiffs because of the abandonment of their lands, grain, works, livestock and for other losses incurred during the greater part of the summer which has passed in order to come to Québec and to stay there. Riverin will be able to have recourse against those whom he would deem appropriate for his reimbursement of the advances, expenses and damages.

On Monday, 8 October 1700, through a request from Jean Hostain, René Beaudin, Jean Moreau, Pierre Guenet and other residents of Mont-Louis, the Council appointed Sieurs Delagrange, merchant, and Denis Roberge, merchant, as arbitrators to appraise the damages and to draw up a report of their decision. In case of disagreement, they would be able to add Sieur de Grandville.

The residents of Mont-Louis had to be patient for a few months more before knowing the outcome of their case. The Council met again on Monday, 21 February 1701 to inform the parties in this case of its decision. Pierre Guenet, who in the meantime, had been named as administrator for the plaintiffs, acted as their spokesperson. The appraisers were no longer the ones which the Council had appointed in October. They were the merchants L'Espinay and Pineau who had received this mission.

Riverin challenged their appraisal which he found too high. The members of the Council did not agree with him. On the contrary, they considered that the amounts awarded were justified and would be deducted from that which the inhabitants owed to the company, with the exception of the twelve livres which Riverin would be held to pay to those who wanted to return to Mont-Louis in order to facilitate their subsistence until spring. Riverin must also pay to the named Sauvage Laine 60 livres owed to him by Pierre Guenet and other plaintiffs for food and expenses which they had been obliged to pay during the course of their case.

RETURN TO THE ROOTS

The end of this lawsuit also brought a final end to the adventure at Mont-Louis for the Guenet family, now back at Saint-Léonard on the Ile d'Orléans. It was there that Jacques, the younger, was born and baptized on 13 April 1701. Jacques, his older half-brother, was his godfather. Had Pierre, Elisabeth and their four children been rescued, the previous year, by the Pasquier grandparents? Or did they settle on the half-arpent still belonging to Jacques and Thomas which had come from an inheritance from their mother Catherine Veuillot? This half arpent of frontage wedged into the land of Pierre Ruel would be sold to him on 4 June 1710 (contract Chambalon) for 60 livres. In 1694 and 1696, Ruel had already acquired the rest of the land which had belonged to the other heirs of Jacques Dubois, except for one-fourth of the three arpents bought from François Dubois by Claude Sallouer in 1697. (16)

The stay on the Ile d'Orléans was only temporary. The family settled at Saint-Michel de La Durantaye about 1703 and remained there until 1712. It was there that Thomas, Anne-Dorothée and Charlotte were born successively. The seigneur Olivier Morel de la Durantaye ceded to Pierre Guenet, through a simple note made privately, a piece of land located on the banks of the Boyer River. This land had a frontage of six arpents and extended as far as the line which separated the former homesteads which stretched along the Saint-Lawrence. It joined on the northeast the lot of René Goupil and on the southwest that of the widow La Madeleine. There was a small house of stakes covered with straw and an old shed. Guenet sold this homestead to Jean Paquet on 30 September 1712 (contract Gaschet), for 200 livres,

100 of them paid in playing card money. In a rider dated on 18 March 1715, Elisabeth Paquet, gave her consent to this sale and Pierre Guenet, resident of the seigneurie of Beaumont, acknowledged receipt of the 100 livres still due.

THE CHILDREN OF ELISABETH PAQUET

After selling his land at La Durantaye, Pierre Guenet, his wife and his children who were still at home went to settle finely at Beaumont. It was there that the family welcomed Louise, the last child. In 25 years, Elisabeth Paquet had brought ten children into the world.

1. Pierre, born on the 10th and baptized at Saint-Pierre, I.O., on 13 January 1690. This son did not live beyond infancy.

2. Elisabeth, born on the 10th and baptized at Beaumont on 20 January 1691. Married at La Durantaye on 2 June 1710, to François Bacquet dit Lamontagne (1680-1744) (François and Anne Philippe). Buried at Saint-Vallier on 7 March 1734. Six sons and three daughters,. This family lived successively at La Durantaye, Beaumont and Saint-Vallier.

3. Charles, born on the 6th and baptized at Beaumont on 7 April 1694. Married in this parish on 4 November 1721, to Geneviève Bizeux dit Larose (Jean and Marie-Madeleine Barsa). Buried at Saint-Charles on 28 February 1758. Four sons and five daughters. This family lived primarily at Beaumont.

4. Pierre, baptized at Beaumont on 19 February 1696. Married in the same place on 25 November 1723, to Marie-Madeleine Roy or Le Roy, born in 1700 (Louis and Marie Ledran). Six sons and four daughters. This family lived at La Durantaye and Beaumont.

5. Marie-Françoise, born on 31 January and baptized on 2 February 1698 at Beaumont. Married in this parish on 7 January 1718 (contract Gaschet, 17 November 1717), to Louis Bechard, born in 1691 (René and Marie-Anne Vaillancourt. Three sons and seven daughters, Family of Beaumont.

111

6.   Jacques, born on the 12th and baptized on 13 April 1701 at Saint-Laurent I.O. Married at Beaumont on 8 April 1723 (contract Gaschet, on the 6th), to Louise Gromelin, born in 1704 (Noël and Marie Balan). A son and a daughter. On 28 December 1722 (contract Gaschet), Jacques exchanged his land on the Boyer River for that of his brother-in-law Louis Bechard and his sister Marie-Françoise, of Rivière de La Durantaye.

7.   Thomas, born on the 2nd and baptized on 15 August 1704 at Saint-Michel de La Durantaye. Destiny unknown.

8.   Anne-Dorothée, born on the 6th and baptized on 19 September 1706 at Saint-Michel de La Durantaye.   Fate unknown.

9.   Charlotte, baptized at Beaumont on 22 October 1709. Married in this parish on 8 November 1728 (contract Dubreuil, 27 October), to Joseph Jolivet (1705-1758) (Aime and Anne Fiset). Died on the 11th and buried at Saint-Charles on 12 April 1757. Four sons and six daughters. This family lived mainly at Beaumont.   However, Charlotte and Joseph were buried at Saint-Charles.

10.   Louise, baptized at Beaumont on 29 June 1714; buried in the same place on the following 11 July.

ALMOST A CENTENARIAN

Pierre Guenet's last stay at Beaumont lasted almost thirty years. The census of 1681 gave him the age of 32. He was said to be 37 at the time of his second marriage in 1689. The census of Mont-Louis in 1699 aged him by ten years exactly. On 19 August 1741, his burial act said he was almost a centenarian. The pastor Joseph Chasle wrote in the registry of Beaumont: (17)

BURIAL OF BONHOMME GUENET

"On the ninth of August in the year one thousand seven hundred forty one was buried in the cemetery of this parish of St Etienne de Beaumont by me undersigned priest pastor of the said parish the body of Pierre Guenet

112

resident of the said place about one hundred years old who had been like a child for two years, he received the sacrament of Extreme unction, the said burial took place in the presence of Joseph Jolivet, Jacques Fournier, Joachim Moleur, who did not know how to write."

A preceding act to the burial notice above in the registry was dated 11 August. It was the baptismal act for Marie-Louise Guenet, daughter of Thomas and of Catherine Leroux. She was the great-granddaughter of the deceased. Thus, at the time of the death of our ancestor, four generations of Guenets were numerous in the cradle of New France. The survival of the family was already assured for centuries to come!

FAMILY NAME VARIATIONS

Guenet has the following known variations: Gainet, Gannet, Genet, Genette, Grente, Guenette, Queneville, Qinnette, Quenet and Rainville.

END NOTES

1) DBC, 1, PUL, p.357 & 358.

2) JDCS, I, June 1664, p. 190 & 194.

3) Albert Dauzat, DENLF, Larousse Selection, 1963, Vol.2, p.1915.

4) JDCS, II, p.180 & 181.

5) André Lafontaine, RANF 1681, Sherbrooke, 1981, p.262, The ages of Thomas and Jacques Guenet have been inverted.

6) RANQ, 1973. *Les terres de l'Ile d'Orléans*, p. 215.

7) Pierre Francheville was born at Trois-Rivières in 1649 from the marriage of Marin Terrier de Francheville and of Jeanne Jallot. He was a brilliant student at the Seminary of Québec. After his ordination in 1676, he exercised his ministry at Beauport, on the Isle d'Orléans, at Rivière Ouelle, Cap-Saint-Ignace, Saint-Thomas and, finally, at Longueuil, where he died in 1713.

8) The record of deaths and illnesses from the Hôtel-Dieu of Québec is not available for this part of 1689.

9) André-Louis de Merlay sojourned at Québec from 1689 to 1694. He was the chief chanter of the chapter of the *"eglise episcopale"*, then chaplain of the Hôtel-Dieu. Following this he retourned to France.

10) The marriage record gives to the spouses ages as 37 and 16 respectively.

11) The abbot Tremblay arrived at Québec in 1687. In 1693 Msgr Laval named him the administrator of the Seminary of Québec. He occupied this post until his death on 9 July 1740.

12) Denis Riverin arrived in New France in 1675 as secretary to the new intendant Duchesneau. At the same time he represented Jean Ouedette who was an employee of the *Compagnie de la Ferme* of the King. Later on he would become a member of the Sovereign Council. He left Canada in 1702 in order to become a part of the *Compagnie de la Colonie* at **Paris.**

13) <u>PRDH</u> Program of research in historical demography. PUM, VI, p. R185.

14) *Mont-Louis se raconte....1984.* p. 39 & 40.

15) Jean Bochart de Champigny was the intendant of New France from 1686 to 1702.

16) <u>RANQ</u> 1973, pp. 226 to 228. Léon Roy, *Les Terres de Saint-Laurent I.O.*

17) Nicolas-Joseph Chasle was born at Québec on 18 February 1694 from the union of Claude Chasle and of Catherine Foi. Ordained by Msgr de Saint-Vallier in 1717. Was pastor of Beaumont from 1718 to 1754. He died at that place on 23 March 1754.

OTHER SOURCES

Cyprien Tanguay, <u>DGFC</u>

René Jetté, <u>DGFQ</u>

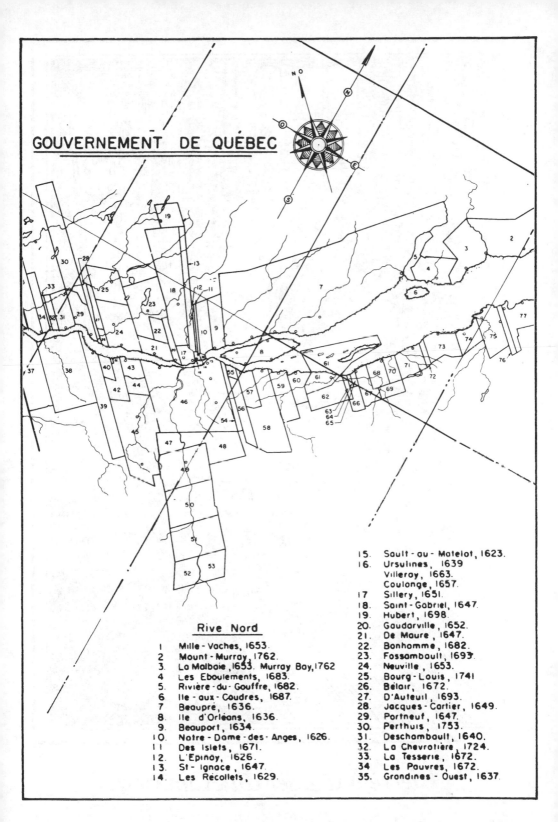

GOUVERNEMENT DE QUÉBEC

Rive Nord

1. Mille - Vaches, 1653.
2. Mount - Murray, 1762.
3. La Malbaie, 1653. Murray Bay, 1762
4. Les Eboulements, 1683.
5. Rivière - du - Gouffre, 1682.
6. Ile - aux - Coudres, 1687.
7. Beaupré, 1636.
8. Ile d'Orléans, 1636.
9. Beauport, 1634.
10. Notre - Dame - des - Anges, 1626.
11. Des Islets, 1671.
12. L'Epinay, 1626.
13. St - Ignace, 1647.
14. Les Récollets, 1629.
15. Sault - au - Matelot, 1623.
16. Ursulines, 1639
    Villeray, 1663.
    Coulonge, 1657.
17. Sillery, 1651.
18. Saint - Gabriel, 1647.
19. Hubert, 1698.
20. Gaudarville, 1652.
21. De Maure, 1647.
22. Bonhomme, 1682.
23. Fossambault, 1693.
24. Neuville, 1653.
25. Bourg - Louis, 1741.
26. Bélair, 1672.
27. D'Auteuil, 1693.
28. Jacques - Cartier, 1649.
29. Portneuf, 1647.
30. Perthuis, 1753.
31. Deschambault, 1640.
32. La Chevrotière, 1724.
33. La Tesserie, 1672.
34. Les Pauvres, 1672.
35. Grondines - Ouest, 1637.

Pierre Métayer dit Saintonge

CHAPTER 7

Pierre Métayer dit Saintonge

uring the time of Louis XIV, French clothing reached the apex of flamboyant style. Men and women rivaled each other in styleishness: it even seems that these men surpassed the women at elegant society gatherings. According to Robert-Lionel Seguin, (1)

"The Canadian usually dresses in the "French" style. He even has some items and clothing accessories which are only found at the home of well-to-do merchants and minor gentlemen in France. Such as rhino graves (a type of breeches), hair wraps and wigs. A special feature: the wardrobe of the men was better adorned than that of his female companion who indulged in fabrics of quality."

With well-off folks, a complete wardrobe could cost more than a house of upright logs built of oak and covered with straw. (2)

Arriving at the end of the seventeenth century, Pierre Métayer dit Saintonge brought with him his skill as a tailor, a very complex trade at that time which required several years of apprenticeship. The men at that time wore stockings and breeches, leg trimmings, jerkins, cuffs, adornments, doublet, neck cloth and frock coat; the women wore scarves, mantles, braiding, simarre, tavayole and many other articles of clothing the identification of which today seems to us to be completely archaic. At the beginning of the eighteenth century, the Canadians found the means to import less fabric from the mother country. They made linen fabric and cloth by using hemp, wool, even bark from tree and nettle.

117

THE MÉTAYERS IN NEW FRANCE

The sharecropper is essentially a tenant farmer. one who works a piece of land by giving half of his produce to the land owner. Several French Métayers crossed the Atlantic in the seventeenth and eighteenth centuries.

1. The earliest seem to have been Denis and Marie Mestayer, brother and sister, originally from Poitou. On 7 August 1650, Denis was a witness to his sister's marriage contract to Mathurin Baillargeon, noted by the notary Gastineau-Duplessis.

2. A few years later, André Métayer dit Cupidon appeared, originally from Lachevrolière in Brittany. He died at the *Hôtel-Dieu de Québec* in 1690 after having worked here for a quarter-century without marrying.

3. Jean Métayer dit Desmarets, discharged captain and commander of Fort Châteauguay, was killed by an Iroquois in 1690 and buried at Lachine.

4. Another Jean Métayer, originally from Poitou, died at Beauport in 1725. For many years he had been a flour merchant at the local mill. (3)

5. Suzanne Métayer, arrived from La Rochelle at the beginning of the 1680's, and was married successively to Philippe Dion in 1683, Guillaume Dupont in 1693 and François Frechet in 1717. She was buried at Saint-Nicolas in 1742, after giving birth to children from her first two marriages.

6. Another Jean Métayer, who died at Montréal in 1748, had been a barge-master at Fort Frontenac.

7. Louis-Charles Le Metaillier, a Normand who settled at Sainte-Anne-de-la-Pocatière where he was married in 1748 to Marie-Joseph Thiboutot, has numerous descendants called Métayer starting in the second generation.

8. Also from Normandie, Marin Métayer who was married at Montmagny in 1749 to Marie-Madeleine Proulx.

9.   Finally, there was Pierre Métayer dit Lagiberne, another Normand who arrived at Louisbourg at the age of sixteen. He was deported to New England, from where he returned with the English troops in 1759 to attack Québec. In 1763, he was discharged and settled at Sainte-Foy where he was married in 1766 to Marie-Joseph Fournier.

10.   The descendants of ancestor Pierre Métayer, our subject, are also known by the last names of Metilly, Metigny, Metiguay, Metivier and Saintonge. (4)

TROOPER DE LA MARINE

Pierre Métayer arrived in this country with the troops of the Marine.   He must have served for a few years as a soldier before beginning to practice his trade of tailor. In the spring of 1704, he said he was ready to take a wife. His marriage record is lost, but it probably took place at Lévis, where his fiancée lived. On 24 May, the notary Florent de LaCetière recorded the marriage contract. Present were Sieur René Leduc, living in the parish of Saint-Joseph in the seigneurie of Lauzon, and the honorable Lady Anne Gentreau, his wife, stipulating for their daughter Geneviève, and Pierre Métayer, master tailor living at Québec, who acted on his own. Also taking part in the meeting were Claude de Ramezay, Chevalier Seigneur of la Gesse and of Boisfleurant, Commander of the Troops of la Marine supported by the King in this country; Alexandré Leneuf, equerry, Sieur de Beaubassin, Lieutenant of a company of the same troops; Louis Le Fournier, equerry Sieur de Figuier, Ensign in a company, and Jean-Baptiste La Coudray, an innkeeper of Québec, all friends of the groom. Geneviève Leduc's attendants, besides her parents, were her brother Guillaume, Gabriel Lambert and Marie-Renée Roussel, his wife, from the Lauzon coast.

The couple would have joint personal property and real estate on the day of their wedding, according to the *coutume de Paris*. Geneviève's parents promised to give them an equipped bed, linens and used clothes. Pierre brought a dowry of one thousand livres, a considerable amount for that era. The preciput would be equal and reciprocal for an amount of 500 livres to be taken by the survivor from the personal property of the community property. The contract was signed in the house of Sieur Leduc on the Lauzon coast in the presence of Jean-Baptiste Del-

119

guel dit Labreche, cook, the Sergeant André Chauvet, the soldier Jean Cheffaut, and Sieurs de Ramezay, du Figuier, Perthuis, La Coudray and Lambert. It was noted that this contract gave no information on the parents of Pierre Métayer, or on their place of residence. Was this a voluntary omission or a simple oversight?

Less than four months later, on 10 September 1704, a boy named Pierre was baptized at Québec, whose father was Pierre Métayer and his mother Marie-Madeleine Pinguet. The baby was buried four days later. This child could be, according to Jetté, the result of a relationship outside of marriage between Métayer and Marie-Madeleine Gatien, daughter of Pierre Gatien dit Tourangeau and Geneviève Pinguet, since no Marie-Madeleine Pinguet, who could be the mother of this child, can be traced. (5)

A LEASED HOUSE

Again in the same year, on 20 October, Pierre Métayer went to the notary Louis Chambalon charged by the merchant Guillaume Jourdain to draw up the terms of the lease of a house which the tenant already occupied on rue Sous-le-Fort where, according to all probability, he had decided to move his tailor's workshop. The landlord was charged to make repairs on the ground floor and to do glazing, while the tenant will make at his expense a small step in the lower chamber in order to reach the upper chamber, at the same time as the improvements that he would decide necessary, including the glazing of the upper floor. During this four-year lease, Métayer was committed to pay annually the amount of 150 livres, payable in two six-month payments. At the end of the lease, he will be able to leave this lodging and take his improvements and his window glass.

ARRIVAL OF THE CHILDREN

The married life of Pierre Métayer and Geneviève Leduc was rather short. They shared the same roof for eight years, almost to the day, and five children were born, all baptized at Québec.

1. Pierre, the eldest, was baptized on 13 July 1705 by the pastor François Dupré. The godfather was named Durbois, probably his uncle Ignace Liénard dit Durbois et Boisjoli, married to Marie-Anne Leduc, his mother's sister. The godmother was not named. Pierre died on an unknown date without marrying.

2. Marie-Anne, born on 30 October 1706 and baptized the next day by Father Dupré. Godfather and godmother: Charles Normand and Marie-Anne Laraut. The father and godfather signed.

3. François, born on 27 May 1710 and baptized the next day by the vicar Charles Hazeur Desauneaux. (6) Called son of Pierre Métayer, master tailor and merchant of this city, and of Geneviève Leduc. Godfather and godmother: Guillaume Fabas and Marie-Magdeleine Moreau. The father and the celebrating priest signed.

4. Nicolas, born on 28 March 1712 and baptized the following day by the vicar Goulvin Calvarin. Godfather and godmother: Nicolas Martin and Marie-Agnes Maufait. (7)

5. Jean dit Jean-Baptiste, Nicolas's twin. Godfather and godmother: Jean Guillotte and Marie-Madeleine Laraut. Everyone signed the act of the double baptism, with the exception of the parents and Nicolas Martin.

THE FAMILY MOVES

The lease of 1704 was not over when Pierre Métayer dreamed of moving his family and his workshop to the Lower Town of Québec. On 11 April 1707, he had a meeting at the home of the widow Letourneau, with the notary François Genaple. (8) The house where the widow lived was the one which was inherited by Marie Marsollet, widow of Mathieu Damours des Chaufours, equerry, former councillor at the Sovereign Council of New France. Marie, who usually lived at Ville-Marie, was passing through Québec and took advantage of this opportunity to lease

> *"by means of a rent in silver from the first*
> *day of the next May until three consecutive*
> *years have passed",*

121

to Pierre Métayer dit Saintonge, tailor, for a portion of the house located in the Lower Town and which belonged to the widow Marsollet and her children. This portion included a cellar, a heated room separated by a dividing wall of boards on the first floor, another room with a gallery on the second floor and a small attic covered only with crosswise planks on the roof. The rent was one hundred livres per year payable in two six-month installments.

At the end of his lease, the tenant had to return the portion of the house in the same condition as when he leased it, except that he will install in the cellar new stairs of the same form as the old one. The roof, they agreed, would be sealed with shingles in places where water dripped on rainy days; the partition of the tambour had also to be narrowed. Finally, Métayer had to agree with the widow Letourneau who still occupied the place, on the subject of the dividing wall which she had installed in the small room *"which looks out on the street which goes down to Cul-de-Sac"*. At the end of the lease, he would be able to take the glass from the windows if he managed to put them in. The said lease was signed in the presence of witnesses Guillaume Fabas dit Saint-Germain, tailor, and Laurant Normandin, innkeeper.

LAST TRANSACTION

During his brief career as tailor, Pierre Métayer always lived at Québec and he seems to be devoted solely to practicing his trade. He never owned any real estate, except after the death of his father-in-law, René Leduc, when he and his wife jointly inherited *"one-third of two arpents of land in width"*, located in the seigneurie of Lauzon, *"being half of four arpents of width"* on the edge of the river, the other two-thirds going to Marie-Anne Leduc, Geneviève's sister, and to their mother Anne Gentreau. On 21 November 1708 (contract Chambalon), Pierre and Geneviève sold their share to Guillaume Leduc, their brother and brother-in-law. This portion of land joined, on the northeast that of the buyer, and on the southwest the two other arpents belonging to Anne Gentreau, widow of René Leduc. This sale also included one-third of the livestock belonging to the estate, and a plowshare. The buyer had to pay the cens and the rents owed to the domain of the seigneurie of Lauzon and to pay 500 livres:

122

350 for the price of the portion of land, 150 for the livestock and the hay, and 20 livres in interests. On 17 November 1709, one year later almost to the day, the sellers admitted having received the 520 livres of the transaction and gave a receipt for it to the buyer.

DIED AT THE HOSPITAL

Less than four years later, Pierre Métayer dit Saintonge died at the Hôtel-Dieu of Québec after eight days of hospitalization. His death was noted on 21 May 1712 in the registry of the patients of the institution. Something unexplained; the two lines which preceded the inscription of this death indicate the presence of "madame Leduc" and "madame St-Onge", who stayed at the hospital eight days and eighteen days respectively. Does this refer to the mother and the daughter? Was there an epidemic which claimed the life of our ancestor and at the same time afflicted his wife and his mother-in-law?

Even if the death of Pierre Métayer is reported to us in an amazing economy of words, it informs us that he was originally from the city of Saintes in Saintonge. Here is an interesting detail which the notary LaCetière did not mention in his contract drawn up on 24 May 1704. Before the French Revolution which radically changed the parish distribution throughout France, the city of Saintes was home to several parishes and faubourgs. In his "Analyse socio-professionnelle de Saintes, in 1742", the historian *François-Julien-Labruyère* noted that the map of Saintes indicated four parishes, those of Saint-Pierre, Saint-Colombe, Saint-Michel and Saint-Maur, backed up to the river Charente. Around this nucleus were the faubourgs of Saint-Vivien, Saint-Macou, Saint-Eutrope, Saint-Pallais and La Bretonnière. The textile industry was the most important one: 22 tailors practiced their art there.

WIDOWHOOD AND REMARRIAGE OF GENEVIÉVE

Geneviève Leduc's period of mourning lasted less than four years. In the meantime, she had a close relationship with her family. On 20 June 1712 (contract Chambalon), her sister Marie-Anne and her husband Ignace Liénard dit Durbois, residents of the seigneurie of Neuville, ceded to the young widow

123

"the third franc of the half" of a plot and house located in the Lower Town of Québec, on the quay of Cul-de-Sac. This portion of property, which Marie-Anne inherited from her father, joined on one side the house of the widow Lavergne, and on the other side, the street which goes from the quay to the rue Demeulle. The sale was carried out for 400 livres which Geneviève paid in cash.

On 22 August 1713 (same notary), Anne Gentreau made a donation to her daughter Geneviève of half of a piece of land with three and a half arpents in frontage on the river, by forty deep, joining the lands of Gabriel Lambert and Guillaume Leduc, on the Lauzon coast. The donation also included the half of a lot and a house located in the Lower Town of Québec, on the quay of Cul-de-Sac. In fact, it refers to the half of the real estate coming from her right to the joint property she had with her late husband. However, Geneviève was only able to profit from life tenancy of these properties after the death of her mother.

During the following months, Geneviève and her brother Guillaume did business together two more times in the presence of the notary Chambalon. On 11 November 1713, Guillaume and his wife Elisabeth Drouin admitted owing Geneviève one thousand livres for a similar sum lent the day before in playing card money and which they promised to repay according to the wishes of the lender. A rider signed by the notary Pierre Rivet on 20 July 1716 (Chambalon having died the preceding month) certified that the loan had been repaid in good and proper form.

On 4 April 1714, Geneviève Leduc took possession, for 416 livres, 13 sols and 4 deniers, of another third franc (or one-sixth) of the same plot and house located on the quay of Cul-de-Sac at Québec, which she had gradually taken possession of since the death of her husband. We learn here that the said lot with only 18 feet in frontage and 30 deep was appraised by the heirs at the tidy sum of 2500 livres. This plot must have been occupied as it was quite suitable for business during this era.

Less than two years later, before Geneviève entered into married life again which, this time, lasted more than twenty years. Her new husband was Joseph Roberge, a tanner by trade, born at Saint-Pierre on the Ile d'Orléans on 2 February 1690 to the union of Pierre Roberge and Françoise Loignon. Thus he was more than fifteen years younger than Geneviève, whom he must have nevertheless considered an excellent match. The canon Goulvin Calvarin, a member of the chapter of the cathedral of Québec, blessed this marriage which took place on 16 January 1716, in the presence of Pierre and Charles Roberge, Guillaume Leduc and Toussaint Fossé.

The following 8 June, in the presence of the notary LaCetière, Pierre and Joseph Roberge, Geneviève Leduc, and her brother Guillaume, the latter as guardian of the minor children of the late Pierre Métayer dit Saintonge, requested that the inventory be made of the property which had belonged to the estate of the latter and his widow, for the preservation of the property which is found in the house on rue Sous-le-Fort, where the said Roberge and his wife live. All this was done in the presence of the witnesses Jean-Baptiste Dessalines and Jean-Baptiste Cardinet.

Following is the list of the utensils and personal property. Note that a buffet contained 2063 livres. Recorded were a milk cow worth 170 livres and some accounts payable and receivable. Geneviève stated that she was owed 10 livres and that she even owed 100 livres for the rent of her house.

SECOND GENERATION

Remarrying at the age of 41, Geneviève Leduc only gave one son to Joseph Roberge, whose first name was Joseph like his father, born on 6 October 1716 and baptized the following day by the canon Goulvin Calvarin. His godfather and godmother were Romain Dolbec and Elisabeth Drouin, the child's aunt. On 17 October 1740, Joseph Roberge, junior, was married at Beauport to Marie-Cécile Lefebvre, daughter of Jacques Lefebvre and of the late Marie-Joseph Parent. The young couple went to live at Lévis, where the majority of their ten children were born (eight sons and two daughters).

In the second generation of the descendants of our ancestor Pierre and his second wife Geneviève, three of the Métayer children also chose to make the absolute bond in order to assure, through marriage, the permanence of their family up to today. They were Marie-Anne, Jean-Baptiste and François. As for Pierre, the eldest, and Nicolas, Jean-Baptiste's twin, we know that they died unmarried, but we are unaware of what became of them after their baptisms.

125

1.   Marie-Anne, the only Métayer daughter, was the first to leave the single state. She did so at Québec on 20 October 1727, by marrying Louis Baugis, son of the late Jean Baugis and Thérèse Parent. Louis was born at Beauport on 12 January 1699. Eight days earlier, the newlyweds had signed a marriage contract in the presence of the notary Jacques Pinguet. Messire Etienne Boullard, who had been the first pastor of Beauport and who became in 1727 vicar general of the diocese of Québec, blessed the union of Marie-Anne and Louis, who would live at Beauport and become the parents of three sons and nine daughters.

2.   Jean dit Jean-Baptiste, twin of Nicolas, was married to Gertrude Huyet dite Champagne at L'Ange-Gardien on 27 May 1736. Gertrude, born at Contrecoeur on 27 February 1709 was the daughter of Etienne Huyet or Huguet dit Poncelet et Champagne, and Barbe Forestier. Etienne, master shoemaker, was originally from Charlesville, in Champagne (Marne). First settled at Contrecoeur, the Huyet family moved to L'Ange-Gardien in 1723. (9) The wedding of Jean-Baptiste and Gertrude was celebrated by the curate Gaspard Dufournel, in the presence of Joseph Roberge, half-brother of the groom, Joseph Roberge, his step-father, and Pierre Leger, René and Pierre Huot. Jean-Baptiste practiced the trade of cooper at Québec. He lived on rue Saint-Joseph, faubourg Saint-Roch. His son and eight daughters were baptized at Québec.

3.   François, second son of Pierre Métayer and Geneviève Leduc, a day laborer living at Saint-Nicolas, was married there on 8 July 1738, to Marie-Madeleine Michel, born at Saint-Antoine-de-Tilly on 22 May 1719, daughter of Pierre Michel dit Taillon and Jeanne Baron. The marriage was celebrated by the curate François Rouillard, in the presence of Joseph Roberge, step-father of the groom, Joseph Roberge, his maternal brother, Jean Métayer, his brother, Charles Desjadons, Pierre Michel, father of the bride and Antoine Nadeau. All the children of the Métayer-Michel couple, four sons, four daughters, and one anonymous, were baptized at Saint-Nicolas.

A week before the marriage, on 30 June 1738 (contract Jean Latour), with the consent of their mother, François Métayer and his brother Jean-Baptiste sold to their half-brother Joseph Roberge, *"voyageur living in the city of Québec",* seven and a half perches of frontal land by forty deep, located on the Lauzon coast, parish of Saint-Joseph. This portion of land was inherited from their maternal grandparents, René Leduc and Anne Gentreau.

However, this contract by Latour was rescinded by a decree from the Sovereign Council of New France on 26 June 1747.

RECOURSE TO THE COURTS

During this era in which they had to build a country, the inhabitants of New France were poor for the most part. And they saved every little bit of their property to obtain fair remuneration for the results of their work. They often had to borrow to pay their debts: their main problem was to pay them back. In this respect the world has hardly changed. To settle litigation, the governmental authority of the time established the courts of first instance and of last resort. These were the bailiwicks or seigniorial courts in the rural regions, and the royal jurisdictions in the cities.

> *"All those who have closely consulted the judicial archives agree that judicial proceedings were much more familiar to the people of the seventeenth and eighteenth centuries than they are to contemporary man"*, wrote André Lafontaine. *"They went to court for everything and under any pretext; the nobles for distraction, the merchants for their business and the peasants for the preservation of their heritage"*. (10)

In cases when they were dissatisfied with the sentences rendered, petitioners and defendants could appeal to the supreme court, whose decision was irrevocable. The Sovereign Council played this role from 1663 until 1716, and the Superior Council from 1717 until the end of the French regime. Before the creation of these courts, litigation was submitted to arbitration by the government first, then, beginning in 1647, to a Council of State formed by the Governor-General living at Québec, the particular governor of Montréal and the superior of the Jesuits. (11)

127

Pierre Métayer, at least once during the practice of his trade as tailor, was summoned to appear before the Provost of Québec. This happened on 19 November 1704 following a claim made against him by the merchant Louis Prat. In a decision rendered on 28 November, the court agreed with the plaintiff and

> *"ordered that he will have credit for seven aulnes of pinchina and the breeches consisting of two aulnes of the same cloth that he had requested from the named Métayer until Henry Leparisien has been heard on the matter in question in the legal proceedings brought by the said Prat".*

The decision was appealed before the Sovereign Council on 22 December, but the court favorably received Prat's opposition, upheld the sentence of the Provost and ordered Métayer to give Prat

> *"a hood and breeches make and complete by the said appealing party paying him the sum of eight livres".*

Métayer also had to pay the expenses of the appeal. (12)

Between 1722 and 1733, Guillaume Leduc became very demanding of his sister Geneviève and his brother-in-law Joseph Roberge concerning the inheritance. (13) Among others, in a decision delivered on 9 June 1728 by the Provost of Québec, Guillaume, after a display of flawless and relevant documents, managed to convince the court to order Roberge to pay him 898 livres out of a total of 1000 livres that he claimed from him. The case was appealed and heard by the Superior Council on 13 April 1733, nearly five years later. The court of last instance dismissed this appeal, except for a few details.

Ten years later, Jean-Baptiste Métayer dit Saintonge, cooper of Québec, would not have any luck in the case brought against him by the mason Pierre Bélanger who claimed 150 livres which he owed him by the terms of a transaction signed between them on 13 December 1742. In a decision announced on 20 March 1744, the Provost of Québec ordered Métayer to pay his debt. The latter instead asked the Sovereign Council to annul this order. The appeal was heard on 14 April 1744, then referred to

128

30 September so that an architect could do the appraisal of the land and the house that Bélanger wanted to seize. The Council agreed with the latter and allowed him, on 16 November, to put up for auction the property of the defendant, who attempted a final recourse before the Council, but without success.

This litigation finally found a happy conclusion by means of an out of court agreement initialed by the notary Hilarion DuLaurent, who intervened on 10 January 1745. After making a statement of his accounts, Bélanger discovered that Jean-Baptiste Métayer and his wife now owed him an amount of 415 livres, 200 of which were repaid immediately with deniers from the merchant Charles Turpin. The debtors promised to pay the 165 other livres in two payments, the last due in March 1746. Joseph Roberge offered security for this arrangement and everyone seemed satisfied.

Jean-Baptiste Métayer would have more luck in his suit against the blacksmith Henry Creste, on 12 December 1747, before the Provost of Québec. Creste's debt was for 74 livres for non-payment of the lease of a small house. Creste was ordered to pay. He did not accept this and appealed the judgment to the Superior Council. The appeal was heard on 8 January 1748. Crest's' appeal was dismissed and he had to pay what he owed.

DEATH OF GENEVIÉVE LEDUC

When Jean-Baptiste Métayer tried his case against Henry Creste, his mother had already left for a better world. Geneviève Leduc died at Québec on 31 May 1747 and her mortal remains were buried the next day in the cemetery of the Hôtel-Dieu. The canon Michel Poulin de Courval, acting as chaplain of the hospital, presided at the funeral at which Joseph Philippon dit Picard and Pierre Chabot dit Lusignan attended as witnesses. The deceased, according to the record, was 72 years old.

One month later, on the first of July 1747, Joseph Roberge had the notary De Laurent draw up an inventory of the property of their estate. The document, which counts nineteen very full pages, certifies that the widower had a right to a child's share of the estate, as provided for in the marriage contract, which was one-fifth of the inheritance of his late wife. The other four-fifths went to Joseph Roberge, junior, and to Jean-Baptiste

Métayer, who had acquired the rights of his brother François and those of his sister Marie-Anne, wife of Louis Baugis. The same document reveals that Geneviève had died in her house on rue Saint-Joseph.

The assets of the estate were appraised by the court crier Pierre Pilote. The latter first visited the tannery where he discovered some horse, cow and seal pelts, and some vats, barrels, cauldrons and millstones. A gross of paper contained various notarized contracts, acts of guardianship, rulings, releases, survey reports, acknowledgment of debts, receipts, one of them was for seven livres for the payment of the coffin of the deceased and another for twelve livres for her burial. Another gross in paper contained a contract by the notary Hiché dated 5 April 1731 concerning the sale of a piece of land and a white house to Charles Leclerc, etc.

REMARRIAGE OF JOSEPH ROBERGE

Joseph Roberge was remarried at Québec on 8 January 1748, to Madeleine Girard, born in this same city on 24 January 1719. An unusual fact, this daughter of Jean-Baptiste Girard and Madeleine Aumier was 44 years younger than Geneviève Leduc. Madeleine gave Joseph another son and two daughters, all three born at Saint-Nicolas.

Another act written by the notary Du Laurent on 2 May 1750 informs us that Joseph Roberge, who had vouched for his step-son Jean-Baptiste Métayer in the out of court settlement reached in 1746 between him and Pierre Bélanger, had become, by virtue of a decision made by the Provost of Québec, purchaser of the house and the lot adjacent to his tannery on rue Saint-Joseph. On that day, a part of this property was sold to Etienne Lavallée for 980 livres, paid in various payments until 1754. The buyer seems to have had some difficulties in paying. On 16 June 1752, the seller had him appear before the Provost of Québec for non-payment of 338 livres which were owed.

In another act by the same notary, dated 28 December 1750, Joseph Roberge sold to his step-son Jean-Baptiste Métayer the other part of the same lot on rue Saint-Joseph, faubourg Saint-Roch, an area of 30 feet by 50, for 700 livres. In the same act, Jean-Baptiste withdrew claims that he might have against his step-father concerning the rights of his brother François Métayer, those of Louis Baugis, his brother-in-law, and those which could have gone to Pierre and Nicolas Métayer, who died unmarried and those of their trustee Guillaume Leduc, also deceased. Finally, a last act by Du Laurent written on 15 April 1752 reveals that Marie-Anne Métayer, widow of Louis Baugis since 12 April 1751, had ceded to Joseph Roberge all her rights to personal property and real estate coming from her late mother and her brothers Pierre and Nicolas, who died as *"boys"*. The sale was made for 250 livres coming from the sale of the furnishings and effects contained in the inventory acquired by the named Lavallée.

Finally, Joseph Roberge, who had taken over from Pierre Métayer some 40 years earlier and who knew how to keep everything going under his firm but benevolent authority, was himself led to his final rest. His passage to the here-after was noted in the registry of Notre-Dame of Québec on the first of August 1756 by the curate Felix Recher, who had been placed in charge of this parish seven years earlier, when he was only 26. The burial act gives Joseph Roberge's age as 65. In reality, he had been made younger by 18 months.

In 1756, the War of the Conquest had already begun. Thus, Joseph Roberge was not a witness to the siege of Québec. Nor was he subjected to the anguish of the defeat of New France at the hands of the invading English.

FAMILY NAME VARIATIONS

In addition to those alternate surnames mentioned earlier in this Chapter, the following additional variations are known: Cupidon, Ladouceur, Lafillasse, Lagiberne, LeMétayer, Levron, Métilly and Saintonge.

END NOTES

1)   "La civilisation traditionelle de l'habitant aux XVIIe et XVIIIe siecles". Fides, 1973, p.459ss.

2)   Andrée Paradis:"L'avenement d'un costume canadien". Revue Cap-aux-Diamants, été, 1988, p.12.

3)   This Jean Métayer did not leave any descendants, contrary to that reported by Msgr Cyprien Tanguay (*DGFC, VI, p.9.*) which gave him paternity from Pierre Métayer dit Saintonge.

4)   Tanguay (Ibid).

5)   René Jetté: DGFQ, p.803.

6)   Son of Léonard Hazeur-Desauneaux and of Marie-Anne Pinguet. Charles would become the first resident priest at Montmagny, from where he died on 6 June 1719.

7)   A Breton priest who arrived at Québec in 1703. Promoted to chanter in 1712 he was one of the directors of the Seminary of Québec, where he exercised the functions of vicar general of the upper town, of Chaplain of the Hôtel-Dieu and of diocesian chief. He died on a mission to the Mississippi on 26 November 1719.

8)   Really Marie-Madeleine Vallée, widow of Philippe Letourneau, who died at Québec during this epoch.

9)   A private contract, drawn up by Father Gaspard Dufournel on 5 May 1723 and deposed for the record by Joseph Jacob on the forst of July 1732.

10)   "Les bailliage de Beaupré and of the Isle of Orléans." Sherbrooke 1987, p. XI & XII.

11)   J. Delalande "Le Conseil Souverain de la Nouvelle-France" Québec, 1927, p.30 & 31.

12)   _____.*JDCSNF*, IV, p.1120 & 1121.

13)   _____.*JDCSNF*, I, 11 August 1722, p.158-159; 27 March 1724, p.214; II, 18 April 1733, p.313.

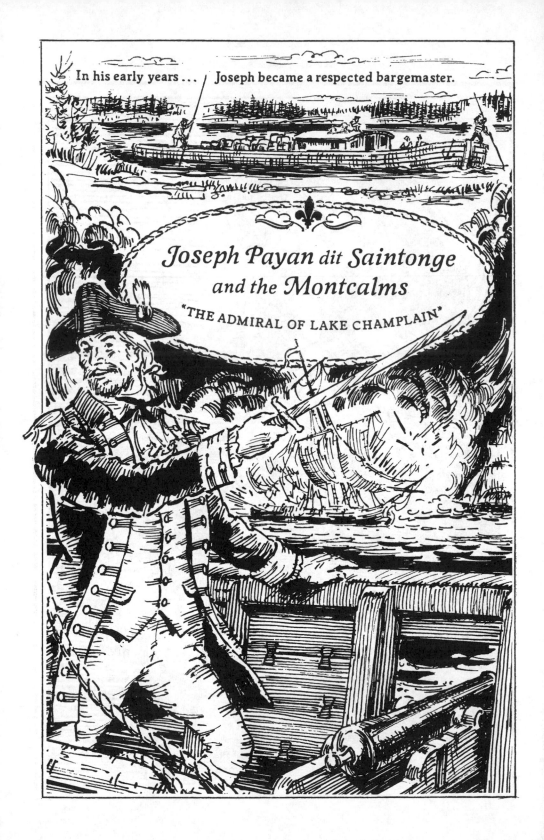

In his early years... Joseph became a respected bargemaster.

Joseph Payan *dit* Saintonge
and the Montcalms
"THE ADMIRAL OF LAKE CHAMPLAIN"

CHAPTER 8

Joseph Payant dit Saintonge

and the Montcalms

oseph Payant dit Saintonge, eldest son of the soldier-shoemaker Jacques Payant, arrived in Québec with the troops of *la Marine* at the end of the seventeenth century, undoubtedly not imagining during his lifetime, that a goodly number of his descendants would trade the surname of Saintonge for that of Montcalm, but this is indeed what happened fifty years after his death. Surnamed *"the Admiral of Lake Champlain"* because of the important role that he played on this lake during the Seven Years War, when he was under the command of General Montcalm and his lieutenant Bourlamaque. Joseph Payant ended his career in 1760, at the same time as the French domination of New France came to an end.

HIS CHILDHOOD

Joseph was born at Québec on 19 February 1700 to the first marriage of Jacques Payan to Louise Morin, and was baptized by messire Pierre Pocquet (1) the same day with the first name of Joseph-Jacques. His godfather and godmother were Joseph Morin and Marguerite Gauthier. Until the end of his life, Joseph would almost always be present at the notable events concerning his family and he would sign his name with a firm and elegant signature, witness to an education superior to the average child during that era.

After the death of Louise Morin in February 1710, Jacques Payan, eight months later, was remarried, to Marguerite Sédillot. At the time of the parish census of 1716, this family lived on rue des Pauvres (2), across from the Hôtel-Dieu. Our ancestor was 57, his wife at least 30. The children of the two marriages were Joseph, Pierre, Charles and Marie-Charlotte. (3)

The house on rue des Pauvres, where Jacques Payan practiced his trade of shoemaker, had been acquired from the master sculptor Denis Mallet in August 1700, a few months after the birth of Joseph, for a perpetual land rent of 12 livres and 10 sols. In October, our ancestor embarked for France *"on business"*. He seems to have stayed three or four years before returning to New France. Meanwhile, Pierre Morin filled the void created by the absence of his son-in-law at his home in Québec.

HIS MARRIAGE AND HIS ESTABLISHMENT

On 2 November 1721, while his father was again staying in France, the 20 year old Joseph, took a wife in his native parish. The nuptial ceremony was presided over by Thomas Thiboult (4), successor to Pierre Pocquet as pastor of Notre-Dame. The bride was the 21 year old Marie-Jeanne Legris, daughter of Jean and of Marie-Geneviève Sédillot, residents of Rivière Saint-Charles. On this same day, during the afternoon, the young couple, their friends and relatives went to the notary Jean-Étienne Dubreuil in order to take part in the reading of the marriage contract. Present were Jean Legris, the father of the bride, Marguerite Sédillot, second wife of Jacques Payan, Guillaume de Guise, cousin, Gilbert Thomas, Louis and Jean Sédillot, maternal uncles of the bride, Adrien Legris, paternal uncle and Pierre Legris, her brother. Joseph, whose dowry had been set at 1,000 livres, would live in community property with his wife. The father of the latter promised to give them, in the following spring, a cow *"well-wintered"* valued at 30 livres.

On 2 February 1724 (contract Dubreuil), Marie LeRoy, widow of Georges Regnard du Plessis, former treasurer of *la Marine* in this country, acknowledged having sold to Joseph Payant a piece of land with 50 feet in frontage by 36 1/2 wide located on rue Saint-Flavien. This land, which Joseph had already occupied for some time, was part of a larger area which the seller and her late husband had acquired from the clergy of Québec. The transaction had been carried out for 285 livres which Marie LeRoy agreed would be paid to her in the form of a rent of 14 livres and 5 sols payable on the first of June each year.

On 20 August 1737, in his records of the fief of Sault-au -Matelot, the intendant Hocquart noted the location of Joseph Payant between those of Pierre Normandeau dit Deslauriers and the widow of Pierre Payment (Françoise Huppé dit Lagrois).

He described it like this:

"Above is Joseph Payant dit Saint-Onge who owns a Place with fifty feet of frontage by thirty six and a half deep charged with Five Sols for the Cens and rents On which is a house in stone with two Stories twenty seven feet long By twenty four feet wide. The Rest of the said Lot is in a Yard." (5)

Joseph Payant kept this property for more than fifty years. He sold it in 1779, more than twenty years after having finally left the city of Québec.

HIS FAMILY

It was probably in this stone house on rue Saint-Flavien that the majority, if not all, of the children of Joseph Payant and Marie Jeanne Legris were born. Seven sons and three daughters were baptized at Québec between 1722 and 1740. Seven of them reached adulthood and were married:

1. Louis-Joseph, born on the 11th and baptized on 12 August 1722. Married at Québec in 1746, to Geneviève Dalerat. Died on the 27th and buried at Saint-Ours on 28 December 1768.

2. Dominique, born on the 22nd and baptized on 23 November 1724. Married at Chambly in 1745, to Marie-Louise Laporte. Buried at Saint-Ours on 29 July 1778.

3. Jean-Baptiste, born on the 2nd and baptized on 3 April 1726. Married at Laprairie in 1755, to Catherine Lerigé-Laplante. Died on the 10th and buried at Laprairie on 12 September 1808.

4. Pierre-François, born and baptized on 11 March 1729. Died on the 26th and buried on 27 July of the same year.

137

5. Jean-Marie, born on the 11th and baptized on 12 June 1730. Married at Kamouraska in 1757, to Rosalie Lebel. Died on the 20th and buried at Kamouraska on 21 November 1803.

6. Marie-Angélique, baptized on 3 February 1732 and buried on the following 4 July.

7. Nicolas, baptized on the first of October 1733. Married at Fort Saint-Jean in 1758, to Marie-Rose Lerigé-Laplante. Died on the 2nd and buried at Laprairie on 4 March 1778.

8. Marie-Jeanne, baptized on 20 May 1735 and buried on the following 23 July.

9. Louis, baptized on 21 September 1737. Married at Laprairie in 1766 to Monique Lefort. Died on the 6th and buried at Saint-Philippe de Laprairie on 8 November 1789.

10. Marie-Joseph, baptized on 22 May 1740. First marriage at Laprairie in 1759, to Jacques or Nafré Delprat; second marriage at Laprairie in 1762, to Ignace-Rigobert Pinsonneau. Date of death unknown.

At the time of the parish census which took place at Québec in 1744, Joseph Payant figured among the seven riverside residents on rue Saint-Flavien. He was said to be 43 years old and practiced the trade of blacksmith. Noted were Marie Legris, his wife, and his children Louis-Joseph, Dominique, Jean-Baptiste, Jean-Marie, Nicolas, Louis, and Marie-Joseph. Living in the same home were Marie-Anne Saint-Onge, younger sister of Joseph, and Thomas Caret. (6)

A few years earlier, in 1726 (contract Dubreuil, 2 April), Joseph Payant had renounced his rights to the succession of his late mother and to that of his father in favor of his brothers and sisters *"both full and half on the father's side"*, in return for a milk cow which his father had promised to deliver to him, on 15 October of the same year, and for four tin plates and a frying pan.

Our ancestor Jacques Payan died unexpectedly ten years later and was buried at Québec on 27 June 1736. It was Joseph who requested that the inventory of the property of his late father be drafted. The document drawn up by the notary Jacques Pinguet on 29 April 1737 reveals that Jacques Payan only left his heirs a few personal effects which were barely sufficient to cover the funeral expenses and the fees for a few masses.

BARGE MASTER

We see from the census of 1744 that Joseph was practicing his trade of blacksmith at that time. He must have, we believe, engaged in this activity mostly in the winter when the river was covered with ice. During the summer he plied the Saint-Lawrence and perhaps other navigable waterways on board his barge. He did this for more than 25 years, at least from 1734 until 1760.

The registries of the Admiralty of Québec, concerning the size of the ships which were built during the year 1734, reveal that on 15 May of this year,

> *"the boat named St Joseph belonging to Joseph Payant d.Xantonge, built on the Isle aux Oyes with a 41 foot keel, a 15 and one half foot Beam and seven feet deep was measured in the presence of the officers of the admiralty by Fabien Badieaux (7) and was found to be of 44 tons according to official report of the said Officers on 7 June".(8)*

The document was signed by the notary Jean-Claude Louet, clerk of the Admiralty of Québec.

FIRST PILOT ON LAKE CHAMPLAIN

Payant was hardly slow to unfurl the sails between the banks of the Richelieu river and ferry goods among the forts on Lake Champlain. According to Philippe Demers (9), from 1731 until 1742, Fort Saint-Frederic was supplied by the boats departing from Sainte-Thérèse and Bleury. In this last year appeared the master of the Québec barge who will have the honor, in 1749, to count among his passengers the famous Swedish naturalist Pehr Kalm and, in 1753, the the military engineer Louis Franquet, who came to inspect the fortifications in the regions of Québec, Trois-Rivières and Montréal. According to Kalm

"The yacht which brought us to Saint-Jean, wrote Kalm (10), *is the first which had been built here, and which had ever navigated on Lake Champlain, because earlier only boats were used for transporting the provisions. The captain was of French origin, but was born in this country; he had built his yacht himself and took some soundings to find a safe route between the forts Saint-Jean and Saint-Frederic".*

"Thus it was in 1742, assures Demers, *that navigation by boat on Lake Champlain resumed. Schooners, chebecs, gunboats, tartans, brigantines and warships of all sorts have been plying these peaceful waters, throughout all our wars".*

"The title of admiral which was given to the barge master, he continues, *surprises us, especially in an act countersigned by several soldiers. Was it given during this era to someone who commanded several armed ships? In 1758, the military operations required the construction of a few barges and undoubtedly the name of admiral was given to the pilot St-Onge who commanded the main barge. In 1759 and 1769, there were three chebecs, a large tartan and some naval officers on Lake Champlain; as a result St-Onge was the name of the pilot and his barge, the barge or schooner belonging to St-Onge."*

But let's not get ahead of the events.

The registries of the Admiralty of Québec report that for the first seven months of 1742, Joseph and his uncle Pierre Payant, caretaker of the ship, had each received a salary of 252 livres: 36 livres a month.

In the same registries of the year 1744 were recorded the expenses made two years earlier, at the time of the building of the King's supply ship *Le Canada*, as well as the wages of the personnel of the said barge. The master on board, Joseph Payant, received 319 livres and 10 sols for the period from the first of April to 3 October 1744. The name of Dominique Payant, Joseph's son, also appears. He received 213 livres for the same time in recognition for his work as sailor. The accounts book consented to fortifÿng the storehouses of Québec and Montréal *"in a state of defence during the war"* mentioned on the date of 5 March 1746 that Joseph had made 583 bows at 9 sols each, which was a supplemental income for him of 262 livres.

During this era, the American colonies endured the jolts of this war between France and England. Louisbourg fell in 1745 under fire from English sailing ships. The peace of Aix-la-Chapelle in 1748 solved nothing. It only increased rivalry between the colonies. After the loss of Acadia in 1755, a new conflict broke out, much more serious, since it resulted in the loss of New France.

THE PROMISED LAND

About ten years earlier, the family of Joseph Payant began its exodus to the promise land, that of the valley of the Richelieu. The first to take root there was the sailor Dominique. On 21 February 1745, the young man, 20 years old was summoned to the house of Jean-Baptiste Besset, at Chambly, where the notary Gervais Hodiesné was ready to read his marriage contract with Marie-Louise Laporte, daughter of François and of Marie-Louise Chedevergue, residents of the seigneurie of Saint-Denis, on Lake Champlain. Louis-Joseph, elder brother of Dominique, was present. The future couple would have community property according to the *coutume de Paris*. Dominique said he owned a piece of land in standing wood with three arpents of frontage facing Lake Champlain, in the seigneurie of M. Foucault. This land was located across from the ile-aux-Noix.(11) The wedding took place the next day, 22 February, in the church of Saint-

141

Joseph de Chambly, in the presence of Joseph Payant, father, Charles Lebeau, Louis Bourbos, Baptiste and Charlotte Bessette, and Baptiste Laporte. The officiating priest was the Récollet Michel Levasseur.

The following year, it was the turn of the eldest, Louis-Joseph, to take a wife. He signed his marriage contract on 8 May 1746 in the presence of the notary Gilbert Boucault de Godefus, at his father's home, on rue Saint-Flavien, at Québec. The young man, who practiced the trade of gunsmith, was 23 years old. In the absence of Joseph Payant, navigator *"presently at Pointe a la Chevelure"* (12), it was his mother, Marie Legris, who stipulated for him and she stated that she had her husband's verbal consent. The bride was the 25 year old Geneviève Daleret, living at the home of Sieur Louis Dunière, businessman. (13) The groom was accompanied by his brother Jean-Baptiste, his uncles Pierre Payant and Jacques Pampalon. The couple would live in community property. Louis-Joseph brought a dowry of 1000 livres. Two days later, on 10 May, at the time of his wedding celebrated in the parish church of Québec by the curate Joseph-André-Mathurin Jacrau, Louis-Joseph Payant, classified as a blacksmith, son of Joseph, navigator, living in this city, and Marie Legris, married Geneviève, living at the home of Louis Dunière, businessman, in the presence of several witnesses, including Jean-Baptiste Payant, brother of the groom, who signed curiously *"Jan Batite paians de Saintonge"*.

During this era, in the winters, Joseph Payant rarely left his native city. On the morning of 24 January 1750, he paid a visit to the notary Hilarion Dulaurent to proceed with the sale to Louis Lebel dit Beaulieu, of a portion of land from the succession of Louise Morin, his late mother. It concerned an area of eight perches in frontage, more or less, by 25 arpents of depth, located at Rivière Saint-Charles. This transaction was reached for 275 livres which the buyer paid in cash.

Three years later, it was also during winter that Marie-Jeanne Legris made her final farewells to her loved ones. On March 1753, her family was present for her last breath and she was buried the next day in the parish cemetery after a funeral presided over by the pastor Jean-Felix Recher, who said she was about 45 years old. In fact, she only needed a few days more to reach her 54th birthday.

A few days later, on 15 March, Joseph Payant dit St-Onge "commander of the barge of the King on Lake Champlain was on the point of leaving to go serve on the said Barge", appointed his brother Pierre to be his general and special administrator to whom he gave the power to receive from the general treasurers of the colonies

> *"all the amounts which will be ordered for him by His Majesty, both for his wages, bonuses in the said capacity and others furnished which can be owed to him, to give all valid receipts and discharges and others during his absence, to regulate and administer all his property and affairs present and to come, and to receive the revenues, rents, owed to him and also to receive all the payments which could be offered to him, accounts with the debtors, farmers and others owed to the said sieur grantor...also the power to lease and to renew the leases of his property, to collect from them all inheritance which could fall to him...to pay the balance or receive it, to accept all donations", etc.*

> *(contract Paul-Antoine-François Lanouiller DesGranges).*

In summary, before going away for the length of the navigation season and no longer able to count on the support of his wife, Joseph had chosen his brother the most capable one to replace him in the administration of his affairs. The following spring on 14 June, Antoine Foucher, notary practicing at Fort Saint-Frederic, noted that Joseph Payant,

> *"captain commanding the schooner called "Le Saint-Frederic", presently at the said fort, agreed to lend to Jean Rousseau dit Ladouceur, resident of the Saint-François coast, the amount of 76 livres which the latter promised to repay to the commander of the post during the following month of July."*

In 1755, it was the turn of Joseph's third son, the 29 year old Jean-Baptiste, to settle in the Richelieu valley. On 4 April, in the presence of the notary Joseph Lalanne, he promised to marry Catherine Lerigé, daughter of the late Pierre, equerry, Sieur de Laplante, and of Marie-Louise Hubert dit Lacroix, living at Laprairie. This marriage contract indicated that Joseph Payant, *"captain maintained in the service of the King"*, was still living at Québec. Also present were Nicolas Payant, brother of Jean-Baptiste, Pierre Demers, first captain in the militia and commander of Laprairie, Joseph Lerigé, equerry, Sieur de Laplante, Catherine's uncle, and her cousin Pierre Hubert dit Lacroix, guard of the King's storehouse at Saint-Jean. The bride and groom would live in community property and Jean-Baptiste's dowry was set at 400 livres. The marriage was celebrated at Laprairie ten days later, on 14 April, by the curate Jacques Delignery (14), in the presence of the numerous friends and relatives of the two families.

It was also in 1755, on 26 May, in the presence of Gervais Hodiesné, that Joseph Payant dit Xantonge, *"captain of the barge of Fort Saint-Jean"*, accepted from Charles Lemoine, baron of Longueuil, captain of an infantry company living on rue Notre-Dame in Montréal, a concession of six arpents in frontage by thirty deep, bordering on one end the rivière de Chambly, on another end the lands not ceded. This land was located in the vicinity of Fort Saint-Jean. It was charged with six sols for the cens, and a rent of one half-minot of wheat for each area of twenty arpents, payable each year on Saint-Martin's Day (11 November). The tenant was committed to have a home on this land, the first to be ceded in the area of the fort.

MILITARY JOURNAL OF NICOLAS DES MELOIZES

On 17 May 1756, King George II of England declared war on France whom he accused of conducting itself in an unjustifiable manner in the West Indies and particularly in North America after the treaty of Aix-la-Chapelle. All throughout New France and New England, the pot had been boiling for a long time. It was felt that someday it was going to overflow, and that Lake Champlain was the place where the invading Americans would try to enter. The French had already built several forts to block this eventuality.

Upon his arrival in Canada some sixty years earlier, the soldier Jacques Payan worked among the troops of *la Marine* then commanded by François-Marie Renaud d'Avene des Meloizes. A grandson of this captain, Nicolas des Meloizes, was also famous in the military. He distinguished himself in Acadia and Ohio. He also took part in the battle of Carillon and that of Sainte-Foy. This last war which New France fought gave him the opportunity to write a military journal in which he sometimes noted the presence and the activities of Joseph Payant on Lake Champlain. (15)

Between 1756 and 1760, Joseph played an important role, not only as transporter of troops and military supplies on the Richelieu River and Lake Champlain, but also as bearer of news and as a messenger. On Friday, 27 August 1756, Nicolas des Meloizes noted in his journal:

>*"The journeys between St Frederic and Carillon have informed us that the barge left yesterday morning from St-Jean arrived in the evening at Fort St-Frederic. M. de Lusignan commander of the said fort sent to M. his son the statement by the captain of the barge in these terms.*

>*"St-Onge reports the news of the taking of Chouaguen where we have only lost eight men, we have taken 1800 prisoners of whom 700 have already left for Québec, 600 on the barge of Dussault; we have taken one hundred pieces of artillery, 3 barges, 3 cases of gold and silver. M. de Montcalm travels to St-Jean today. There are one hundred ships all prepared. There are 120 savages who are coming and are at Saint-Jean; a lot of people have been placed on all the roads to prevent the enemy from learning about the capture of Chouaguen.*

>*"The English lost four hundred or five hundred men. M. Hiché comes with the savages and Perthuis interprets, they have the letters. The Te Deum was sung at Montréal. Xaintonge said he saw the letter*

145

which M. the General wrote on this matter to M. de Sacquepee. In addition, we took six hundred ships at Chouaguen. A barge was sunk at the entrance of the river of Chouaguen".

On Monday, 30 August, Nicolas des Meloizes added:

"St-Onge says that a man named flame (Nicolas Flame), sergeant of our troops and who found himself at the festivities at Montréal brought with all speed to St-Jean letters from M. de Vaudreuil which he gave to M. de Sacquepee, that this officer immediately celebrated in his fort which required a similar news and that he had delivered the letters to the barge fearing that it would be too long on the way, that he preferred to send them by the savages; that Madame de Sacquepee upon her return to St-Jean from a piece of land that she had at la Chine had spoken to M. de Villiers coming from Chouaguen who had told him about the matter...The barge had to leave in the morning for St-Jean."

Nicolas des Meloizes took up the writing of his journal again in 1759. On Friday, 13 October, after the fall of Québec, the confrontations on Lake Champlain continued, he added:

It happened during the night of the 12th and 13th that two sailors who told M. de Bourlamaque that the barge commanded by St-Onge had been pursued by an English boat and a skiff with cannon, that it would have surely been taken if the boat had not run aground. St-Onge entered the Mississippi river where he still is. He is the one who fired the cannon heard yesterday to warn us and the chebecs so that they not be taken. He thought that they had been attacked."

In his work concerning the Admiral of Lake Champlain, the judge Philippe Demers gave his version of these events which he titled *"L'alerte of 12 October 1759"*.

However, he wrote, *our hero plays a considerable role in the events of the day. The brilliant victory of the French at Carillon had not discouraged England, because the capture of Louisbourg was ample compensation. Resolved to finish it, England decided to attack the colony by way of the the river and Lake Champlain...*

"Amherst having gathered an army of 11,000 men and being assured of an artillery, an amount which Abercrombie lacked, went on to seize Carillon and Saint-Frederic in a period of a week. Hebecourt who had been left at Carillon with 400 men, seeing the struggle lost, emptied the storehouses and retreated after blowing up the two forts under the nose of the invaders. Thus Amherst saw the fruit of his victory lost to him. He was indeed master of the key to the lake, but he could not venture out with the barges; the schooner and the three armed chebecs stood in his way. Fortunately, he had the saw mill by the falls; but warships were not built in a few days. It was only on 10 October that his navy was ready and he decided to advance his army in pursuit of two powerful brigantines.

"During this time de Bourlamaque entrenched himself on l'Ile-aux-Noix. Having had news of the movements of the enemy, he sent the barge and the chebecs on reconnaissance, with orders not to allow themselves to be cut off; the essential thing was to get back to the river before the enemy. The schooner, being the weakest, kept to the rear and stopped during the evening of the 11th at the entrance of the chan-

nel which separated the grand l'Ile from Contrecoeur, in order to monitor the bay of Saint-Albans.

"During this time the three chebecs got as far as the four Iles des quatre vents, now known by the name of the Four Brothers. During the night, the English brigantines of the advanced guard of the army which followed them, probably from the east side, passed the three French ships without being discovered.

"At daybreak, Saint-Onge fortunately noticed across the Iles aux bois blanc, now the Sister Islands, a brigantine with twenty pieces of cannon of 18 and a gun-ship as strong as his schooner which were preparing to attack him. He immediately committed himself to the channel of the grande island. The brigantine gave him chase and he would have been captured, when it ran aground, and the schooner slipped away towards the Mississippi bay, all sails spread to the wind.

"During this time, the chebecs, commanded by M. de Laubaras, vigorously attacked the rear guard of the English which had only made it to the Iles des quatre vents, taking a barge from it and took twenty prisoners. The wind having turned to the northeast, the brigantine managed to free itself and proceeded in its turn to attack the French ships which took refuge in the bay of Tsonnanthouans. In the night, de Laubaras seeing himself blocked, sank two of his ships and beached the other, after having dispatched two boats to Bourlamaque to warn him and to report to him about the prisoners. On the morning of the 13th, he set out for Montréal with all his people, about sixty men. This calamity disappointed de Bourlamaque very much. In a letter to Lévis, he

complained bitterly of the inability of Laubaras and concluded: I would not give him command of la galiote Saint-Cloud".

On the l'Ile-aux-Noix, everyone believed that St-Onge's schooner was captured or burned; however, she waited for three days north of the Ile-a-Lamothe for a favorable wind, consequently she was the only one to return to port. The experience of the old pilot was worth more than the science of all the naval officers."

On Wednesday, 17 October, Nicolas des Meloizes added to his military journal:

"Good weather. M. de Lepervanche left at daybreak with 8 soldiers and 8 militia men and provisions for four days to take supplies to the barge and an order to St-Onge to return.

"At eleven o'clock, an officer and six Englishmen arrived who had been on board the St-Onge planning to go to one of their vessels..."

Thursday 18 October.

"Calm weather and very cloudy. The schooner commanded by St-Onge arrived at ten o'clock in the morning, towed by barges on orders of Mr de Lespervanche. It left yesterday in early evening from above the Isle de La Mothe from where nothing is seen. M. de Langy left the barge at sunset to push his exploration further."

SAD END OF A CAREER

Again according to Demers, the naval career of Payant ended at the Ile-aux-Noix on 25 August 1760. The English army, with a strength of between eight and nine thousand men,

149

debarked on the 14th on the right bank of the Richelieu, a mile and a half above the fort. The army was accompanied by five ships armed with cannon, two floating batteries and six boat hulks also armed with cannon. Bougainville had established some blockhouses on each side of the mouth of the south river, but he was forced to abandon them. He contented himself with ordering St-Onge's barge to anchor across from this place.

> *"On 25 August,* concluded Demers, *the English, who had secretly brought a company battery of 8 pieces, opposite the tartan, suddenly showed themselves. The commander of the French ship was killed after giving the order to cut the cable; the panic stricken sailors managed to swim to the island, and the wind from the west carried the tartan towards the enemy who seized it. De Bougainville immediately sent a warning to St-Onge to get to open water. But it was too late; already the enemy had turned their artillery on him. The channel in this area turns almost into a right angle from east to west; in addition,the wind was contrary; this explains for us how, in spite of the experience of the pilot, the schooner ran aground on a sand bank which was located precisely north of the mouth of the south river. It was easy for Major (Robert) Rogers and his men to cross the small river to take our pilot and his barge. (16) The event was of the greatest consequence, since it allowed Haviland to move his troops from the west side, on the Bilodau farm, to north of the fort; this forced Bougainville's army to retreat.*

> *"Payant, about sixty years old, understood that his career was finished. The flag that he had served had crossed the ocean again; the beautiful lake that he had defended was, in 1763, through an unfortunate proclamation, abandoned to the state of New York. In the future, he had to content himself with the*

*title of former sailor and to retire to
Chambly where he lived for several years
more.*" (17)

THE MIGRATION CONTINUES

In spite of the war, the migration of the Joseph Payant
family towards the Richelieu valley did not slow up. A lone son,
Jean-Marie, took the opposite direction, that of the lower river.

In the beginning of 1757, Jean-Marie was already established at petit Kamouraska. On 15 March, he and the notary
Joseph Dionne met at the home of Jean-Baptiste Dupère, a major
in the militia, in order to proceed with an exchange of lands with
Joseph Bouchard, another inhabitant of petit Kamouraska. One
of these lands had five arpents in frontage, the other eight.
Bouchard kept for himself the small house that he already occupied and required an additional amount of 500 livres.

On 24 April, Jean-Marie married Rosalie, the daughter of
his neighbor Jean Lebel and Marie-Madeleine Dupère. This wedding was celebrated by the pastor Joseph Trutaut. The next day,
25 April, the notary Dionne drew up the marriage contract of the
new couple. As a dowry, Rosalie brought a piece of land with
four arpents in frontage and in standing wood located in the
neighborhood of the one which Jean-Marie had just acquired in
his exchange with Joseph Bouchard. The descendants of the
paternal line of Jean-Marie Payant and Rosalie Lebel have all
adopted the surname of Saint-Onge. They are numerous not only
in the region of Kamouraska, but also in New Brunswick and in
the state of Maine.

In 1758, it was Nicolas's turn to take a wife. On 21
March, he and the notary Joseph Lalanne met at the home of the
notary Jacques Lecomte, at Lapraire, to conclude the marriage
contract with the 20 year old Rosalie Lerigé, daughter of Paul
Lerigé, equerry, Sieur de Laplante and of Louise Hubert-
Lacroix. (18) Nicolas, 24 years old, was accompanied by his
father, Joseph, *"captain of the barges maintained in the service of
the King"*. The wedding, presided over by the Récollet Felix de
Berey, took place on 4 April at Fort Saint-Jean, in the presence
notably of M. de Sacquespee, commandant of the said fort.

The following year is the one in which Marie-Joseph, the youngest of the family and the only survivor of the three daughters of Joseph Payant and Marie Legris, took a husband.

The marriage contract was reached on 2 February 1759 according to the terms drafted by the notary Gervais Hodiesné. Present was Guillaume Delprat, grenadier of the regiment of Bearn in garrison at Longue Point, the future husband. He was the son of the late Nafré Delprat and dame Marie Jobert, merchant living in le Bourget, parish of Castelmelan, (19) diocese of Montauban, in Quercy, and stipulated for himself, whereas Joseph Payant dit Xaintonge, *"captain of the King's ship on Lake Champlain living at Fort Saint-Jean"* represented his 18 year old daughter, who was living with him. The dowry of the groom was 3000 livres.

The wedding took place on 5 February at Notre-Dame de Laprairie with the pastor Jacques Delignery presiding. The latter noted that Guillaume, soldier-grenadier of the company de Dalquier, in the Bearn regiment, was the son of Jacques Delprat and Marie Jaubert, of the parish of Castelmeran, diocese of Montauban. Joseph Payant was said in this act to be a resident of Laprairie. Two banns were dispensed with, as authorized by the Sulpicien Étienne de Montgolfier, who had just been named superior of his community at Montréal.

The union of Guillaume and Marie-Joseph only lasted for a few months during which they barely had the opportunity to see each other because of the war. Delprat died at the Hospital General of Québec, probably as a result of injuries suffered during the conflict. He was buried in the cemetery of the said hospital on 19 November 1759, under the surname of Belfleur. In a second marriage, Marie-Joseph, called widow of Jacques Delprat dit Bellefleur, was married at Notre-Dame de Laprairie, on 22 February 1762 (contract Lalanne, on the 20th), to Ignace-Rigobert Pinsonneau, a coureur des bois, son of the late Paul and of Marie-Joseph Tessier. It was again Father Delignery who signed the act. The Pinsonneau-Payant couple settled at Rivière de la Tortue. We lose track of them after 1763.

The last son of Joseph Payant to take a wife was Louis, the youngest. He was almost 29 years old when he appeared at the home of the notary Claude Hautraye on 6 September 1766 for the reading of his marriage contract with Marie-Monique Lefort, daughter of the late Jean-Baptiste and of Marie-Marguerite Favereau. Joseph Payant, senior, was present as well as his sons Jean-Baptiste and Nicolas. The groom brought a dowry of 1,000 livres. On 8 September, the priest Delignery blessed their marriage in the church of Notre-Dame de Laprairie.

Alexis and Augustin Payant, sons of Jacques and of Françoise Rivard, thus nephews of Joseph Payant, also went to settle later in the Richelieu valley. Augustin, born in 1750 at Saint-Pierre-les-Becquets, was married at Saint-Charles-sur-Richelieu, on 21 January 1774, to Geneviève Boucher, daughter of Michel and of Josephte Lambert. Alexis, also born at Saint-Pierre-les-Becquets in 1751, joined his destiny to that of Marie-Cécile Ledoux, daughter of Gabriel and of Cécile Gareau St-Onge, on 12 February 1776 (contract François-Pierre Cherrier, on the 9th), at Saint-Ours. Augustin's family lived at Saint-Charles and at Saint-Marc, whereas that of Alexis settled at Vercheres, near Contrecoeur.

FINAL DEPARTURE FROM QUÉBEC

After the death of his half-sister Marie-Anne, on 29 May 1757 at the age of 31, Joseph Payant's paternal love prevailed over the fraternal ties which bonded him to the other members of his family. Marie-Anne, last child of the marriage of Joseph and his second wife Marguerite Sédilot, was only ten years old when her father died in 1736. Her mother had died the preceding year. Through fate, Joseph became the adoptive father of the orphan.

In 1758, the war intensified on Lake Champlain and his duty as commander of the royal barges no longer left him any respite, Joseph believed it his duty to devote all his time to the defense of the colony against the invading English. On 23 February, he had the notary Jean-Claude Panet draw up the official report of the assets of the community property which existed between him and the late Marie Legris, because he did not stay

"very much in this town but at Fort Saint-Jean where he was employed in the service of the King, the personal property had been in a house located in this town on rue Saint-Flavien since the death of his wife".

153

Two days later, Joseph admitted having received from M. Panet the amount of 734 livres and 18 sols for the contents in the said report. Finally, on 27 February, still living at Québec on rue Saint-Flavien, he went to the home of the same notary to ask him to renew a proxy already signed in the presence of the notaries Lanouillier and Sanguinet on 15 March 1753, authorizing his brother Pierre to proceed with the sale by auction of two houses which he owned on rue Saint-Flavien.

On 9 April 1758, Joseph Payant returned to his loved ones. On that day, he paid a visit to his friend the notary Joseph-Lalanne to ratify the purchase of a piece of land with three arpents in frontage, acquired from Charles Laplante, living on the Saint-Joseph coast, in the seigneurie of la Prairie de la Madeleine. Joseph was described as an *"officer of the navy maintained by the King"*, living at Saint-Jean. This land contained *"a bit of shed"* sixteen feet both in width and length and enough grain to seed twelve minots. It was bordered by those of Jean Lefort, Maurice Demers, Clément Bougie and Ange Laplante. The seller had acquired this land from his father in the presence of the same notary, on 16 December 1754. He had just resold it for 300 livres paid in cash.

BILLS OF EXCHANGE FOR FRANCE

On 25 September 1761 was recorded in the records of Simon Sanguinet an *"Etat des lettres d'Echange (sic) du Tresor* which Sieur St-Onge, sailor, produced to take to France for his account: namely He had remitted the said 3rd Exercice of 1757 livres concerning the General expenses.

No 2, a letter from Imbert to M. Vaudesir (20) on 6 October was an order from St-Onge payable on 17 June 1760 for 1250 livres.

An item of the same to M. Vaudesir on 6 October payable on 7 August 1759 on order from St-Onge for 2500 livres.

No 2, a letter of the same to M. Perichon (21) on 1 October payable on 28 July 1762 by order from M. Payan for 540 livres.

No 3, an item on 1 October 1758 payable on 28 July 1761 on order from M. Payan for.......902 livres.

An item on 1 October payable on 31 August 1760 on order from M. Payan for 1000 livres.

If there is no error, the present Statement above amounts to six thousand One Hundred ninety-two livres five sols at Montréal on 25 September 1761.

They were signed by Le Chevalier De Lacorne and filed in the records of Notary Sanguinet.

Did these letters of exchange concerning the general expenses of the sailor Joseph Payant dit St-Onge during the main years of the conflict which resulted in the defeat of New France at the hands of the English, ever reach the treasurer-general of the Navy in France? Had they been entrusted to the chevalier de Lacorne? We know that the latter embarked at Québec on 15 October 1761, but he perished in the shipwreck of the *l'Auguste* off the coast of Cap-Breton the following month.

LANDOWNER

Had Joseph Payant already worked a piece of land at Québec? The proxy given to his brother Pierre in 1753 lets this possibility be foreseen. Did he still practice his trade of blacksmith during the winter? The first concession which was granted to him seems to be the one located on the banks of Fort Saint-Jean in 1755. A concession that he was barely able to work because of its proximity to Lake Champlain, principal theater of the confrontations between the French and the English in the Richelieu valley.

On 24 February 1763, exactly two weeks after the signing of the Treaty of Paris which brought an end to the Seven Years War, Joseph Payant dit Xaintonge *"previously captain of the*

155

ships at present living on the St Joseph coast" acquired in the presence of the notary Hodiesné two pieces of land belonging to Marie-Agnes Grenier, widow of Jean-Baptiste Girou. One was located on the St-Joseph coast, consisting of an arpent and a half in frontage by thirty deep, of which an area of 24 arpents was cleared on which was built a small house fifteen feet square, and half of an old barn fallen into ruins. The other land, located on the Sainte-Geneviève coast, also measured an arpent and a half in frontage to a depth of twenty. There were about four arpents of cleared land there, the rest covered in standing trees and burned wood, and also half of an old barn. Everything was acquired for 1000 livres, 200 of them paid in cash, the rest had to be paid the following May. Joseph Payant did not let this account drag on. He paid the balance of 800 livres on 14 March. The same day, he resold the same two lands to François Girou for the same amount of 1000 livres. For the Girous, it seems that it was a matter of taking back possessionregretted having sold them?

The following year, 13 July 1764, Joseph Payant put his land at Saint-Jean up for sale. It had been ceded to him in 1755 by the late Charles Lemoine, Seigneur and Baron of the censive of Longueuil. It was bought by John Macombe, equerry, a merchant living at Albany, for the modest amount of 100 livres tournois which the seller admitted having received *"before the signing of the documents"*. The record was signed by the seller, the buyer and the notaries André Souste and Pierre Mézières.

Joseph still had the land acquired in 1758 from Charles Laplante. On 26 October 1768, he relinquished it to the benefit of Pierre de Laplante, equerry, living on the Saint-Joseph coast in a contract signed before Lalanne, with only the charges of the cens, rents, arrears and seigniorial duties. Joseph was also classified there as an equerry, an officer of the navy living on the Saint-Joseph coast. During the ten years that he owned it, Joseph hardly worked it. No buildings had been built and only a little bit of land was plowable.

Joseph Payant would soon become a septuagenarian and the lot on rue Saint-Flavien at Québec still remained to be sold, at least in part. Since the death of his wife in 1753, he was only legally owner of half of this lot; the other half had to be divided among the other legal heirs, his children. The family had to wait until 1779 to find a buyer.

The transaction was made on 3 May at the home of the notary Antoine Foucher, at Montréal, in the presence of Joseph Payant, *"former captain in the navy of his very Christian Majesty"*, living at Montréal, on rue Notre-Dame, widower of Marie Legris; Jean-Baptiste Payant, navigator, living at Laprairie, his son, Louis Payant, living at Saint-Philippe, and Rose Laplante, widow of Nicolas Payant, living at Sault-Saint-Louis. The latter acted as guardian of her children heirs of Marie Legris, their maternal grandmother concerning the rights acquired from the late Dominique Payant, her brother-in-law, heir with the same right. Among the heirs was still found Geneviève *"of name unknown"*, widow of Joseph Payant and guardian of the minor children born to her and the said deceased, heirs like the others. All these people admitted having sold to Sieur Eustache Toupin, king's courier, living at Québec, all the rights to the property belonging to the male and female sellers, consisting for the Sieur Joseph Payant of half of the lot located on rue Saint-Flavien, consisting of 51 feet in frontage by 40 deep, with no buildings. Each child inherited one-sixth of the half through division, including the share of Jean-Marie, resident of Kamouraska. Marie-Joseph Payant, sister of the heirs, was not mentioned, which leads to the belief that she had died.

The said land was part of the censive of the clergy of foreign missions of Québec, to whom the buyer will be liable for the cens and seigniorial rents. He also had to pay the sum of 900 old chelins: 450 to Joseph Payant and 75 to each of the children. Immediately after this sale, Toupin stated that he had resold the said land to Pierre-Stanislas Bédard to whom he had lent his name to conclude this transaction.

On 13 and 17 February 1783, at the time of the marriage contract and the religious ceremony of his grandson Jean-Baptiste to Marie-Joseph Caille, Joseph Payant signed the two acts as he had often done in similar circumstances. It seems likely that these two signatures were the last which have come down to us. When, where and in what circumstances did Joseph die? Mystery!

However, there is an important detail which, in spite of intensive research, we have not yet managed to clear up. In the margin of a copy of the contract for sale of the land at Saint-Jean

157

to John Macombe, the notary Pierre Mézières indicated that he had sent it a second time to the seller on 23 November 1785. Does this mean that Joseph Payant was still living on this date?

THREE GENERATIONS OF JEAN-BAPTISTES

At the end of the eighteenth century, the Montcalms had not yet appeared on the horizon. We must pass through three successive generations of Jean-Baptistes to see them appear.

1.   They were: Jean-Baptiste I, third son of Joseph. Born at Québec in 1726, he was married at Laprairie on 14 April 1755, to Catherine Lerigé, daughter of Pierre and of Louise Hubert-Lacroix. He died at Laprairie in 1808.

2.   Jean-Baptiste II, third son of the preceding. Born at Laprairie in 1760. Married for a first time at Laprairie on 17 February 1783, to Josephte Caille, daughter of Pierre and of Josephte Daniau. Remarried in the same place on 6 July 1801, to Angélique Brassard, daughter of Claude and of Angele Barrette. He died at Laprairie on 4 December 1825.

3.   Jean-Baptiste III, eldest son of the preceding. Born on 6 May 1784 at Saint-Philippe de Laprairie. Married at Laprairie on 13 February 1809, to Louise Longtin, daughter of Jerome and of Louise Barrette. He died at Saint-Isidore in 1858. This family which settled at Châteauguay was the first to adopt the surname of Montcalm.

Joseph Payant probably knew, if only briefly, his great-grandson. The patriarch was always present at the great events which the members of his family experienced, especially those of his family at Laprairie. His relationship with this Jean-Baptiste's line seems to us to be particularly close. Before the remarriage of his daughter Marie-Joseph in 1762, Joseph was already living at Laprairie. For more than twenty years, the former sailor would have the opportunity every day to entertain his descendants with tales of his career as barge-master and the role that he had played in the victories and in the defeats of the regiments placed under the supreme command of Montcalm, to whom he assuredly had a very great admiration. The glorious death of the general and that of very dear friends opened in the book of his memories some wounds which never healed. These

158

memories were never written down, but according to tradition, they were passed down by word of mouth from generation to generation.

FIRST MENTION OF THE SURNAME OF MONTCALM

The first mention of the surname of Montcalm appeared in the registries of Saint-Joachim de Châteauguay. When he married Louise Longtin at Laprairie on 13 February 1809, Jean-Baptiste was already settled at Châteauguay. There on the Saint-Regis coast, he owned a piece of land with three arpents in frontage, including an area of four arpents of plowable land, and three other cleared arpents. There was a trough and a house covered with boards, a stone chimney and some mounted frames with glass, a barn covered with straw, as well as a stable of logs also covered with straw. (22)

The surname of Montcalm was mentioned for the first time on 3 March 1830, on the occasion of the burial of Florence. The curate Pierre Grenier (23) recorded the following act in these terms:

> *"On the third of March one thousand eight hundred thirty We undersigned priest pastor have buried in the local cemetery Florence who died the day before yesterday, fifteen years old, legitimate daughter of Jean-Baptiste Payant dit Montcalm farmer of this place and of Marie-Louise Longtin. Present were Augustin Plante and Joseph Bourdeau who did not know how to write."*

On 9 March and 18 August 1831, the same pastor reported the baptism and burial of Marguerite-Rosalie, legitimate daughter of Jean-Baptiste Payant dit Montcalm and Louise Longtin. He did the same at the time of the baptism of Jean-Noe, on 27 August 1832. The same year, the registries of Saint-Joachim noted the burials of numerous victims of the cholera epidemic. It does not seem, however, that the name of Montcalm had been adopted quickly by the Payant families. The census of 1851 for the parish of Saint-Isidore mentioned the family of Jean-Baptiste Payant senior, 67 years old, who lived with his wife Louise Longtin, 61, and their son Jean-Baptiste, 38,

159

married to Julienne Rayaume (Rheaume), 30. There was no mention of the Montcalm surname. Twenty years later, in 1871, the census of the same parish indicated that Jean-Baptiste and Julienne had done away with the Payant last name and replaced it with Montcalm. Mentioned there were their children Gedeon, Avila, Chery, Casilde, Emma, Cordelie, Victorine, Noe and Mathilde.

A college colleague, Omil Perrier, from Saint-Denis-sur-Richelieu whose paternal grandmother Amanda Montcalm married his grandfather Calixte Perrier at Moose Creek (Ontario) on 20 June 1887, states that in the family there is an oral tradition passed on by his father and which is summarized in the following manner:

> *"The introduction of the last name of Montcalm comes from the pastor of the parish of Saint-Joachim de Châteauguay. On the occasion of the baptism of two children of Jean-Baptiste Payan dit St-Onge, Marguerite-Rosalie on 9 March 1831 and Jean-Noe on 27 August 1832, the pastor P. Grenier himself added to the family name the surname of "dit Montcalm".*

> *"He was struck, it seems, by the fact that the child who had just been made a "Christian", would be called "paien"(heathen)... because the people in the local area pronounced Payan as "paien". He did not want to subject them to this manner of speech and looked for a means to avoid this. Let's not forget that at that time one easily added another last name to a family name and that it often became the only and unique name of the family.*

> *"The pastor closely looked at the father and even invited him to turn to the side.-- Monsieur Payan, you truly have the profile of the Marguis de Montcalm! And without futher ceremony, he wrote in the registry: Payant dit Moncalme (without the t but with a final e)".*

"We can believe, concludes Perrier, that the other children, when grown, willingly chose only to keep the surname of Montcalm; it sounded well at that era, given the reputation of the great Marquis and the Francophilia of the 1850's; may we recall the Franco-English alliance during the Crimean War and the visit of the frigate La Capricieuse to Québec in 1853." (24)

This introduction of a new surname in the Payant family seems to me to be a whim, but one which occurred nevertheless! If this is the case, the officiating priest, perhaps unconsciously, was able to cause problems with the rule that the civil registries must contain nothing other than that which is stated by the concerned parties.

However it happened, I believe that the oral tradition, especially that emanating from the tales of Joseph Payant, a witness to the naval battles fought on Lake Champlain, who undoubtedly did not miss an opportunity to recite the exploits of Montcalm, his hero, embellished his memory, and played a preponderant role in the choice of the surname of Montcalm.

The majority of the present Montcalms descend from the Payant-Longtin couple and from their three sons Jean-Baptiste, Jean, Noe and Médard.

Joseph Payant, another son of Jean-Baptiste and Josephte Caille, also counts some Montcalms among his descendants. This Joseph, married to Flavie Robidoux at Saint-Constant on 19 February 1827, lived mainly at Laprairie, but also at Saint-Constant and Montréal.

CLAIM WITHOUT BASIS

About ten years ago, some Canadian Montcalms living in Ontario claimed, without proof, to descend from the victor of Carillon. In its edition of 13 July 1945, the newspaper *LeSoleil* noted their presence at Québec where they had come to visit *"the*

historic sites and particularly Montcalm's house". On the following 21 July, the newspaper *Le Droit* also reported their visit to
Ottawa in these terms:

> *"Our French-Canadian families seem for
> some time to have a taste for reconnecting
> themselves to their ancestors. As proof, the
> number of them visiting our institutions,
> societies and family genealogies. Another
> typical fact no less convincing is the matter
> of these families who no longer doubt their
> descendance from the Marquis de
> Montcalm."*

Historians, biographers and even some descendants of the
families related to that of the general who died at Québec on 14
September 1759 have proved that the Canadian Montcalms have
no family tie to the famous personnage. (25) On 8 October
1975, Msgr Rosario Montcalm, from Holyoke, wrote to Roland
J, Auger, then director of *Service de genealogie de Québec,* em-
phasizing that, two years earlier, to his great astonishment he had
learned from Father G. Robert Gareau, a well known genealogist
at Montréal, that the Canadian Montcalms had for their ancestor
a certain Jacques Payan, a simple soldier.

> *"As you can see,* wrote Msgr Montcalm,
> *there does not seem to be a connection to
> the family of the Marquis de Montcalm. I
> have no idea why the name of Montcalm ap-
> peared in our genealogy. If you can inform
> me I would appreciate it. All that I know is
> that, when my grandfather, Cheri Montcalm,
> left Saint-Isidore de Laprairie to go to Gen-
> tilly, Minnesota, U.S.A., about 1878, he
> brought his parents and his children with
> him. Jean-Baptiste, the great-grandson,
> died on 2 December 1886. Later, about
> 1890, Cheri and his family left Minnesota to
> come here to Holyoke. Since that time and
> since their departure from Canada, it seems
> that my parents and grandparents never used
> the name "Payan".*

On 19 January 1976, I myself wrote to Msgr Montcalm to ask him for information on his family. Several months later, I was still waiting for his response. One day, when I was in my office at the parliament, my wife called me and said" "You have visitors!" --"Stay there. I'm coming." A few minutes later, to my surprise I made the acquaintance of Msgr de Montcalm and one of his sisters. "You bring me information on your family?, I asked him. "I come seeking it", was his response. I apologized to Msgr Montcalm for waiting more than 20 years to give him this answer. Regular correspondence for four years with a nun from Edmonton, Sister Simonne Lapointe, s.g.m., whose grandmother was a Montcalm, compelled me in someway to offer this story that I have wanted to write for a long time.

SCATTERED FAMILIES

According to intensive research conducted in these last four years by Sister Lapointe, the Montcalm families are now very scattered. Nearly 300 households have been listed in the censuses of the United States and as many in Canada. They have also been discovered in Australia, Ireland and France.

In the United States, the Montcalms are present in some 25 states, mainly in Michigan. They also live in New Hampshire, Vermont, Arizona, California, Delaware, Florida, Georgia, Illinois, Indiana, Kansas, Kentucky, Louisiana, Maine, Massachusetts, Minnesota, Missouri, Nevada, New York, Tennessee, Texas, Virginia, Washington and Wisconsin.

In Canada, we find them mainly in Québec in nearly 50 municipalities. In Ontario, there are some in 25 cities and towns. They are also found in Alberta, Saskatchewan, Manitoba and British Columbia.

FAMILY NAME VARIATIONS

Several thousand descendants of Joseph Payant dit Saintonge live today in North America.

Those of the paternal line, are for the most part, Saintonge or St-Onge. Other variations are: Aubé, Baril, Barthélemy, Biosson, Boisonneau, Bourdigal, Buveteau, Centau, Charlopin,

163

Chatignon, Chaussard, Chesne, Chotard, Cochery, Défelteau, Gareau, Groton, Jacquenot, Joly, Lecoq, Letard, Loubat, Martineau, Ménard, Métayer, Payan, Pélissier and Roudier.

A few hundred have kept the original last name of Payan or Payant (with a t), a spelling introduced by Joseph in the second generation. Other variations are: Desforges, Laliberté, Noyan, Paillard, Payen, Payet, Saint-Amour, Roby, Ruby and Saintonge.

The Montcalms still are not very numerous and their name is singularly free of variations, but they are everywhere, or almost so. Let's not forget that it has barely been more than a century since they added their new last name. They are proud of it. Even if they now know that they have no family tie with Louis-Joseph de Saint-Veran, Marquis de Montcalm. They are also very proud of Joseph Payant, their true ancestor, the captain of royal barges who bravely fought under Montcalm from 1756 to 1759.

END NOTES

1. This priest arrived in country in 1691. He was the third pastor of Notre-Dame-de-Québec from 1707 to 1711. following Henri de Berniéres and François Dupré. He died at the Hotel-Dieu on 16 April 1711.

2. Today known as the *Cote du Palais*.

3. André Lafontaine., *RAVQ 1716 et 1744,* Sherbrooke 1991, page 21.

4. Thomas Thiboult arrived in Canada in 1710. The following year he was named administrator of the parish of Notre-Dame having become the pastor two years later. Named superior of the Seminary in 1723, he died the following year. His body was entombed in the cathedral.

5. André Lafontaine., Op. Cit., p.357.

6. Ibid., p.170. Thomas Caret (or Carré), master-mason, was originally from Paramé in Brittany.

7. Jacques-Fabien Badeau, was a ships master-carp[enter.

8.   An international unit of volume for ships, equivalent to 2.83 cubic meters.

9.   Georges Ducharme., <u>L'Admiral du lac Champlain, Joseph Payant dit St-Onge</u>, Montréal, 1929. p.5ss.

10.   <u>Voyage in Amerique</u>, Montréal, Berthiaume, 1880.

11.   François Foucault (1690-1766), the king's magazine guard at Québec, first councillor to the Sovereign Council, then Seigneur of a vast domain of 3 leagues in frontage on the Richelieu river. Dominique Payant was one of his first concessionnaires.

12.   Situated near to Fort Saint-Frédéric, it was later known as "Crown Point" to the English.

13.   Baptized at l'Ange-Gardien on 18 March 1721, Geneviève was the natural daughter of Marie-Angélique Dalleray, daughter of Juseph and of Jeanne Moreau.

14.   Born at Montréal in 1701 and ordained a priest in 1727, he was the son of our ancestor Constant Lemarchand, Sieur de Lignery, originally from the region of Tours, France.

15.   <u>RAPQ, 1928-1929</u>, pages 1 to 3, 12, 13, 80 & 81. *A military journal* by Nicolas d'Avène des Méloizes, chevalier, seigneur de Neuville au Canada, from 19 July 1756 to 30 October of the same year, and from 8 May 1759 to 30 October of the same year.

16.   This quote is taken from the Memoires of Major Rogers.

17.   Thisa series of events leads us to believe that irt was not only at Chamblay, but in the neighboring parish of Laprairie, among others, that Joseph Payant ended his days.

18.   The name of the mother of the spouse was not Louise Hubert-Lacroix, but Barbe Dupuy. It was an error of the notary Louise Hubert-Lacroix, having married Pierre Lérigé, brother of Paul.

19.   Really Castelmayran (Tarn et Garonne).

20. Jacques Imbert (1708-1765), agent of the general treasury of the Marine. He was in charge of receipts due the King. Claude Baudart de Vaudésir, Baron of Sainte-James, general treasurer of the colonies of France.

21. Noel-Mathurin-Étienne Perichon, treasurer-general of the Marine of France.

22. These details are mentioned in the conventions of marriage signed the same day by the notary Edmé Henry.

23. Priest born at Québec in 1791 from the marriage of Gabriel Grenier and of Marguerite Rose. Ordained on 21 April 1816, he was successively pastor of Fraserville, Sainte-Anne-des-Plaines, Beauport, Châteauguay (1825-1833) and Varennes, from where he died in 1834.

24. Les Montcalm au Canada. Communication of 30 Nobember 1996, p.4.

25. On the subject of the descendants of the eldest and youngest branches of the Montcalm family in France, see copies of a letter sent from Brooklyn on 18 January 1897, by the Marquis Loise de Montcalm. This letter has been published in L'Eventment of Québec on the 23rd of the following January and reproduced in L'Ancetre of January 1997, p. 187.

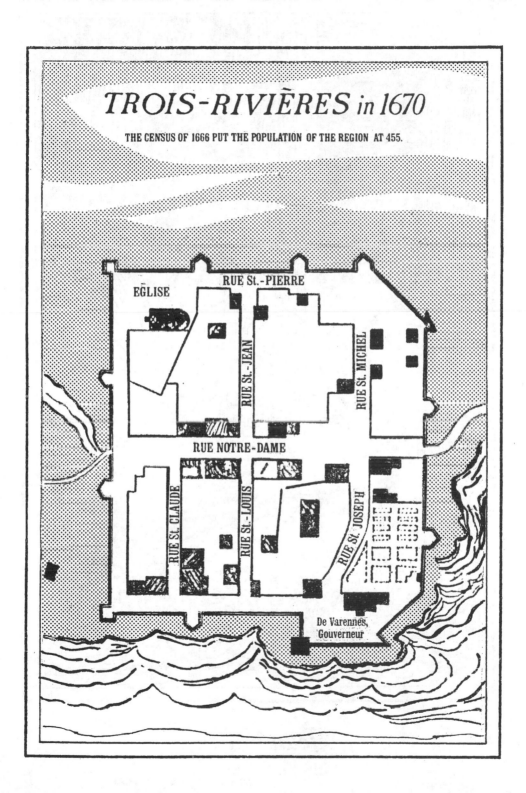

TROIS-RIVIÈRES *in 1670*

THE CENSUS OF 1666 PUT THE POPULATION OF THE REGION AT 455.

EGLISE

RUE St.-PIERRE

RUE St. JEAN

RUE St. MICHEL

RUE NOTRE-DAME

RUE St. CLAUDE

RUE St.-LOUIS

RUE St. JOSEPH

De Varennes, Gouverneur

Jean Vallée

CHAPTER 9

Jean Vallée

everal colonists bearing the surname of Vallée and others with the last name of Lavallée settled in New France during the French règime. Let us note Pierre Dubois-Morel dit Lavallée, originally from Perche; François Le Gantier de la Vallée-Rane, from Maine; Jean Friloux dit Lavallée, a Parisian; Jean Vallée dit Sansoucy, from Poitou; Louis Lavallée, from Flandré; Jean Lavallée dit Petit-Jean, of unknown origin, and Isaac Pasquier or Paquet dit Lavallée, from la Vendée. Even though Marcel Trudel did not mention them in his *"Catalogue des immigrants 1632-1662"*, the brothers Pierre and Jean Vallée were indeed present in the region of Québec before 1662. They were the first French Vallées to settle in America.

According to Nicole Priollaud, (1) the last name of Vallée was the name of an inhabitant of a house located in a valley. The author cites a Geoffroy Vallée, born at Orléans and died in 1574. This person was hanged on the gallows two years after being sentenced to death for denouncing religious doctrines in his writings and professing to be a deist. A certain Jacques Vallée, Sieur des Barreaux, who lived at Châteauneuf-sur-Loire from 1599 to 1673, left a less enviable reputation. He was called the king of debauchery. The ancestors Pierre and Jean Vallée left a better memory among us. The present account especially recalls the memory of Jean, the younger of the two, and that of his son Charles and his family, who are counted among the pioneers of Sainte-Anne-de-la-Pèrade, in the Mauricie. (2)

ORIGINALLY FROM SAINT-SAENS

Pierre and Jean Vallée were originally from Saint-Saens, in Normandie. Located between Rouen and Dieppe, this seventeenth century hamlet has become a picturesque small town in the department of *la Seine-Maritime*. Albert Dauzat (3) states that this topographical name takes its origin from the name of Sidonius, an abbot who lived in Normandie in the seventh century. Well, this Sidonius whom the Catholic church celebrates on 14 November is better known today by the name of Saint Saens. (4)

The charming town of Saint-Saens is located on the banks of the Varenne river, near the forest of Eawy. It is a summer resort town dominated by a modern church in the Roman style, where one can admire some stained glass windows from the sixteenth century illustrating the life of Saint-Louis, the Passion and the Pentecost. The forest which borders the valley is planted in oaks and beeches which grow quite near the houses. (5)

THE FRENCH FAMILY

Maurice Vallée (6) was the one who rediscovered the true place of origin of the Vallée brothers in France. In 1906, Mary Louise Dalton, in the *"Missouri Historical Society Collections"* (vol. 2, no 7), had already suggested the name of Saint-Saens, after consulting the genealogists Arthur Doughty and Placide Gaudet. However, the authors of the genealogical dictionaries, probably relying on the marriage record of Pierre Vallée, which took place at Beauport on 12 January 1665, had until then persisted in mentioning, as place of origin, the parish of Saint-Jean in the city of Rouen.

It was in the micro films of Saint-Saens that Maurice Vallée found the family of Pierre Vallée and Marie-Madeleine Du Mesnil, the parents of Pierre and Jean Vallée. They had been baptized there, the first on 6 June 1636, the second on 29 August 1640. Eight other children completed the French family of the Vallées: Marie, the eldest, born in 1630; Louis, the youngest, in 1645. There is a possibility, however, without absolute certainty, that Pierre, the father, was remarried in 1646, to a certain

Suzanne Savary, and that three more children were added to the household. If this is the case, the writer of the act neglected to make the connection with the first marriage.

IN NEW FRANCE

We know, from a baptismal act recorded in the registry of Trois-Rivières on 28 December 1657, that a Pierre Vallée was godfather of an Amerindian child called Pierre, born to the marriage of 8aetagon and Kokis8mi8ek8e. (the numeral 8 stands for the French "oui") The godmother was Madeleine Hertel, daughter of our ancestor Jacques and Marie-Marguerite. A few months later, this Madeleine married the master surgeon Louis Piard. It seems likely that Pierre Vallée was Jean's brother. Had they crossed the Atlantic at the same time? Perhaps. One thing is certain, the two brothers had been confirmed together by Msgr de Laval at Château-Richer on 2 February 1662. Two years later, on 5 April 1664, Jean Vallée was cited in a decision of the Sovereign Council of New France, after hearing a case in which Gilles d'Anjou was sued by the surgeon Jean Madry, the latter stating

> "to have lost a Summons or Memorandum by him decreed between the defendant and a man named Jean Vallée, in which the said Vallée was obliged to acquit the said defendant of the demands which René Mezeré could ask of him." (7)

JEAN MARRIES

On 7 January 1666 (contract Vachon), Jean Vallée, living in the seigneurie of Lirec on the Ile d'Orléans), who was said to be about 26 years old, showed his intention of setting up a home.

The couple met in the house of Paul Chalifour, resident of the seigneurie of Notre-Dame-des-Anges. Joachim Martin, who also settled at Lirec, vouched for his sixteen year old sister Marie, the bride to be. Pierre Vallée, master surgeon at Beauport, accompanied by his wife Thérèse Leblanc, and

169

Léonard Leblanc, master mason in the village of Fargy, were the guests of the groom. The Martins, for their part, had invited the master carpenter Paul Chalifour and his wife Jaquette Archambault, the master cutler Pierre Paradis and his son Jacques. Joachim Martin endowed his sister with a half-arpent of his land at Lirec and Jean Vallée brought a dowry of 300 livres. The husband and wife would live in community property and make a mutual donation to each other.

According to all probability, Marie Martin, whom Silvio Dumas classified as among the *"daughters of the king"*, had only been in the country for a few months. Born at La Rochelle, in the parish of Notre-Dame-de-Cogne, it was at Québec, however, that she was confirmed on 9 November 1665. She was the daughter of Jacques Martin and Marie Le Maistre. Her marriage to Jean Vallée was celebrated in the parish of *La Visitation de Notre-Dame de Château-Richer*, on 4 February 1666, in the presence of witnesses Pierre Vallée and Joachim Martin. The pastor Thomas Morel gave the nuptial blessing.

THE SETTLEMENT

The same year, Jean and Marie were in the census of the Ile d'Orléans. They were listed in it again the following year. The censustakers found them there in possession of a plot of land with six arpents under cultivation and one domestic animal. (8) According to Léon Roy, (9) a concession not traced from the seigneur Charles de Lauzon-Charny had been made to Jean Vallée before 10 December 1664, at Saint-Pierre on the Ile d'Orléans. On 20 September 1669 (records of Auber), Jean exchanged this land in return for another belonging to Antoine Guyonne (Dionne). The act reveals that the two colonists agreed to cede to each other their homesteads and their buildings, that of Sieur Vallée had three arpents in frontage on the river, abutting the line or route planned in the middle of the island, bordering on one side Jean Guy and on the other Joachim Martin. The said homestead owed the seigneur twenty sols for the rent, one sol for the cens for each arpent of frontage and two capons, all must be brought to the seigneurial manor each year on Saint-Remy, the first of October. The concession offered by Antoine Guyonne was two arpents of frontage on the river; it was wedged between the lands of Antoine Lefort and Laurent Benoist and included the same obligations to the seigneur. Furthermore, Guyonne was

170

committed to clear an area of six arpents of the land that he had just relinquished. The contract was signed in the presence of Jean Guy, resident of the island, and the master surgeon Gabriel Ballestaquin du Chesne.

THE CHILDREN

The Vallée-Martin couple only had three children:

1. Marie-Madeleine was born at Saint-Pierre on 21 July 1668 and baptized two days later in the parish of Sainte-Famille. Her godfather and godmother were Jean Guy and Anne Martin, wife of Jacques Raté. On 12 February 1685 (contract Genaple, 13 December 1684). Marie-Madeleine married Philippe Letourneau, widower of Marie-Madeleine Simon, and brought into the world a son and a daughter, Philippe-Lucien and Marie-Joseph, both of whom died at an early age. After the death of her husband, another son, the result of an adventure with a soldier, was born but only lived a few days.

2. Charles, born at Saint-Pierre on the 7th and baptized at Sainte-Famille on 23 February 1670. Godfather and godmother: Charles Lefrançois and Anne Petit, wife of Joachim Martin. Future pioneer of Sainte-Anne-de-la-Pèrade.

3. Elisabeth, born on 27 March at Saint-Pierre and baptized at Sainte-Famille on 4 April 1672. Godfather and godmother: Jean Chaudreau and Elisabeth Anger, wife of Laurent Denis. Married at Québec on 22 May 1692, to Jean-Joseph Belon or Blon, a sergeant originally from the region of Blois, Orléanais. Elisabeth had a daughter, Marie-Anne, who died in the cradle, and a son, Jean-François, whose fate in unknown.

LAST TRANSACTION

On 13 February 1671, Madeleine Bélanger, widow of Bertrand Chesnay, Seigneur of the fief of Lotinville, had the notary Fillion draw up an inventory of the property left by her late husband. Jean Vallée was mentioned among the debtors. A decision handed down on the following 20 March by Claude Bermen reveals that he owed the heirs 143 livres, 2 sols and 6 deniers. (10)

The following year on 10 July (contract Vachon), Jean Vallée acknowledged having sold to Joseph Choret his land on the Ile d'Orléans, with its two arpents in frontage on the river, increasing to three arpents in the middle of the island. On one side, his neighbor was still Antoine Lefort; on the other side was found a part of the land destined to be the site of the future church of Saint-Pierre, thus a part of the land of Mathurin Bellouard. There was a habitable house, stable, yard, garden, plowable lands, meadows, woods and pastures, all belonging to the seller from a contract of exchange with Antoine Guyonne, drawn up by the notary Auber on 20 March (sic) 1669. The deed of concession had been originally granted to Guyonne on 3 December 1662 by the seigneur Charles de Lauzon-Charny, in a contract signed in the presence of the notary Vachon.

The price of the Vallée-Choret transaction was set at 500 livres, plus 20 livres for the pot of wine; *"he will be paid in pelts of legal tender in this country, except that the seller will keep all the grains still in the ground, and the house which he will occupy for another year with his family."* In return, Vallée allowed Choret to use his kneading trough, a cauldron, a hoe, and other things. Jean Vallée signed the contract (with initials), with his brother Pierre, the clerk Daniel Avissé and the notary. On 22 July, Marie Martin appeared before the notary to agree to the transaction made a few days earlier by her husband.

This sale will be profitable to Jean Vallée. It allowed him to acquire another piece of land at less cost, on the Ile d'Orléans. On 27 January 1673, in the company of the notary Vachon, he went to the home of Guillaume Paradis where Jean Chaudreau said he was ready to proceed, in good and proper form, with the sale of his land at Saint-Pierre. This property with two arpents in frontage on the river *"at the North passage"*, was bordered on one side by the concession of Thomas Lesueur, on the other side by that of René Dubois. It included all the *"appurtenances"*, plowable lands, meadows, woods, pastures and shed. This concession had been made to Chaudreau by the seigneur of Lauzon-Charny, on 9 December 1661. The said land was sold for 190 livres *"to be paid in silver, pelts or solvent notes upon the first ship to arrive from France this year"*. It seems that Chaudreau returned to his country after spending a dozen years on American soil.

MYSTERIOUS DEATH

Chaudreau and Jean Vallée lived simultaneously in New France for almost the same number of years. If, for the first, it was a return to the mother country, the disappearance of the second still remains a mystery for us. Did he die during a hunting trip? Did he drown? Did someone forget to record his death in the parish registry? No one knows this yet.

On 22 June 1673, his widow, Marie Martin, begged the notary Vachon to draw up an inventory of her property, both in her name and as mother-guardian *"chose by the court in the presence of monsieur the judge of the provost of Beaupré and the l'Ile d'Orléans"*, of her minor children Marie-Madeleine, about five years old, Charles, about three years old, and Isabelle about three months old. Joachim Martin, brother of the widow, was chosen as substitute guardian.

After he bought the land from Chaudreau, Jean Vallée had not had time to build his house. The family had to move into a house belonging to Antoine Poullet. This was the location of all the personal property inventoried and appraised by Nicolas Labbé, Louis Moreau and Mathurin Bellouard. They began their work with the traditional description of the utensils. There was a cabin *"made of carpentry and joining"*, two chests, the linens, the contracts and deeds, two pigs, two sows, two cows, a bull, and the accounts payable and receivable. We learn that the deceased had not had the time to pay the 190 livres that he owed Jean Chaudreau, and that this amount only covered the appraisal of the work carried out on his concession, consisting of two arpents of harrowing, the cut wood, three-fourths of a cleared arpent and about seven arpents of land plowed and ready for sowing. There was no house, no barn, no shed yet. Thus, a heavy task was awaiting Jean Vallée when death surprised him a few months before he would have celebrated his 33rd birthday.

JACQUES CHARTIER DIT LAFONTAINE - AN ENIGMATIC PERSON

Marie Martin, unfortunate to have lost her first husband in the prime of life, barely had time to console herself with her second husband, the enigmatic Jacques Charier dit Lafontaine.

173

During this era, the remarriage of a widow or a widower with children was done hastily. A few sweet nothings and some fine promises had probably won the heart of the young woman, who saw in this suitor a good adoptive father for her three tots.

Alas! Jacques only brought anxiety and bitter disappointment to Marie's home.

By 1673, Charier had been in the colony for at least seven or eight years. The censuses of 1666 and 1667 identify him in the region of Montréal, where he was the servant of the merchant Jean-Baptiste Migeon de Branssat. The latter was then fulfilling the post of clerk for the Company of the West Indies. He would soon become the fiscal administrator of the residents of Montréal. He would also became a seigneur, civil and criminal judge for the bailiwick of this city, and finally, sub-delegate of the Intendant Jacques Demeulle. (11) In 1668, on 27 May (contract Basset), still at Montréal, Charier made an attempt to settle down. He bought from Jean Aubuchon dit Lesperance two arpents of land located on the Saint-Louis slope, a sort of knoll which extended above the river, with a wind mill on its summit. In the eighteenth century, this knoll was used as a foundation for the citadel of Montréal. (12)

Charier found a simple cabin there for his use. The plot had been ceded to Aubuchon by Maisonneuve, governor of the island, on 24 January 1654. Charier obtained it for 200 livres.

In 1669, he settled at Québec. On 30 September, he and Aubuchon met with the notary Becquet, in order to reach an agreement on the cancellation of the contract signed at Montréal sixteen months earlier. Aubuchon thus took back possession of the two arpents on the knoll on the Saint-Louis slope after Charier was unable to pay for them. On 2 May 1670, Charier again went to Becquet. He acknowledged having been hired

> *"by a noble-man Charles Aubert de la Chesnaye, merchant of Québec, to work at his trade of mason from the 15th of the present month until the following first of October, in the service of Jean-Baptiste Legardeur de Repentigny, in his seigneurie of la Prairie de*

la Magdelaine, near the island of Montréal.
He will carry out all the work which will be
indicated to him, for 25 livres per month."

Did Charier honor this contract? If he did make the trip to la Prairie, he had already returned to Québec at the beginning of August.

BEFORE THE COURTS

On the 9th of this month, he appeared before the Sovereign Council of New France to be interrogated and confronted by other witnesses summoned for the trial of Catherine Gemier, widow of Louis Dupin, accused of witchcraft. Not satisfied, the Council decided on 26 August, to continue for a year with the legal opinions relating to this matter *"in the legal proceedings of the substitute of the general prosecutor"* and to summon the said Gemier as many times as it deems appropriate, *"on penalty of conviction"*.

What was the outcome of this accusation of witchcraft against Catherine Gemier? We don't know. A judgment rendered by the Sovereign Council on 5 October 1671 informs us that Charier had known this Catherine for some time, even before the death of her husband on 29 November 1669. In fact, on 3 September of the same year, in a contract signed in the presence of Gilles Rageot, (13) Jacques Charier bought, for 1800 livres, Dupin's land located in the parish of Sainte-Famille on the Ile d'Orléans. This amount had to cover the expenses of a journey to France that Dupin was ready to make.

Shortly after selling his land, Dupin fell ill and had to keep to his bed. He then received a visit from Charier and the notary Vachon, who offered to take him to the hospital by canoe. On the way, the trio stopped at Beauport, at the home of the notary. The dying man was urgently beseeched to change the terms of the contract for sale drawn up by Rageot, in case the journey to France was compromised. Charier insisted that Dupin make him a donation of his part of the land. The latter refused, but agreed to sign a receipt for 900 livres. This receipt was drawn up on 22 October 1669 by the notary Fillion. It stipulated that this amount would be given to Dupin only when he goes to France; if he died during the journey, the said receipt will remain *"in force and in power"*.

175

Taking advantage of the precarious condition of the patient, it seems that Charier managed to take this concession from him, but Dupin had the time to change his mind. On 23 November, he asked the missionary priest Thomas Morel to draft his will for him in which he states that he understands that

"all the affairs,deals, claims and contracts
that he had had with the said Charier be
broken and annulled".

He preferred to give his part of the homestead to Antoine Brault, a son from a first marriage of Catherine Gemier. He insisted, however, that she keep his share of the 900 livres. On 28 March 1670, another agreement was reached between the parties who agreed to annul the sale of the homestead. But Charier was slow to carry it out.

On 10 April, the intendant Claude Bouteroue ordered Charier to give the dame Gemier his half of the homestead. In view of his hesitations, Catherine began other proceedings, this time at the Provost of Québec. The case was heard on 1 and 20 July 1671. The plaintiff wished not only that she be given back her share, she also claimed the income that Charier had been able to draw from it after he took possession of the land. For his part, the bishop seigneur of Québec had already seized eighteen minots of wheat, both for the lots et ventes and for other debts. The remainder was found in the hands of the farmer René Dubois, who wanted to be paid for the work that he had done. In spite of the appeal filed by Charier concerning the decision of Bouteroue, the Sovereign Council at its session of October 1671 dismissed Charier, upholding the decision of the lower court, this time, ordering the plaintiff to pay the costs of her suit. (14)

A MAN IN DEBT

The Charier-Gemier episode did not end with the decision of the Sovereign Council. Before taking up his trade as mason again, the work on the land of Louis Dupin had left Charier with some unpaid debts. On 26 April 1672 (contract Rageot), we learn that he was now living at Québec. He admitted owing monsieur Dudouyt (15) 212 livres for both the seigneurial rents for the land in the seigneurie of Lirec and for the money which had been lent to him and for merchandise provided. This

176

amount included a debt of 108 livres which had dragged on since April 1670, and a debt of 22 livres contracted by Catherine Gemier and which Charier had promised to pay to monsieur Dudouyt.

On several other occasions, the Provost of Québec mentioned the debts of Jacques Charier. On 16 December 1672, in spite of the summons that he had received from the bailiff Jean Levasseur, he neglected to appear before this tribunal to respond to a debt of 17 livres to Louis Lefebvre dit Batanville. On 4 June 1673 (contract Becquet), Charier admitted having given to Bertrand Chesnaye de la Garenne, merchant of Québec, 44 livres which was part of a larger amount which the grantor stated was owed to him by André Mesnier dit Lagasse, resident of the seigneurie of Saint-Joseph.

On 18 July 1673, the Provost took advantage of the presence of Charier to settle a few matters concerning him. First, he was obliged to kneel and confess that he had maliciously and sternly spoken against the honor of Louis Lefebvre and he was ordered to publicly apologize. At the same time, the court ordered Charier to repay Lefebvre the 17 livres that he owed. It was agreed that André Mesnier would pay this amount to the plaintiff by deducting it from that which he himself owed to Charier who, on the same occasion, was also ordered to pay the six francs owed to Philippe Nepveu. In addition, Charier was also sued by the surgeon Timothée Roussel for a chimney he made with which his client was not satisfied.

Again on 18 July, the litany of the suits continued to fade away in the absence of Charier, who asked the bailiff Levasseur to represent him. It was now Guillaume Fournier who claimed a hammer, a trowel, some shirts and a pair of French shoes. Louis Moreau also entered the scene and demanded that Charier give him the 44 livres and 10 sols which he owed him. And finally, on the following 15 September, when Charier was conspicuous by his absence, Étienne Ardouin asked the tribunal to order him to repay 53 livres.

A MEETING THAT HE DID NOT MISS

Charier did not miss the next meeting. On 4 December, he forgot his debts. Instead, he went to find his friend the notary Vachon, who had also summoned the young 24 year old widow who was pleased to welcome to her home an adoptive father for her three young children. In 1673, Jacques Charier was living at Saint-Pierre on the Ile d'Orléans. This new parish only counted a few tens of inhabitants. A small chapel served as a meeting place for prayer and to receive travelling missionaries. There was no registry yet. Baptisms, marriages and burials normally took place, or at least were recorded, in the mother parish of Sainte-Famille, located thirteen kilometers further to the east.

The marriage contract written by Vachon noted that Jacques Charier dit Lafontaine, master mason-stone cutter, was the son of Jean Charier, also a master mason, and the late Anne Abert, his father and mother from the parish of Saint-Pierre in the town of Saint-Jean d'Angely, diocese of Saintes, in Saintonge. For her part, Marie Martin, widow of Jean Vallée, was said to be the daughter of the late Jacques Martin and the late Marie Bonneau(sic) her father and mother from the parish of Notre-Dame de Cogne in La Rochelle. Among the friends and relatives gathered for this occasion, we note Pierre Vallée and Joachim Martin, respectively brother-in-law and brother of the young widow. The couple would live in community property according to the *coutume de Paris*. Charier was obliged to support the Vallée children until the age of 15 and promised to endow his bride with 600 livres and to pay each of the Vallée daughters 84 livres and 4 sols and the same to the son when he reaches the age of majority for all the claims that they would be able to have to the estate of their late father.

The marriage was celebrated the next day, 5 December, at Sainte-Famille. Messire Benoit Duplein, (16) the official priest, noted that Henry de Berniéres, grand vicar of the diocese of Québec, gave them permission to marry during Advent and dispensed with the publication of the three proscribed banns. The witnesses were Jacques Doublet dit Delisle, Maurice Crespeau andThomas Lesueur, neighbors on the north side of the island.

178

On 2 March 1674 (a rider to Vachon contract), it was Jacques Charier who, in the name of his wife, received from Joseph Choret 468 livres and 10 sols, deducted from the 520 livres from the contract of sale of Jean Vallée's land, dated 10 July 1672. A second rider dated 8 May 1674 indicates that Charier had also received the balance of 51 livres (sic) and 10 sols, in complete payment of the total amount required at the time of the transaction.

The married status of Marie Martin's new spouse did not free him from his previous debts. On 12 March 1675, he was present to hear Bertrand Chesnay ask André Mesnier for the accounts concerning what he owed to Charier. Two weeks later, Louis Moreau also wanted to remind Charier that he had a debt to him. The latter was not present this time but, just the same, he was ordered to pay 10 livres with expenses.

In the meantime, Jacques and Marie had the joy of welcoming into their family their first son. He had the first name of Jacques like his father. The infant was born on 19 September 1674 and he was baptized eight days later at Sainte-Famille. This Jacques would become a *coureur des bois*, but disappeared while still young under unknown circumstances. Louise, his sister, born on 11 August 1676, was baptized at Québec two days later. Her existence would be shorter than that of her brother since at the end of October 1677, she was no longer alive. Jacques Charier thus left no descendants in New France.

THE MASON'S WORK

In the year 1676, Jacques was in the service of Nicolas Dupont councillor at the Sovereign Council, who asked him to practice his trade as mason and stone cutter in his fief of Neuville; the commitment was made at the home of Becquet on 24 January. The notary described the work which he would have to complete for the construction of a house with two stories with the length and width which the seigneur will indicate. Charier was charged with building a chimney, doors and windows like those which had been made the previous year at his house in the Upper Town of Québec by the stone cutter Lerouge. (17) The corners of the buildings (sic) would be similar in cut and polished stone. Charier had to work with another competent mason. The two men would begin work on the first of June and work there without stopping for a salary of 70 sols for each toise of wall and six livres for cutting the doors and windows. The two masons would be fed by Sieur Dupont as long as the work lasted, even on Sundays and holidays, on days of bad weather or others, except in the case in which there will be lack of work on their part.

Charier received from Dupont an advance of 60 livres; he also received four minots of wheat when he began the work. Finally, the two masons would receive their pay as the work progressed and was deemed well made by other competent workers. On the following 8 March, Charier worked with René Gervais, a mason living at Lorette. The latter had to be suitably equipped with tools and would earn 25 livres a month, paid half in silver, half in *"corn"*. The contract was firm for a duration of five months, until the next All Saints Day.

GUILTY OF THEFT

Was Jacques Charier able to complete this commitment? It seems that he was not. Some six months earlier, he had been compelled by the Sovereign Council to return to Québec in order to give testimony at the time of the trial of Catherine Gemier, accused of witchcraft. This time, the circumstances were far more dramatic for him: he had to answer to an accusation of theft.

During that era, the smallest theft constituted a very serious offense and could even lead to the gallows. But it also could happen that the Sovereign Council, deciding that the punishment imposed by a lower court was excessive, commuted the sentence by punishing the guilty party much less severely. (18)

On Monday, 19 October 1676, following a request made by the prosecutor of the Provost and in accordance with a decree dated on the preceding 3 August, the commissioner de Villeray (19) had Jacques Charier led before the highest court of the land to answer an accusation of *"theft and larceny"*. On 7 and 8 September, three witnesses came to recount what they knew about this theft. After these witnesses were heard, the accused was himself interrogated on 10 and 11 September, it was a matter of *"his confessions and denials"*. On the 14th and the 17th, the court heard *"the named le Picart soldier, Delisle and his wife and*

Eustache Lambert". (20) These different details were collected and compared with those made by Charier. On 14 October, the commissioner de Villeray made his report and again questioned the accused who had been placed *"on the Witness Stool"*.

On the 19th, the court said it was ready to render a decision. It declared Charier

> *"duly attained and convicted of having forced the lock of the door of a certain cellar belonging to the widow of Eustache Lambert, took and removed stealthily some pelts belonging to the said widow; for this reason and other causes resulting from the lawsuit, condemned and condemns him to be whipped and beaten with rods until blood flows, at the public square and the usual places in the Upper Town and Lower Town, and after this is done, he will be branded with a fleur de lys by the said executioner with a hot iron on the right shoulder; in addition ordered to pay one hundred fifty livres in a fine and the expenses of the trial; this being done, ordered that the used clothes and furnishings which will be found to have been placed or sent by the said Charier into the hands of Jouin, Laverdure and Sr Martin will be brought to the clerk of the court in order to be sold at public auction in the square of the said Lower Town, the proceeds of which to be taken as payment for the expenses and cost of the suit after the tax which will be made by the consular commissioner, and if they are not sufficient from the other property of the said Charier."*

The report of this trial which was called *"extraordinarily done"* was signed by the intendant Duchesneau. (21)

The consequences of this trial and the execution of the sentence had to be very humiliating for Charier. It was also a catastrophe for him, ruin for his family and a dishonor that he would be unable to overcome. A few days after the fateful sentence, on 2 November, he met with the notary Rageot and admitted owing Antoine Caddé 33 livres and 15 sols *"for food and deposit given to him"*, an amount that he was committed to pay to the creditor of his own accord. Already laden with debts, one more or less barely weighed in the balance. After this last acknowledgment, he went away to hide his shame; we know not where. He was only spoken of as absent. Did he return to France? Was he to become a *coureur des bois*? Where was he?

On 10 November, the butcher Michel Lecours appeared at the Provost of Québec and claimed from Marie Martin a cow which was to be delivered to him.

POOR MARIE MARTIN

The poor woman, now left to herself, and alone with five young children, found support and comfort with her brother Joachim. It was to him that she entrusted the care of the animal which Lecours claimed. On 5 March 1677, after a respite of a few months, Lecours intervened again with the tribunal and insisted that the cow be delivered to him. Regretfully, Marie had to comply.

The flight of Jacques Charier left Marie completely destitute. Deprived of sufficient resources, she decided to leave her land on the Ile d'Orléans. On 25 October 1679, (22) Louis de Niort de la Noraye, acting in the name of François Berthelot, Count de Saint-Laurent, (23) reminded the *"widow of Jean Vallée"*belongs to her at Saint-Pierre

> *"belonging to the domain of the said Count St-Laurent for lack of which it would be joined to his with expenses without prejudice for the arrears of the cens and rents of the past until this day".*

The defendant stated that she had not been able to do so up to now, but she offered to submit to this obligation within a year. On 23 January 1680, Marie was again summoned to appear before the magistrate of Beaupré at the request of Louis de Niort, who claimed from her 6 livres and 3 sols for the arrears of the cens and rents. Seeing the absence of the defendant, the magistrate ordered an adjournment *"to the first day of the hearing"*.

We are unaware of the aftermath of these interventions by la Noraye, but we only know that in 1681 the "widow of Jean Vallée" and her family were still living at Québec. The general census taken that year mentioned their settlement in the Upper Town, between Michel Durand and Edme Tinon. Magdeleine, Charles and Elisabeth Vallée were 14, 12 and 9 years old, respectively. Jacques Charier, junior, was 7 years old. (24) The family had definitely left the Ile d'Orléans.

Two years later, on 19 October 1683, a contract drafted by the notary Genaple, noted that Marie Martin was the *"wife of Jacques Charier, absent from the country"*. This was, it seems, the first mention of the second husband since he had disappeared seven years earlier. Did she have any news of him? We don't know.

On that day, Marie accepted from Guillemette Hébert, widow of Guillaume Couillard, *"living and usually making her residence at the Hôtel-Dieu of this city where she was presently confined to her sick bed"*, a plot of land located near the hospital, with 5 toises in width on the road which passes along side the cemetery in order to enter the enclosure of the bishop's palace, by 16 toises high, in the direction of Pierre Groleau and Jean Marchand going up the grand chemin, and only 13 toises on the side of Jean Giron. On the other end was a small slope which was near the grand chemin which goes to the Hôtel-Dieu. The said land belonged to the widow Couillard, through inheritance from Louis Hébert, her father.

Marie Martin only had to pay the annual rent of 20 sols, but she was committed to build a house there within a year.

On 21 January 1684 (contract Rageot), Marie Martin, *"widow in a first marriage to Jean Vallée, at present the wife of Jacques Charier, absent from this country"*, managed to sell her land at Saint-Pierre to Nicolas Goulet, a laborer from Beaupré.

Joachim Martin was present and represented the interests of the minor children of the late Jean Vallée. The land was sold for 200 livres, to which were added 2 sols *"for the pins"*, with all the appurtenances included, 5 to 6 arpents under cultivation and the remaining in felled and standing trees. The buyer was obliged to pay with 10 minots of wheat, 50 minots of oats, 25 francs and a note "marketable and solvent", on the next Saint-

Jean-Baptiste Day, 50 francs on All Saints Day and the balance of 100 francs the following year. Attached to this record of sale was another act signed by the notary Chambalon dated 23 October 1694. It indicated that Elisabeth Vallée, wife of Jean-Joseph Blon (Belon), her absent husband, was appointed general and special administrator for Marie Martin, her mother, who gave her the power to receive all the moneys owed by her debtors and to give the receipts required until the debts were completely paid.

In 1694, Elisabeth, the youngest of the Vallée children, was still living in the Upper Town of Québec, probably with her mother. From her marriage to Jean-Joseph Blon, she had a daughter, Marie-Anne, born in 1691, and died the following year, and a son, Jean-François, born in 1693. Marie-Madeleine, the eldest daughter of Marie Martin, married Philippe Letourneau in 1685 and also lived at Québec. And Charles, who had left the maternal home at least three years earlier, had settled at Sainte-Anne-de-la-Pèrade, where he had just taken a wife.

Jacques Charier, junior, had also left. On 31 July 1691 (contract Genaple), the Jesuits hired him to work at their mission at the Outaouais, for four consecutive years beginning with their departure the following month. On the same occasion, they also had hired another adolescent, 15 year old Pierre Chappeau, son of Madeleine Duval and the late Pierre Chappeau. Marie Martin was also present at the hiring of her 16 year old son.

Father Pierre Raffeix, administrator of the missions, required that the two lads show themselves to be

"good and faithful servants in all that will be asked of them lawfully for their service with neither of them being able to leave or abandon it through his fault".

Each will receive 120 livres the first year, 135 the second and 150 for each of the following years. Everything will be paid at Québec, therefore, to the mothers. The two young men had attended school; they signed with a fine hand at the bottom of their contract.

184

Upon his return from the Outaouais, Jacques dreamed of settling in the region of Québec. On 15 October 1696 (contract Charles Rageot), he bought a piece of land from Hubert Simon dit Lapointe. It had an area of about 60 arpents on the Saint-Michel coast, at Sillery. This land joined on one side another piece belonging to Hubert Simon, on the other side that of Thierry de Lestre dit le Vallon. It had been ceded in 1663 by the Jesuits to René-Louis Chartier de Lotbinière, civil and criminal lieutenant-general of the Provost of Québec, who in his turn ceded it to Hubert Simon some 16 years later (contract Rageot, 5 April 1679). It was charged with one sol for the land rent for each arpent of land and of wood, as well as two deniers and two live capons for the entire concession. On 15 April 1697, Jacques Charier, classified as a *"garcon voyageur,"* claimed from Hubert Simon one perche and six feet of additional frontage in addition to the two arpents mentioned in the transaction. Simon replied that the land sold only consisted of two arpents in frontage, *"just as he had (bought) had it from monsieur de Lotbinière"*, with the same appurtenances. The claim by Charier was heard in the Sovereign Council on the following first of July, but the young man neglected to appear. It seems that the case ended there. (25)

DOUBLE MYSTERIOUS DEATHS

In 1704, the two Jacques Chariers, father and son, died. Where and when did these deaths occur? This is a mystery. In an act by Chambalon dated 2 July, Marie-Madeleine Vallée, wife of Philippe Letourneau, declared herself authorized by the Provost of Québec, dated the preceding 28 June, to receive from her mother, widow in a first marriage to Jean Vallée, and in a second marriage to the late Jacques Charier, 60 livres for all her rights and claims as heir to the late Jacques Charier dit Fontaine, her half brother. She immediately gave a receipt for the same amount to her mother.

Finally, on 21 January 1705 (contract Genaple), Marie Martin, heir to the assets of the late Jacques Charier her son, sold to Michel de la Roche dit Lafontaine, resident of the Saint-Michel coast, the land acquired from Hubert Simon dit Lapointe in 1696. This property was located near the Sainte-Geneviève hill, in the seigneurie of Sillery. It joined, on the southwest, the land of the heirs of the late Hubert Simon and, on the northeast, the assigns of the late Thierry de Lestre. To the south stretched the Saint-Michel route. The land was sold with everything that it included of wilderness, standing wood and appurtenances, for 550 livres, for which the seller admitted having received payment from the hands of the notary Florent de la Cetière, in three installments: 130 livres from the notary Jacques Barbel (receipt on 6 June 1704), 247 livres in French currency being 329 livres 8 sols in local money, paid by Sieur de la Cetière to the dame Roy, proxy for the notary Janvrin du Frené of Montréal, to whom the seller owed the same amount; and finally, 85 livres from Sieur Touray du Chesneteau, from the receipt of 8 January 1705. All these amounts joined that of the 112 sols which the seller owed the notary for expenses and procedures totaled 550 livres for the sale price. The buyer promised to pay this amount in the form of an annual rent of 27 livres and 10 sols, committing all his property present and in the future. In a rider, the seller said she relinquishes to the buyer the perche and the six feet which had been the subject of the lawsuit attempted by her son in April 1697, however, without this addition being secured.

The census taken in Québec in 1716 did not mention Marie Martin, nor her daughters and sons-in-law, nor any of their children. Marie seems to have descendants today only by her son Charles, settled at Sainte-Anne-de-la-Pèrade, the only one of her children who would survive her.

She ended her days with the pensioners of the *Hôpital General de Québec,* on 10 July 1729, about 80 years old, as noted by the burial record.

CHARLES VALLÉE PIONEER OF RAPIDE-NORD

The establishment at Sainte-Anne-de-la-Pèrade by Charles Vallée was not fortuitous. Twenty years old, or perhaps less, the young man who had been for a certain time the servant of Eustache Bacon at Château-Richer, (26) left the region of Québec to try his luck at Sainte-Anne; it was there that Mathurin Tessier and his family had lived for several years. (27) Tessier was married in 1670 to Elisabeth Letourneau, daughter of David and of Jeanne Baril. After a brief stay at Champlain in 1676, Mathurin went the following year to Sainte-Anne at the request of the seigneur Edmond de Sueve, who offered to make him his farmer on his domain of *la rivière Sainte-Anne.* A little later, Jeanne Baril, accompanied by René Bin dit Lacroix, her second

186

husband, also settled at La Pèrade. René died about 1680. On 12 January 1681, Jeanne was married a third time, to Julien Bion dit le Breton, originally from Brehan-Loudeac, in Bretagne. That year, the general census mentioned that Julien and Jeanne lived at Sainte-Anne, with Philippe and Jacques Letourneau, two sons from Jeanne's first marriage. Her daughter Elisabeth also lived in the area. Jeanne Baril thus managed to surround herself with her three children.

In 1682, Philippe returned to the region of Québec where he was married the following year to Marie-Madeleine Simon She died prematurely. On 12 February 1685, at Québec, Philippe married Marie-Madeleine Vallée, Charles's sister. The Vallée and Letourneau families, who lived on each side of the north arm of the Saint-Lawrence, within the boundaries of the Ile d'Orléans, probably had known each other for several years. The marriage of Philippe and Marie-Madeleine only reinforced the ties which already existed. The reception of the young Charles at Sainte-Anne must have been very warm. Fortified by references furnished by Mathurin Tessier, his mother-in-law Jeanne Baril and the Letourneau children, the seigneur Edmond de Sueve would be favorably convinced to grant a piece of land, if only verbally, to Charles Vallée.

This land, we learn in a contract written on 18 August 1691 by the notary Michel Roy dit Chatellerault, was located in the immediate neighborhood of the homesteads which Edmond de Sueve ceded that day to the fabrique of Sainte-Anne. It was a matter of

> *"two homesteads with two arpents in frontage by forty deep, next to each another, bordering on the front by la rivière Sainte-Anne, on one side above Charles Vallée and on the other side below Philippe Estienne"*

According to Raymond Douville, (28) one of these lands was given for the use of the parish priest; the future church had to be built on the other one. Charles Vallée did not live long enough to see this project completed.

MARIE-URSULE GENDRA

It was instead in the small Saint-Nicolas chapel, which barely measured twenty feet long by fifteen wide, that he appeared on 3 February 1694 to marry Marie-Ursule Gendra, (29) daughter of Pierre and of Marie Charpentier, in the presence of Sieur de Sueve, Jacques Letourneau, Pierre Gendra and Catherine Châtellerault, a friend of the bride. A few days earlier, on 24 January, the same people along with a few others, gathered in the house of Jean Grimard at Batiscan to see the young couple make a promise of marriage before the notary Trotain. On the same occasion, Pierre Gendra and his wife committed themselves to house the couple in their house for a year, in addition to giving them a two-year old steer. Everything was appraised at 200 livres. For his part, Charles promised Ursule the customary dowry of 300 livres and both made a mutual donation of all their property. On 5 February, the celebration took place at the home of Jeanne Baril where the engagement of her son Jacques Letourneau to Angélique Guyon took place. Charles Vallée and Pierre Gendra were witnesses. On the 8th, everything ended with the religious ceremony of the wedding of Jacques and Angélique.

THE BEGINNING OF RAPIDE-NORD

In his work entitled "La route du bois du Merle et les debuts du Rapide-Sud", Raymond Douville also traced the beginning of the chemin du Rapide-Nord, which corresponds today with the route which leads to Saint-Casimir. (30) He recounts that in the 1680's, Pierre Gendra and Antoine Guibord had verbally obtained concessions in this place which they did not immediately develop. The first to settle there was Gendra. By virtue of a notarized act written by Michel Roy on 6 March 1687, the seigneur de Sueve gave it to him officially, while noting that the recipient had owned this concession *"for about seven to eight years"*.

As for Guibord, in December 1688, he sold his two lands to Jacques Letourneau, who was committed to give the seigneur 90 livres *"for a cabin and some work carried out on this land"*. Jacques was going to settle on the side of his sister Elisabeth and his brother-in-law Mathurin Tessier, who sold his concession at Rapide-Sud on 30 January 1689, in order to acquire the one which had already been ceded to him at Rapide-Nord.

After his marriage, Charles Vallée left his concession bordering the lands of the fabrique, if, however, he still lived there, to go lodge at the home of his father-in-law for a year. The area pleased him and he returned among the people whom he knew well, the Tessiers, Letourneaus, Guilbaults, and others.

IN THE LAND OF THE OUTAOUAIS

A year after his marriage, Charles and a few other young men formed an association which retained the services of François Desloriers, living at *rivière des Roches (Grondines)*, as voyageur and domestic servant, for two full years. A contract was signed to this end on 6 April 1695, at the home of the notary Louis Chambalon at Québec. The commitment would take effect as soon as the group left Montréal to go to the land of the Outaouais. (31) The other associates were Philippe Letourneau, Jacques Cordeau dit Desloriers, Charles Desloriers and Pierre Masson. The latter and Vallée were not present for the signing of this contract.

Charles Desloriers promised to serve the association during all the journeys, for all the works and services which will be ordered of him with complete loyalty required. In return, the partners were committed to feed him beginning on the day on which he will leave Québec and to give him each year 200 livres in salary, in currency of the country, in addition with providing him two cloaks and six shirts which he will be able to trade to his profit the second year. The contract stipulated that it will be possible to add a third year of service. In this case, Desloriers would have to return to Montréal the following year if the association deems it suitable. He would be able to return to the Outaouais to take up his service.

FIRST CONCESSION AT RAPIDE-NORD

Did Charles Vallée spend two years in the land of the Outaouais? We only know that his companion Pierre Masson was in Montréal the following year. On 21 August 1696, the notary Claude Maugue announced his return to the Outaouais in the company of Pierre Laguerre and Jean Pépin, but for the account of the merchant Edmond Chorel. In the spring of 1697, on 10 April, Charles Vallée was found among his family to receive a concession of nine arpents in frontage on the Sainte-Anne river, to an undetermined depth. This act, probably drawn up by Michel Roy, is lost. We know of this land's existence, however, by the brief description made of it on 5 November 1742, by the notary Arnould Balthazar Pollet, in the inventory of the property left by Charles Vallée.

A FINE FAMILY

It was there, on the banks of the Sainte-Anne river, whose murmuring waters coax the strip of forest, that the fourteen children of Charles and Marie-Ursule were born. We see that some two and a half years passed between the births of Pierre-Charles and Marguerite, probably because of the prolonged absence of the head of the family.

1. The eldest, Pierre-Charles, born on 7 July 1695, was baptized the same day. On 24 January 1724, he was married to Marguerite Campagna, originally from Sainte-Foy. She died in 1736, and Pierre-Charles was remarried on 30 June 1738 to Marguerite Guilbault. The two wives gave birth successively to fifteen children, all born at Sainte-Anne. Pierre-Charles died there on 23 March 1769, at the age of 71.

2. Marguerite, born on the 19th and baptized on 20 January 1698. Probably died in infancy.

3. Pierre, born and baptized on 29 March 1699, Married at Lachine on 9 November 1730 to Marie-Joseph Prejean. This couple lived mainly at Montréal (cote Saint-Paul), where the majority of their children were born. Pierre was actively involved in the fur trade, as witnessed by the records of the notaries Adhemar, Porlier, Le Pailleur and Souste. He hired numerous *coureurs des bois* who traveled for his benefit to among other place the Outaouais and Michilimakinac. Marie-Joseph Prejean died at Montréal on 9 May 1794. The burial act refers to her as a widow.

4. Marie-Anne, born and baptized on 30 March 1701. Remained a spinster.

5.   Elisabeth, born and baptized on 28 February 1703. Married on 18 May 1722 to Pierre Gervais.   This couple raised ten children at Sainte-Anne.   Elisabeth died on 29 November 1768.

6.   Jacques, born and baptized on the first of January 1705.   Married at Sainte-Geneviève-de-Batiscan on 6 February 1729 to Marie-Catherine Veillet.   This couple lived at Sainte-Anne and raised a dozen children there.   Catherine died in 1766 and Jacques was remarried on 15 September 1767 to Marie-Anne Guilbault.   He died on the first of March 1781.

7.   Michel, born and baptized on 10 May 1707.   Married at Québec on 14 March 1738 to Marie-Madeleine Morand, remarried in 1740 to Pierre Godard.   Michel died on 27 May 1738, before the birth of his daughter in December of the same year.

8.   Marie-Joseph, born about 1708.   Married on 22 February 1729 to Denis Tellier.   This couple lived at Cap-Santé where their five children were born.   Marie-Joseph was buried at LaPèrade on 27 March 1743.   By this date, she was already a widow.

9.   Marie-Angélique, born on the 27th and baptized on 28 October 1711.   Married on 16 July 1731 to Jean Massicot, widower of Louise Trotier.   From this union seven children were born between 1733 and 1754.   This family lived at Batiscan and Sainte-Geneviève-de-Batiscan,   where Marie-Angélique died on 10 January 1797 at the age of 85.

10.   Marie-Renée, born on the 21st and baptized on 26 January 1715.   Married on 3 October 1738 to Antoine Massicot, brother of Jean. Marie-Renée and Antoine were buried at Sainte-Geneviève-de-Batiscan in 1740; she on 27 April, he on 13 September.   They had only one daughter.

11.   Dorothée, baptized on 16 May 1717.   Married on 26 June 1738 to Alexis Leduc.   At least eleven children were born to this union.   Dorothée died on 27 March 1774.

12. Louis, baptized on 12 September 1720. Married at Deschaillons on 11 January 1745, to Marie-Louise Maillot. Eight children, all born at Sainte-Anne. Louis was remarried on 26 February 1770, to Marie-Joseph Guilbault.

13. Jean-Baptiste, baptized on 27 May 1723. Not mentioned in the division of 1742.

14. Marie-Jeanne, born on the 23rd and baptized on 24 June 1724. Married on 26 June 1741 to Jean-Baptiste Leduc. Three children. Marie-Jeanne died on the first of September 1748 and Jean-Baptiste was remarried on 20 October 1749, to Marie-Joseph Beaudoin, who gave him thirteen more children, all born at La Pèrade.

THE LANDS OF CHARLES VALLÉE

In 1709, the surveyor Jean-Baptiste de Couagne, duly authorized by the Count de Pontchartrain, (33) minister of the king, and by his colleague, Gedeon de Catalogne, drew up the map of the lands belonging to the government of Trois-Rivières, from the outlet of Lake Saint-Pierre to Sainte-Anne-de-la-Pèrade. That year, eleven pieces of land had already been distributed along the *chemin du Rapide-Nord*, those of Gilbert Leroux dit La Seigne, Jacques Letourneau, Pierre Jendro (Gendra), Joseph Gouin, Edmond Tessier, Louis Guilbault, one named Dumoulin, Jean Guilbault, Charles Veillet, François Guilbault and Pierre Levesque. The name of Veillet is wrong. It indeed refers to Charles Vallée whose land was the largest of all those at Rapide-Nord.

Charles would acquire a second concession the following year, bordering the Sainte-Anne river. While the notary-surveyor Hilaire Bernard de la Rivière carried out the survey work in this region, Charles took advantage of this to have himself ceded another piece of land. This one had eight arpents in frontage by twenty deep. The contract was dated 24 March 1710. Bernard de la Rivière stayed at Sainte-Anne for fifteen days, from 14 to 29 March. (34)

After the death of his wife Marie Charpentier, on 28 May 1713, Pierre Gendra ceded, on 30 June 1714 (contract Normandin), to his sons René and Antoine, and to his son-in-law

Charles Vallée, an arpent in frontage by twenty-five deep, each had his share of the six arpents of the estate that he had had with his deceased wife. The recipients had to pay him *"each on their own"*, 166 livres, 3 sols and 4 deniers. On 22 February 1716 (contract Trotain), this act of sale was modified with the introduction of Jean Gendra, another of Pierre's son, as part of this division. Therefore, each would receive more than three-fourths of an arpent, an area equal to that from the division of the three arpents coming from Marie Charpentier.

VISIT FROM THE ADMINISTRATOR COLLET

In 1720, the Duc d'Orléans, at that time regent of King Louis XV, decided to make changes in the parishes of New France so they would adapt better to their new needs. The general administrator Mathieu-Benoit Collet received this delicate mission of visiting them and submitted his remarks and his recommendations. He made this trip on 4 February 1721. On the 9th, he left the Grondines, accompanied by his clerk Nicolas-Gaspard Boucault, and went to Sainte-Anne. Upon their arrival, the two men were received by a welcoming committee of which Charles Vallée was part. The parish was also represented by the pastor Jacques Lesclaches, the co-seigneur Pierre-Thomas Tarieu de la Pèrade, the militia ensign François Garièpy, the co-seigneur François Chorel Dorvilliers, the seigneur Louis Gastineau de Sainte-Marie, the militia lieutenant Joseph Gouin, Pierre Roy, Jean Charest, Louis Baril, Edmond Tessier and Antoine Gendra.

The official report of this meeting noted that in the seigneurie of Tarieu, there were fifteen inhabitants whose concessions were twenty-five arpents deep, the portion of Dorvilliers counted fourteen heads of family, that of Sainte-Marie had the same number and that of la Pèrade, thirteen. There were fifty-six heads of family in all, not including the sieurs of la Pèrade, Dorvilliers and Gastineau. Concerning the ease or difficulty of going to church, noted Collet, the representatives stated that there was no church in the area where any of the residents of the parish could get to more easily, nor one that was closer. Everyone said they were very content to belong to this parish. (35)

Some six years after this visit, a young Breton surgeon named Yves Phlem dit Ivon arrived at Sainte-Anne. After marrying at Sainte-Famille on the Ile d'Orléans and staying briefly at Saint-Nicolas, Yves had bought in 1727 a piece of land from Jean Gendra, at Rapide-Nord. Hoping to enlarge his domain, on 29 March 1732 (contract Rouillard), he bought from Charles Vallée another piece of land with an arpent and a half in frontage on the Sainte-Anne river, by twenty-five deep, for 300 livres, of which 200 had already been paid and the balance promised on the next Saint-Michel's Day. This land bordered, on the northeast side, the three-fourths arpent already belonging to the buyer, and on the southwest side, the land of Antoine Gendra. Located in the censive of the seigneur de la Pèrade, the said land was charged with five sols in rent.

Finally, in order to make this transaction more lucrative, Vallée, taking advantage of Phlem's presence in the neighborhood, had added at the bottom of the contract a sort of health-insurance clause, requiring that the surgeon care for them, he and his wife, in sickness and infirmity, and that he also provide them the remedies which they would need for the rest of their lives. On the following 15 August, Vallée stated that Ivon no longer owed him anything and gave him a receipt for the amount mentioned in the contract.

DIVISION OF THE SECOND LAND

The land sold to Phlem in 1732 was made up, in fact, of two pieces of three-fourths of an arpent which was part of the land of Pierre Gendra. One had been bought by the the latter, the other was the part of the inheritance which each of the children had received after the death of Marie Charpentier. In 1736, Charles Vallée began, during his lifetime, to divide the concession acquired in 1710, to his benefit and to that of his son Michel. On 30 March (contract Pollet), Charles and Marie-Ursule sold him two arpents in frontage *"being the fourth part of a land of eight arpents by twenty deep"*, located at la Rapide of the Sainte-Anne river, bordering on the southwest Joseph Grandbois and on the northeast the six arpents belonging to the sellers. The buyer had to pay the cens and the rents and other seigneurial rights. The 150 livres required of the buyer had al-

ready been paid and a receipt had been given.   The mason
Georges Niof and his eldest son Joseph-Antoine served as witnesses to this contract.

DONATION AND MARRIAGE

On 17 June 1741, a double event took place in the Vallée
family. The notary Joseph Rouillard was summoned to *la Rapide
de Sainte-Anne* in order to record the notes in his records. ☿Vallèe
Charles&Marie-Ursule   ☿Charles and Marie-Ursule acknowledged, during the afternoon, first that they had given to their
youngest daughter Marie-Jeanne and to her future husband Jean-
Baptiste Leduc, all their personal property and real estate
provided that the latter be obliged to feed them in their house for
the rest of their days. They must also support them in illness,
etc. After their deaths, the personal property and real estate will
return to the heirs. Another clause stipulated that Marie-Anne,
another of the donors' daughters, must be fed and supported by
the recipients. All while continuing to work in their house as she
had always done; she will also be free to leave when it seems
good for her benefit. The donors also wanted to be able to go to
mass in a carriage or by canoe, as, undoubtedly, they had always
done.

During the afternoon of this same 17 June 1741, the
family and friends had the opportunity to take part in the
betrothal of the 26 year old Jean-Baptiste, and Marie-Jeanne, who
glowed with the freshness of her 17 years. Charles and Marie-
Ursule gave their consent to their daughter, while Alexis Leduc
acquiesced to the request of his brother Jean-Baptiste. Jean Tessier, Marie-Jeanne's godfather, was present. The couple would
live in community property and they received a dowry from
Charles and Marie-Ursule of a piece of land with two arpents in
frontage by twenty deep, located between the homestead of the
donors and that of Michel Vallée. According to the custom,
Jean-Baptiste included in the contract a *"prefixed dowry"* of 600
livres. We know the following: the wedding took place on 26
June. After giving birth to four children, Marie⌐Jeanne died on
the first of September 1748, at the age of only 24.

195

DEATH OF CHARLES VALLÉE

In spite of the short duration of her marriage, barely seven years, Marie-Jeanne would know the sorrow of seeing her parents take their last journey. Charles Vallée died first, suddenly, on 24 October 1742 and was laid to rest the next day in the small cemetery of Sainte-Anne. The act written by the pastor François Rouillard (36) indicates that the deceased had not had the time to receive the last rites, despite the haste that he took to administer them to him. The majority of the residents of the parish attended the funeral.

On 29 October, Marie-Ursule Gendra made a request of Louis-Jean Poulin de Courval, civil and criminal lieutenant at the seat of the royal jurisdiction of Trois-Rivières, begging him to issue an order concerning the selection of a guardian and a substitute guardian for the 22 year old Louis Vallée, the only minor child still under the guardianship of his parents. The notary Pollet presided over a family gathering of Marie-Ursule Gendra, her sons Charles and Jacques, Pierre Gervais, Jean Massicot, Alexis and Jean-Baptiste Leduc (married respectively to Elisabeth, Angélique, Dorothée and Jeanne Vallée), Michel Gendra, full cousin, and Louis Vallée. Marie-Ursule refused to become guardian and the gathering then appointed Jean Tessier as guardian and Jean Massicot as substitute guardian.

THE INVENTORY

The notary Pollet drafted the official report of this act of guardianship on 2 November. The next day, he took an inventory of the property which had belonged to the late Charles Vallée and his wife. This document totals more than twenty pages. It demonstrates that living a little more than a half-century at Sainte-Anne, 48 years of them spent at Rapide-Nord, the colonist had not only raised a fine family, but also, through his industry, his unflagging work and good management, was successful in amassing an impressive amount of property of all kinds.

Having ascertained that by virtue of the act of guardianship, Louis Vallée was now entitled *"to become the heir of his late father in the continuation of the property and the rights of the parties"*, the notary made the description of the assets of the community: personal property, real estate, utensils, used clothes and clothing, gold and silver coins and non-coins, letters, deeds, papers, documents and other items remaining after the death of Charles Vallée occurring, about eleven days earlier, in the house where his widow lives. He added that these assets had been shown and described to him by Marie Gendra, Jean-Baptiste Leduc, Marie-Jeanne and Louis Vallée. Everyone present took an oath

> *"made in front of the Crucifix and on the place which they claim in paradise (and) comply when they would find themselves opposed to one another in the difficulties such a situation presents which had been explained to them by the notary".*

The said assets were taken by Pierre Roy, lieutenant of the militia of Sainte-Anne and Pierre Laguerre, resident of the same place. They are valued *"in their soul and conscience with due allowance for the present time..."*, in the presence of Sieurs Jean-Baptiste Brunsard, tax collector, Me Tailhandier living at Batiscan and Alexis Morand, resident of la Rapide of the Sainte-Anne river, witnesses.

The actual inventory began by the description of the personal property left in the care of Jean Tessier. During the afternoon, they displayed numerous articles found in every homestead of that era; farming instruments, gun, tools and the deceased's used clothing which included, among other items, a white cloak of mazamet, a cloak and a jacket of destinne, another ensemble of macrame, and so forth.

The inventory continued on 5 November, at one o'clock in the afternoon. A cane, a cape, a pair of breeches, a pair of mexan stockings, two hats, a calf skin, some pieces of sea cow and moose hide, a tuque, a shirt of linen from Rouen, shoes with buckles, mittens, ten shirts, a jacket of mazamet, a cloak of drugget, etc. The deceased was thus well provided with clothing of all sorts. The livestock included 23 domestic animals: oxen, cows, sheep and pigs. The property inventoried was valued at a total amount of 746 livres and 10 sols. Wheat, peas, beans, bran, hens, butter, grain, cabbage and tobacco would be divided among the heirs.

197

The papers and documents found in the Vallée home consisted essentially of three documents:

1.   The marriage contract written by Trotain on 24 January 1694.

2.   The contract of concession drafted by Michel Roy on 10 April 1697.   This land located at Rapide-Nord had nine arpents in frontage; this was the location of the house in which Charles Vallée died. It was a building surrounded with squared stakes, covered with boards, with a stone chimney set in the middle. There was also an old barn sided with stakes, a stable of split, round stakes, and a stable built of split, round stakes resting on the ground. The three buildings were covered with straw.

3. A contract of concession signed by the notary-surveyor Hilaire Bernard de la Rivière on 24 March 1710. The said land, also located on the banks of the Sainte-Anne river, had eight arpents in frontage by twenty deep. There was a barn there sided with stakes and covered with straw.

The inventory was concluded on 6 November. They made the description of the *"debts owed to the community"*, they amounted to a total of 118 livres and 15 sols. As for the *"debts which the community owed"*, they totaled 41 livres and 10 sols. (37)

ABANDON AND DIVISION

Concurrently with the inventory, the notary Pollet drew up two other acts: that of 5 November in which Marie Gendra relinquished her property to her children, and that of 6 November in which the heirs divided it. In the first, the widow said to relinquish all her personal and real property *"now and for ever"* to Charles and Jacques Vallée, Alexis Leduc (husband of Dorothée Vallée), Jean-Baptiste Leduc (husband of Marie-Jeanne Vallée), Jean Massicot (husband of Angélique Vallée) and acting for Pierre Vallée, absent), Denis Tellier (husband of Marie-Joseph Vallée), Jean Tessier (trustee for Louis Vallée currently in the pays d'enhaut), Jacques Massicot (guardian of the minor daughter of the late Antoine Massicot and the late Marie-Renée Vallée), Jean-Baptiste Brunsard dit Langevin (administrator of Marie-Anne Vallée), Madeleine Morand (widow of Michel

198

Vallée, assisted by Pierre Godard dit La Mothe, her second husband, who authorized his wife to represent her only daughter, Marie-Madeleine Vallée). By this act, Marie-Ursule Gendra stated that all those who were mentioned could dispose of her property *"as property belonging to them to begin to use it starting today"*, in exchange for a pension of 24 minots of wheat, a fat pig ready to be butchered, twelve pounds of butter, twelve pots of eau-de-vie *"Guildine"* and six pots of wine. After her death, her heirs must have her buried in the cemetery of the place where she dies and have 72 low requiem masses said for the repose of her soul. In the meantime, she will live at the home of whomever it seems good to her, and in the place where she will live, she must be supported according to her condition and to divide the rest of her pension, if necessary, among the heirs.

The second act mentioned the dividing and distribution of the two lands located at la Rapide on the river and in the seigneurie of Sainte-Anne. The heirs had chosen Pierre Roy and Pierre Laquerre to visit and appraise these lands and for each to accept his reimbursement for the evaluation made by the arbiters and appraisers. Twelve notes were made, rolled and tossed into a hat, then drawn out by lot by a disinterested person in the presence of the parties involved. Once the drawing was over, everyone moved on to the second piece of land, which had six arpents in frontage, on which it was stated that the portions were of nearly equal value. They proceeded, however, to certain adjustments and they gave each other reciprocal releases.

Finally, on 12 June and 11 July 1744 (acts by Pollet), Louis, Marie-Anne and Ursule Vallée, Alexis and Jean-Baptiste Leduc, and Pierre Gervais, proceeded with the exchanges of portions of land resulting from the division made two years earlier. On 17 January 1745 (same notary), Pierre-Charles Vallée acknowledged having received, for himself and for his brothers and sisters, brothers-in-law and sisters-in-law, all the documents concerning the inventory, the divisions, requests, election of trustees, conclusion of inventory and other papers explaining their rights and income coming from the late Charles, senior. They said they were satisfied with the administration that had been made by Jean Tessier and accepted its general release.

DEATH OF MARIE-URSULE GENDRA

At the time when the Vallée children and the spouses carried out the last modification to the two lands left through inheritance by their father and father-in-law, Marie-Ursule Gendra was spending her last years. On 13 April 1747, the pastor Rouillard wrote in the registry of Sainte-Anne an act which he titled *"Burial of the bonne femme Vallée"*. This expression, used from time to time during that era in the parish registries, was not pejorative; it meant that the woman whom they had buried was a good and brave woman. The widow of Charles Vallée was said to be about 70 years old. In truth, if we base her age on the census of 1681, they had aged her by a few years. Her funeral took place according to

> *"the ceremonies of the Church, after having been assisted by the Sacraments of the Eucharist and Extreme unction. The said burial was made in the presence of the majority of the parish"*.

Marie-Ursule had died the day before.

Good and brave woman, poor and rather unobtrusive, Marie-Ursule was the daughter of the first colonist of Rapide-Nord. Pierre Gendra had occupied his land since 1687, ten years before Charles Vallée acquired his own concession there. (38)

Like so many of the daughters of the king of whom Raymond Douville speaks, they were present at Sainte-Anne at the very beginning of this parish. Marie-Ursule Gendra belonged to this breed of women who, in addition to supporting their brave husbands, encouraged them, and sustained them, *"produced the seed of the future"*. (39)

FAMILY NAME VARIATIONS

Vallée has only three known variations: Blois, Lavallée and Sansoucy.

END NOTES

1) "Votre nom appartient a l'histoire". Edition Sylvie Messinger, 1992, p.324.

2) On the subject of Pierre Vallée, see "Nos Ancetres" Vol.20, pp. 166 to 174, by Gérard Lebel, C.Ss.R.

3) "Dictionnaire étymologique des noms de lieux de France". Larousse Sélection, Vol.2.

4) "Dictionnaire des saints" by Marteau de Langle de Cary et G. Taburet-Misoffe. Librairie generale francaise., 1963, p.341.

5) "Normandie" Guides blue, 1961, p.180.

6) _____. MSGCF, spring edition, 1994, p.35 & 36.

7) _____. JDCS, tome 1, p.166.

8) André Lafontaine, RANF 1666 et 1667. Sherbrooke 1985, pp. 39 & 211.

9) _____. RAPQ 1953 1955. "Les terres de l'Ile d'Orléans (Saint Pierre), p.14.

10) Lionel Laberge, "Histoire du fief de Lotinville 1652-1690" p.105 & 274.

11) OpCit (8), p. 39 & 211, - DBC,1, p.519.

12) Marcel Trudel, Le Terrier du Saint-Laurent en 1663, p.471 & 472.

13) This record is no longer to be found in the acts of this notary.

14) The facts reported here are substantially contained in the "process-verbal" of the Provost of Québec (1st and 20 July 1671) and of the Sovereign Council (JDCS, 1, p.628-629, 26 August 1670, and on pages 664 to 666, 5 October 1671.

15) Jean Dudouyt (1628-1688) priest, then canon and vicar-general of Québec, was at this time the administrator of the estate of Msgr de Laval.

16) Originally from the region of Lyonnais, Benoit Duplein arrived at Québec in 1671. The parish of Sainte-Famille was his first assignment. This was followed by duties at Sorel, Contrecoeur, Saint-Ours, Vercheres, Lavaltrie, Chamblay, Cap-Saint-Ignace and Batiscan. He died at Montréal on 3 October 1689.

17) This matter concerns Jean Lerouge (1639-1712), mason and surveyor, better known for his work of surveying the lands of New-France.

18) On this subject please refer to the work entitled "Le Consiel Souverain de la Nouvelle-France by Jean Delalande (Québec, 1927, p.262.

19) Louis Rouer de Villeray (1629-1700) arrived in Canada about 1650 as a soldier. Billeted at Trois-Rivières, Pierre Boucher appointed him as a special prosecutor. He was also secretary to Governor de Lauson, notary, keeper of supply records, prevost-judge, Seigneur and conselor to the Sovereign Council. (DBC,1,p.593-596).

20) This matter concerns Eustache Lambert, junior. The father died in July 1673.

21) _____. JDCS, 1, p.81 & 82.

22) André Lafontaine, "Les bailiages de Beaupré et de l'ile d'Orléans" (Sherbrooke, 1987, p.455, 471 and 472.

23) François Berthelot, who had never set foot in New France, having acquired the l'ile d'Orléans in 1675 and which gave him the new title of "Comte de Saint-Laurent".

24) André Lafontaine, RANF 1681, p.206.

25) _____. JDCS, IV, p.104.

26) Ibid (24).

27)   Jacques Saintonge, <u>Nos Ancetres</u>, *"Mathurin Tessier dit Maringouin"*, **Vol 6, Sainte-Anne-de-Beaupré, 1986, p. 157 to 163. Also <u>Le Nouvelliste</u>** *"Nos familles et leur origines"* **28 June 1980.**

28)   *"Les premiers seigneurs et colons de Sainte-Anne-de-la-Pérade 1667-1681".* <u>Le Bien Public</u>, **Trois-Rivières, 1946, p. 112.**

29)   **The scribes of that time often wrote the name** *Gendra* **(without s). The name of Gendron appeared later.**

30)   **Collection** *"Notre passé",* **Cahier #46, <u>Le Bien Public</u>, p.16.**

31)   **The** *Outaouais* **were a tribe of the Algonquin nation, living in the region of Georgian Bay. They came regularily to Montréal for the fur trade.**

32)   **Lacking contrary information, all of the baptisms, marriages and burials of the children of Charles Vallée and of Marie-Ursule Gendra took place at La Pérade. The better part of the records on this family have been placed in the Tanguay and Jetté dictionaries, or in the records BMS of Sainte-Anne.**

33)   **Louis Phelypeaux de Ponchartrain (1634-1729), chancellor of France from 1699 to 1714.**

34)   **This act was mentioned in the inventory of 1742, but was not found in the records of the notary de la Rivière.**

35)   _____ . *RAPQ 1921-1923* **"Verbal record of the prosecutor-general Collet on the district boundaries of the parishes of New France, as annotated by the abbot Ivanhoe Caron", pages 275-277.**

36)   **François Rouillard, son of Jean and Jeanne Lavasseur, was born at Sainte-Foy on 3 May 1701. Ordained a priest on 11 June 1726, he was the pastor at Saint-Nicolas and at Sainte-Antoine-de-Tilly. He arrived at Sainte-Anne in 1742 and died there on 15 December 1760.**

37)   **These debts are mentioned in two places, at the end of the inventory and after the regulation put out by the civil and criminal prosecutor for the appointment of the guardian of Louis Vallée.**

38) Raymond Douville: <u>"La route du bois du merle"</u>, p.16. Antoine Guibord also had obtained two concessions at Rapide Nord about the same time as Pierre Gendra, but they were not truly recorded.

39) Raymond Douville: <u>"Nos premières méres de famille"</u> Le Bien Public, 1976, p.3.

René Venet (Loisel)

CHAPTER 10

René Venet (Loisel)

*f there is a city which speaks to the heart of the Canadians,* wrote Robert Hollier in 1967, *it is indeed La Rochelle"*. It is the homeland of the Beauchamp, Levesque, Papillon, Rheaume, Trudeau, Gendron, Cormier, Caron, Bédard, Caille, Nolin, Paradis, Perron, and many other great Canadian families. (1) It is also the home of René Venet, the majority of whose descendants adopted the last name of Loiselle more than two centuries ago.

La Rochelle, a city more than a thousand years old, located on the Gascogne Sea ten leagues from *Saintes* towards the northwest and across from the *ile de Ré*, in ancient times bore the name of *Rupella, Rochella, Raccula or Rocella,* according to the *"Dictionnairé universal francais et latin* published in Paris in 1734. (2) For René Venet's contemporaries, it was *"a rather large city and very commercial"*. It also had a good port, a Presidial, a Sovereign Court for the *Salines du ponant* (west), a *Cour des Monnaies* and a diocese of *Bordeaux*, which had been moved from *Maillezais* in 1649.

Tourists today can still admire the *Vieux-Port* framed between the towers of *la Chaine* and Saint-Nicolas (14th century), a dungeon 35 meters high and the door of *la Grosse Horloge*; also a surrounding wall with battlements dating from the fifteenth century. La Rochelle was the first French fishing port on the Atlantic. To go to Paris, the people of La Rochelle in the eighteenth century had to travel a distance of some 115 leagues (460 kilometers) across *l'Aunis, la Saintonge, le Poitou, la Touraine, l'Orleanais and l'ile-de-France.*

According to Roland-J. Auger, La Rochelle holds, for several reasons, (3)

207

"a very important place in our history. If from an administrative point of view, it did not have the importance of Paris, it exceeded the influence of this last city by its intense commerce with Canada, by the influence of the colonists whom she directed to New France, and also by the considerable number of Canadians who settled there temporarily or to live".

The disasterous siege of La Rochelle by the English in 1627 and 1628, emptied the city of three-fourths of its inhabitants. From the 20,000 that they had been, only 5000 survivors remained.

"The disappeared residents, wrote the historian Auger, were replaced by newcomers almost all of them Catholic, in such a way that the two flourishing Protestant churches at La Rochelle merged into one. The Catholic church, on the contrary, reduced before the siege at the chapel of Sainte-Marguerite, witnessed the rebirth of its former parishes of Notre-Dame de Cogne, Saint-Jean du Perrot, Saint-Sauveur, Saint-Barthelemi, Saint-Nicolas and Saint-Pierre in the faubourg of Laleu".

THE WEDDING

In 1722, René Venet was at Pointe-Claire to marry Marguerite Bigras. On 10 August, the pastor Jean-Baptiste Breul (4) drew up the short marriage contract for this couple which reads as follows:

"Marriage agreement made between Renay Venet and Marguerite Bigras in the presence of Joachim Merlot, Michel Bouvet and Jacques Viaume and me the undersigned. The said Venet and Marguerite Bigras take each other with their rights, joint ownership in all property present and in the future the property will go to the last survivor, the said

Venet gives one hundred arpents as a dowry to Marguerite Bigras his wife and two hundred livres for the preciput the said Merlot, Bouvet and Viaume have stated not to know how to write. Written at Pointe Claire this 10th day of August 1722." Signed: Breul, priest.

The next day, in the church of Saint-Joachim de Pointe-Claire, the same priest blessed their union. He informs us that Renay Venet was the son of Laurent Venet and Françoise Masson, his father and mother of the parish of Notre-Dame de La Rochelle (Aunis) and that Marguerite was the daughter of François Bigras and Marie Brunet, her father and mother of the parish of Pointe-Claire. The witnesses were Charles Parent, François and Alexis Bigras. The ancestor François Bigras dit Fauvel, Marguerite's father, was also originally from La Rochelle. He had been baptized in the parish of Saint-Nicolas on 8 September 1665. Having immigrated to Canada when he was not yet twenty years old, he had recorded his marriage contract with Marie Brunet on 25 August 1685. The latter, daughter of Mathieu Brunet and Marie Blanchard, was then only eight years old. The wedding, we can understand why, had to be delayed until 31 August 1693. Marguerite, fifth of the thirteen children of François Bigras and Marie Brunet, was born at Lachine on 23 November 1701 and was baptized three days later.

THE CHILDREN

René Venet and Marguerite Bigras had eleven children, seven sons and four daughters. The majority of the baptismal acts mentioned that the father was a "day laborer".

1. René, later known by the first name of Louis, was baptized at Pointe-Claire on 8 July 1723 by the Sulpicien Jean-Baptiste Breul. Godfather and godmother: André Roy and Angélique Bigras.

2. Thomas, baptized at Pointe-Claire on 9 March 1725 by messire Breul. Godfather and godmother: Thomas Pilon and Madeleine Brunet. Buried on 7 November of the same year, at the age of 9 months.

3.   Nicolas, born at Montréal about 8:00 o'clock in the morning on 29 August 1727 and baptized the same day by the Sulpicien Charles de La Goudalie.   Godfather and godmother: Nicolas Lefebvre and Marie-Agnes Mongrain who signed with the pastor.

4.   François-Marie, born at 8:00 o'clock during the evening of 30 August 1730 and baptized at Montréal the next day by the Sulpicien Mathieu Falcose.   Godfather and godmother: François Trottier and Marie-Joseph Lefebvre.

5.   Marie-Joseph, born at Montréal on 6 July 1732 and baptized the next day by the Sulpicien Jean Bouffandeau. Godfather and godmother: Jacques Lefebvre and Marie-Joseph Danis.

6.   Antoine, born at Montréal on 14 May 1734 at 3:00 o'clock in the morning and baptized the next day by Jean-Baptiste Breul. Godfather and godmother: Antoine Boyer (originally from the ile de Ré) and Magdeleine Langlois. Buried on 15 June 1741 at the age of 7 *"in the cemetery far from the church"*.

7.   Jacques, born at Montréal and baptized on 10 March 1736 by the Sulpicien Jean Bouffandeau, a priest from the seminary of Montréal.   Godfather and godmother: Jacques Cartier and Marie-Thérèse Boutin.   Buried on 17 November 1737 at the age of 20 months *"in communion with the Holy Roman Church"*.

8.   Marguerite, born at Montréal on 26 August 1737 and conditionally baptized the next day by Jean Bouffandeau. Godfather and godmother: Jean-Baptiste Cavelier and Marguerite Parant, wife of Toussaint Cavelier.   Died on 6 July 1739 and buried the following day at the age of 22 months, *"in communion with the Holy Roman Church"*.

9.   Marie-Louise, born at Montréal on 28 January 1739 and baptized the next day by Jean Bouffandeau.   Godfather and godmother: Joseph Raimond and Louise Duplanti-Heri.   Buried on 18 January 1742 at the age of 3 years and 4 months *"in the cemetery far from of the church"*.

10.   Marianne, born at Montréal on 30 October 1740 and baptized the following day by the Sulpicien Benoit Favré,   a priest from the seminary of Montréal.   Godfather and godmother: René Venet and Marianne Tuot dit Duval.

11. Gabriel, born *"this morning"* on 18 January 1743 and baptized the same day by Jean Bouffandeau. Godfather and godmother: Gabriel Descary and Marie-Joseph Langlois.

A VOYAGEUR SON

On 19 January 1754, the notary Jean-Henry Bouron drew up a contract which reveals that Louis Venet, resident of the faubourg of Québec in the city of Montréal and classified as a "voyageur", was preparing to marry Marie-Amable Boulaguet, daughter of Étienne Boulaguet dit Saint-Amour and of Marie-Louise Custos. The groom, who then found himself in the house of Gabriel Dumont dit Poitevin *"commonly called Plaisance"*, was said to be the widower of Françoise Chancellor. When and where had he contracted this first marriage? Had it been made during a trading journey? A mystery. There is no trace of this union in the parish registries of this era.

The second marriage which was about to take place received the approval of two important people: Jean-Victor Varin, councillor of the king, commissioner-director and sub-delegate of the intendant at Montréal. (5) Among the friends and relatives gathered for the occasion, let us note the presence of René Venet, father, Jean-Baptiste Villeneuve, Jean-Baptiste Marsolet, junior, Pierre Leduc, Gabriel Dumont and Catherine Custons, uncle and aunt of the bride, Antoine Parent, maternal uncle, Jacques Barette, Jacques Jourdan and Pierre Mezière.

Louis Venet stated that he had been unable to draw up the inventory of the property belonging to the community which he had with his first wife. It was then that the people present exhorted him to fulfill this formality *"as soon as he possibly could"*. It was stipulated in the contract that the couple would live in community personal property and real property according to the *coutume de Paris*. Marie-Amable received a prefixed dowry of 300 livres to be taken from Louis's property. Finally, the couple stated that they were giving each other their property and rights coming from the succession of their fathers and mothers.

211

Two days later on 21 January, the nuptial ceremony, presided over by the Sulpicien Jean-Baptiste Breul, the same one who had baptized Louis-René Venet in 1723, took place in the church of Notre-Dame de Montréal. The celebrating priest received the mutual consent of the couple and declared them united

> *"according to the regulations and customs observed by the Holy Church in the presence of Me Jean-Victor Varin equerry Sr de la Mare, commissioner-director in Canada, monsieur Maitre Jacques Joseph Guiton Monrepos, lieutenant-general of the royal jurisdiction of Montréal, M François St Ours equerry lieutenant of the infantry and Mr Jean-Henry Bouron, royal notary".*

Those signing were: Marie Amable Laget (sic), Varin, Guiton Monrepos, Guillemin de St-Pierre, M.P. Lagauchetière, Deligneris, St-Ours, De Couagne, Joncaire Dautrice, Bouron, Gabriel Dumon, Mezière, Breul and Jourdan. Curiously, this marriage act did not mention the first wife of Louis-René. Why? Was it an oversight? Did they voluntarily ignore this fact?

The ancestor Étienne Boulaguet was originally from the parish of Saint-Jacques de la Boucherie, in Paris. He was married at Montréal, on 20 November 1731, to Marie-Louise Custos, daughter of Pierre-Jacques and of Marie Bouvier. Born in 1733, Marie-Amable was their eldest daughter. Seven more children would come to join the family, three sons and four daughters. At least four of them died in the cradle.

Three months after his wedding, Louis-René Venet was hired by Philippe Dagneau, equerry, Sieur de La Saussaye, officer of the troops at Louisbourg, present at Montréal. The contract, written on 22 April 1754 by the notary François Simonnet, directed the servant to leave, at the first request, for the post at "Chiningue" or the boundaries of this place and to return when the voyageurs come back from the said place. Venet must, as leader of the canoe, take care that the merchandise and the pelts, as well as the food and the tools for the journey be conveyed to the trading posts which will be indicated to him. In short, he had to do everything that would be asked of him legally and honestly without being able to leave his service, under penalty of forfeit-

212

ing his wages, 600 livres, resulting from his commitment. Did Louis-René know his eldest daughter, Marie-Louise, born in October of the same year, who died on 11 November and was buried the next day in the cemetery of the poor at Montréal?

That need be no obstacle! Fascinated with large spaces covered with virgin forest where streams, rivers and lakes interweave, the soothing effluvium of which penetrates deep within, Louis-René left again the following year. On 18 March 1755, in the presence of the notary Louis-Claude Danre de Blanzy, who revealed that our servant was now living in the faubourg Sainte-Marie, began in the service of Thomas Dufy Desauniers (6) to lead a canoe loaded with merchandise as far as the post of Michilimakinac and to return by the usual convoys with the pelts acquired by trade. Everything with the same conditions and reservations enacted at the time of his previous journey for 300 livres, 108 of which had already been received, the remaining 192 had to be paid upon the return of the employee to Montréal *"in money having legal tender in this country"*.

In the meantime, a second child was born in January 1756, from the union of Louis-René and Marie-Amable. The young René only lived for six months. He died on 9 July and was buried the next day in the cemetery of the poor at Montréal.

THE NAME OF LOISEL

Then, as if by chance, the name of Loisel appears in the family of Louis-René and Marie-Amable, at the birth of Louis, their third child. The Venets were then living in the parish of Saint-Laurent, where the baptism took place. The act drafted by the Sulpicien Pierre Sartelon reads as follows:

> *"The thirteenth of May one thousand seven hundred fifty-seven I baptized Jean Louis born in the morning legitimate son of Louis Loisel dit Venet and of Marie Amable Bouillaler (sic) dit St Amour living in this parish. Godfather was Maurice Donait and godmother Marie Louise Custeau who stated not to know how to write."*

It is difficult to explain how the Venet last name has today almost entirely disappeared while the Loisels from this family have multiplied from generation to generation.

Other children were born to the union of Louis-René and Marie-Amable and baptized with the last name of Venet or Venette, notably André-René, born in the evening of 10 July 1758 and baptized three days later at Saint-Laurent. Another short life, since Louis-René died on the following 16 August and was buried three days later.

The family returned to live at Montréal a few years later. The registries of the parish of Notre-Dame mentioned at least three more premature deaths:

Marie-Marguerite, born in 1765, died on 24 August 1766 and buried the next day in the cemetery of the poor, about 15 months old;

Jean, born in 1766, died on 7 June 1767 and buried in the cemetery of the poor the next day at the age of 8 months;

Marie-Charlotte, born in 1770, died on 5 October 1771, whose mortal remains were buried in the same cemetery the next day. She was 11 months old.

At his marriage celebrated at Saint-François-Xavier de Kahnawake on 3 May 1779, *"Louis Loisel, son of Louis Loisel dit Venette and the late Marie St Amour"*, seems to begin the Loisel/Loiselle line. On that day, he married Louise Bourice (Boulerice), daughter of Jean-Baptiste and the late Marie-Josephte Cullerier, in the presence of the two fathers, Pierre Comte, John Stacy, Jean Duranleau and several relatives and friends.

THE ANCESTOR'S OTHER CHILDREN

Of the eleven children brought into the world by René Venet and Marguerite Bigras, we already know that five of them died in the cradle.

We are unaware what fate was reserved for three other sons, Nicolas, François and Gabriel, born respectively in 1727, 1730 and 1743.

Marie-Joseph, born in 1732 and Marie-Anne, born in 1740, took husbands at Montréal. The two marriages were celebrated by the Sulpicien Louis Jollivet, appointed by the pastor Antoine Deat.(7) Jollivet was the same one who, on 25 June 1760, delivered in the same church of Notre-Dame, the funeral eulogy of Msgr Henri-Marie Dubreuil de Pontbriand, sixth bishop of Québec. The latter had died at Montréal on the preceding 6 June.

Marie-Anne, the youngest of the daughters, was married first. The nuptial ceremony took place on 6 November 1758. The marriage record indicated that the groom, the 31 year old Jacques Duperon, was the son of the late Jacques Duperon and the late Catherine Becheret, of the parish of Sainte-Anne-de-Vervins, diocese of Laon. (8) It also mentioned that the 18 year old Marie-Anne Venet, was the daughter of René Venet and Marguerite Bigras. The father of the groom was present, as well as Étienne Girard, a cousin, Joseph Gaultier, Joseph Braseau and Suzanne Demers.

Less than two years later, on 4 February 1760, the 27 year old Marie-Joseph, married Gabriel Grenier, 36, son of the late Jean-Baptiste Grenier and Geneviève Lachance, his father and mother from the parish of Saint-Pierre on the Ile d'Orléans, in the presence of René Venet, father of the bride, Georges Vary, Jacques Duperon, Louis Venet, brother of the bride, who all stated not to know how to write. The marriage of Gabriel and Marie-Joseph lasted fifteen years because her remains were buried in the cemetery of the poor on the first of March 1775. She had died the day before at the Hôtel-Dieu of Montréal.

DEATHS OF RENÉ AND MARGUERITE

This period of mourning would soon be followed by others: those of our ancestor René Venet and his wife.

After working hard at Montréal for more than a half-century, René Venet surrendered his soul on 2 May 1776 at the *Hôpital General de Montréal*. The Sulpicien Claude Poncin (9) recorded what follows in the registry of the hospital:

"The third day of May one thousand seven hundred seventy six by me undersigned priest buried in the cemetery of this hospital the body of René Venet who died yesterday at the age of eighty-two. Present were Jacques Larchevesque and Jean Baptiste Poirier who stated not to know how to write."

Two years later, Marguerite Bigras, in her turn, was buried in the soil of the cemetery of the poor at Montréal. Again, it was Claude Poncin who presided at the funeral and wrote the record which is in the registry of the parish of Notre-Dame.

"On the twenty-third day of August one thousand seven hundred seventy-eight by me undersigned priest buried in the cemetery of the poor the body of Marguerite Bigras who died yesterday at the age of eight-five, widow of René Venet. Present were Edme Guil-laume Lucat and Pierre Baron verger and undersigned."

Marguerite, at her death, was in fact 76 years and 7 months old.

The descendants of René Venet and Marguerite Bigras are numerous mainly in the region of Châteauguay and Beauharois, following Louis Loisel, laborer, and of his wife Marie-Louise Boulerice. They are found there all through the nineteenth century. In the eighth generation, André Loiselle, son of Isaie and of Philomene Loiselle, from Saint-Clement de Beauharnois, went to settle in Alberta in 1929. Two years later, at Morinville, he was married to Gilberte Leduc. The majority of this couple's children remained there. But the mother, who became a nun in the convent of the *Soeurs du Precieux-Sang* after the death of her husband, and two of her sons returned to Québec.

Those with the last name of Loiselle have become con-fused with the descendants of two others named Louis Loisel, both Normands who came to New France, the first in the middle of the seventeenth century, the second fifty years later. Homage must be paid to these valiant pioneers! (10)

FAMILY NAME VARIATIONS

Over the years the following known family name variations have appeared:

LOISEL: Choisy, Cloisel, Loiselle, Lorsil, Loysel, Sinode, Venet and Vinet.

LOISELLE: Campbell, Lisotte, Loisel, Loisell, Loizel, and Wisell.

VENET: Other than Venette, Vinet and Vinette, no other variations have been found.

END NOTES

1) Robert Hollier, "La France des Canadiens", Éditions de l'Homme, Montréal, 1962, p.107 & 108.

2) Tome 5, p.1098.

3) Préfacier du livre intitule "Émigration rochelaise en Nouvelle-France" by Pcrc Archange Godbout (ANQ., 1970, p.vii).

4) Jean-Baptiste Breul was born in the diocese of Puy, in France, in 1677. He was ordained a Sulpicien in 1710 and embarked the same year for New-France, where he lived for more than 45 years. He was successively the pastor of Repentigny, Saint-Sulpice, Pointe-Claire, Longue-Pointe and L'Ile Dupas. He died at Montréal in 1756. The contract of marriage in question has been attributed to the records of Michel Lepailleur 26 August 1722.

5) Jean-Victor Varin de la Marre (1699-1786), fiscal-controller of the Navy in Canada and counsellor to the Sovereign Council of Québec. An ambitious and corrupt man, he succeeded in amassing a fortune estimated at 4,000,000 livres. On his return to France he was arrested, found guilty of prevarications and condemned to exile. (DBC, IV, p.813 to 815. Named to the post of LGeneral civil and criminal of the jurisdiction of Montréal in 1741, Jacques-Joseph Guiton de Montrepos became an incorruptible judge. He returned to France after the capitulation of Montréal and was called as a witness to the trial of Bigot and his gang. (DBC, III, p. 290 & 291).

217

6)   Thomas-Ignace Trottier Dufy Desauniers (1712-1777), merchant, church warden, militia captain, about whom Vaudreuil, Montcalm and Lévis had said *"This officer is one of those who are the most distinguished in the corps of militia in Canada"*. (DBC, **IV**, p.802 & 803).

7)   Antoine Déat, born in France in 1696, was the pastor of Notre-Dame de Montréal for more than 37 years. He was a speechmaker of great eloquence. He gave up his pastorship in 1760 and died at the Seminary of Montréal in 1761. (DBC, **III**, p.181).

8)   Vervins is a commune in the Department of the Aisne, located near the Belgian frontier, 38 kilometers from Laon and 180 from Paris. Its church dates from the 12th century.

9)   Born in France in 1725, Claude Ponsin was ordained in France by the Sulpiciens and arrived in Canada in 1750. He began his ministry in the parish of Notre-Dame, then became in 1755, assistant chaplain of the General Hospital of Montréal, then under the direction of Marguerite d'Youville. He died at Montréal in 1811 at the age of 86 years. (DBC, **V**, p.748).

10)   See "Nos Ancetres", Volume 18, by Gérard Lebel, p.120 to 128.

FRANCHE COMTÉ   CENTRE

PAYS DE LA LOIRE   LIMOUSIN

Index of Names

Baret
    Benoit, 86, 90
Barette
    Jacques, 211
Baril, 163
    Jeanne, 186, 187, 188
    Louis, 193
Baril-Duchemy
    François, 52
Baron
    Jeanne, 126
    Pierre, 216
Barrette
    Angele, 158
    Louise, 158
Barsa
    Marie-Madeleine, 111
Barthélemy, 163
Bastien
    Jeanne, 54
Batanville
    Louis Lefebvre dit, 177
Baudouin
    Anne, 83, 84
    Marie-Joseph, 192
    Marie-Magdelaine, 45
Baudry
    François, 86
    Josephte, 40
Baugis
    Louis, 126, 130
Bazin
    Pierre, 32, 34, 75
Bean
    Peter, 6
    Peter & Glenna, 7
Beaubien
    Michel Trottier dit, 39
Beauceron
    Jean Lescarbot dit, 84
Beauchamp, 207
Beaudin
    René, 107, 109
Beaudoin

Laurent, 14
    Marie-Joseph, 192
Beaudon
    Marie, 47
Beaupré
    Claude, 75
Beauregard, 43, 58
Bechard
    Louis, 111, 112
Becheret
    Catherine, 215
Becquet
    Romain, 95
Bédard, 207
    Pierre-Stanislaus, 157
Belair
    François, 30
    Jean-Baptiste, 84, 88
Bélanger
    Madeleine, 171
    Pierre, 128, 129
Bellegarde
    Pierre Gerbault dit, 52
Bellemare
    Joseph, 25
    Laurent & Angélique, 33
    Louis, 33
Bellerive
    Catherine, 46
Bellisle
    Henry, 85
Bellouard
    Mathurin, 172, 173
Belon (Blon)
    Jean-Joseph, 171
Benoist
    Laurent, 170
Benoit
    Marguerite, 54
Bergeron
    André, 6, 11
    André & Ginette, 3
    Antoine, 76
    Ginette, 11

234

Pichette
Joseph, 34
Pierre
Pierre, 103
Pilet, 59
Pilon
Thomas, 209
Pillard
Louis, 21, 68, 78
Pilote
Pierre, 130
Pines
Einerman, 25
Pinguet
Jacques, 126
Marie-Anne, 132
Marie-Madeleine, 120
Pinsonneau
Ignace-Rigobert, 138, 152
Plante
Pierre, 26
Plessis
François, 40
Plessis-Belair
François, 29, 40
Poirier
François, 20
Jean, 19
Jean-Baptiste, 216
Josette, 19
Marie, 29
Marie-Anne, 19, 21, 22, 27, 30, 32
Poirier dit Lajeunesse
Jean, 20
Poitiers dit Saint-Gemme, 22
Poitras
Andrea, 107
Poliquin
Jean, 98
Pollet
Arnould Balthazar, 190
Pombert
Charles, 54
Ponchartrain

Count de, 192
Ponsin
Claude, 218
Pontbriand, Msgr de
Louis-Michel, 77
Portugais
Pierre daSylva dit, 56
Poulin
Maurice, 64
Pierre, 59
Poulin de Courval
Michel, 129
Poullet
Antoine, 173
Poussard. 59
Poutre
Marie, 63
Prat
Louis, 128
Pratte
Charles, 34, 37, 75
Prejean
Marie Joseph, 190
Presseau
Fabien, 97
Prévost
Marie-Madeleine, 43
Prioilaud
Nicole, 167
Pronovost, 59
Proulx
Marie-Madeleine, 118
Provençal
Jean Leroux dit, 22
Prudhomme, 58
Puymegé
Count de, 63
Puyperoulx de LaFosse
Antoine, 48

Q
Quinnette, 113
Quintal
Augustin, 46, 48

243

245

247

LE DRAPEAU FLEURDELISÉ
DE 1608 À 1759

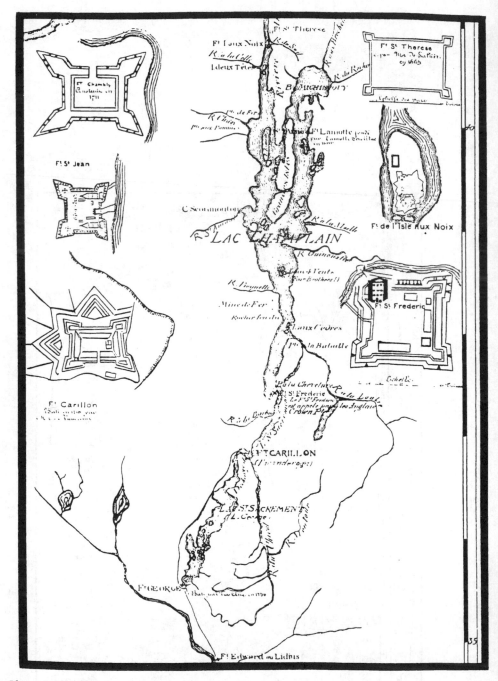

Le lac Champlain, à l'époque de la conquête
Carte tracée vers 1758 sur un plan préparé par Franquet en 1752.

BIBLIOGRAPHY

ACGS.The Genealogist. American-Canadian Genealogical Society, Manchester, NH. 1973.

Adhémar, Antoine., Records. Montréal (1668-1714),
Trois-Rivières (1674-1699).

Adhémar, Jean-Baptiste., Records. Montréal (1714-1754).

AFGS. Je Me Souviens. American-French Genealogical Society, Pawtucket, RI. 1978.

AGE. Jehn, Janet B., *Newsletter.* Acadian Genealogical Exchange. Covington, Ky. 1972.

Allaire, Jean-Baptiste-A., Dictionnaire biographique du clergé canadien-francais. Montréal: Saint-Hyacinthe, 1934.

Ameau, Séverin., Records. Trois-Rivières (1651-1702).

Anctil, Noël., Généalogie de la Familles Canadiennes-Francaises (1985).

ASAB. Annals of Sainte-Anne-de-Beaupré. Lévis: Redemptorist Press.

ASQ. Archives of the Séminary of Québec.

Apvrilleau, Barthélemy G., Records. Québec (1613-1697).

Arsenault, Bona., Histoire et Généalogie des Acadiens. Montréal: Editions Lemeac Inc., 1978.

Auber, Claude., Records. Québec, (1652-1693).

Aubin, Henri., L'Ile d'Orléans a Saint-Pierre (1985).

Audet, Bernard., Le costume paysan dans la région de Québec au XVIIe siècle, ed. Montréal: Lemeac Inc., 1980.

251

Audet, François-Joseph., Le Régiment de Carignan. *The Royal Society of Canada*, proceedings and transactions of., Third Series - Volume XVI, Hope & Son, Ottawa. May, 1922.

Audouart, Guillaume., Records. Québec (1647-1663).

Auger, Roland-J., La Grande Récrue de 1653. *SGFC,* Publication No.1. Montréal: 1955.

FCAG. Auger, Roland-J., French Canadian and Acadian Genealogical Review. Québec: 1968-1981.

Badeau, François., Records. Québec (1654-1657).

Baillargeon, Noël., Le Séminaire de Québec sous l'episcopat de Mgr de Laval. Québec: Les Presses de l'Université Laval, 1972.

Baillargeon, Noël., Le Séminaire de Québec de 1685 a 1760. Québec: Les Presses de l'Université Laval, 1977.

Bancheron, Henri., Records. Québec (1646-1647).

Barbel, Jacques., Records. Québec (1703-1740).

Baret, Guillaume., Records. Montréal (1709-1744).

Barolet, Claude., Records. Québec (1728-1761).

Basset, Benigné., Records. Montréal (1657-1699).

Beaubien,Charles-P., Le Sault au Récollet. Montréal: Beauchemin & fils, 1898.

Beaucarnot, Jean-Louis., Les Noms de famille et leurs Secrets (1988).

Beauce. Recueil de généalogies des Comtes de Beauce, Dorchester et Frontenac, 162-1946. 11 Volumes. Beauceville: College du Sacre-Coeur, 1949-1955.

Beaudet, Lionel., Recensement de la ville de Québec pour 1716. Québec: Côté & Cie, 1887.

Beaudoin, Marie-Louise., Les Premières et les Filles du Roi à Ville-Marie, Montréal (1980).

Beaumont, Charles., Généalogie des familles de la Beauce. Ottawa: 1905.

Beaumont, Charles., Généalogie des familles de la Côte de Beaupré. Ottawa: Parmelee, 1912.

Becquet, Romain., Records. Québec (1663-1682).

Bellemare, Raphaël., Les Bases de l'histoire d'Yamachiche, 1703-1903. Montréal: Beauchemin.

Bellemare, Joseph-Elzéar., Histoire de la Baie Saint-Antoine dite Baie-du-Febvre, 1683-1911. Montréal: La Patrié, 1911.

Bellemare, Joseph-Elzéar., Histoire de Nicolet 1669-1924. Arthabaska: 1924.

Benoît, Pierre., Records. Montréal (1702-1706).

Benson, Adolph B., The America of 1750: Peter Kalm's Travels in North America. New York: Dover Edition, 1966.

DNCF. Berger-Levrault, Dictionnaire national des canadien français, (1984).

Bergeron, Adrien., Le Grand Arrangement des Acadiens au Québec. 8 Volumes. Montréal: Editions Elysée, 1981.

Bermen, Laurent., Records. Québec (1647-1649).

Bernard, Antoine., Le Drame Acadien. 1936.

Bernard de la Rivière, Hilaire., Records. Québec (1707-1725).

Bérneval, Les filles venues au Canada de 1658 à 1661. BRH, Vol. XLVII, 1941.

Bertrand, Camille., Histoire de Montréal.

Biosseau, Nicolas., Records. Québec (1730-1744).

Biron, J.-Hector., Pointe-du-Lac de Père en Fils 1738-1980, (1981).

Blais, Herve., Nos Missionaires Récollets (1615-1629); (1670-1849). Volume 33, No.1. Montréal: 1980.

Blanche, Claude-Pierre., Dictionnaire et Armorial des noms de famille de France. Paris: Fayard, 1974.

Bois, L.-E., L'Ile de Orléans, Notes sur son etendue. Ses premiers etablissement. Sa population. Les moeurs de ses habitants. Ses production. Québec: A. Cote et Cie, 1895.

Boisseau, Nicolas., Records, Québec (1730-1744).

Bouchard, Georges., Vieilles choses, vieilles gens.

Bouchard, Léonard., Le Cap-Tourmente et la chassé aux oies blanches. Montréal: Fidés, 1976.

Bouchard, Léonard., Morts tragiques et violentes au Canada 17e et 18e siéles. 2 Volumes. Québec: Audiovisuelles, 1983.

Bouchard, Russell., Les armuriers en Nouvelle-France. Québec: Ministère des Affaires culturel, 1978.

Boucher de la Bruère, Montarville., La naissance des Trois-Rivières, 1928.

Boujonnier, Flour., Records. Trois-Rivières (1651).

Bourdon, Jacques., Records. Montréal (1677-1720).

Bourgine, Hilaire., Records. Montréal (1685-1690).

Boyer, Raymond., Les crimes et châtiments au Canada du XVIIe au XXe siècle.

Brother Robert-Edmond., Repertoire des Mariages de Saint-Georges de Cacouna 1813-1966, (1967).

BRH. Bulletins des Récherchés Historiques (Les). (1895-1968). 70 Volumes from 1895 to 1965. No longer printed.

Brymner, Douglas., Rapport des Archives du Canada. Ottawa, 1892, p.VIII.

Cabazier, Pierre., Records. Montréal (1673-1693).

Cambray, Alfred., Robert Giffard, premier seigneur de Beauport et les origines de la Nouvelle-France. Cap-de-la-Madeleine: 1932.

Campeau, Lucien., La prémier mission des Jésuites en Nouvelle-France (1611-1849) et Les commencements du college de Québec (1629-1670). Cahier d'histoire des Jésuites No.1. Montréal: Editions Bellarmin, 1972.

Careless, James M.S., Canada - A Story of Challenge. Toronto: Macmillan of Canada, 1958.

Caron, Ivanhoe., Aux Origines d'une paroisse, Saint-Ignace du Cap-Saint-Ignace. Société Royale du Canada (1939).

Caron, Joseph., Records. Trois-Rivières (1744)

Caron, Marie-Ange et al., Mosaïque Rimouskoise: Une Histoire de Rimouski. Committee des Fetes du cent Cinquantième anniversaire de la pariosse Saint-Germain de Rimouski, Rimouski 1979.

Casgrain, Henri-Raymond., Histoire de l'Hôtel-Dieu de Québec. Québec: Léger Brousseau, 1878.

Casgrain, Henri-Raymond., Une Paroisse Canadienne. Québec: Léger Brousseau, 1880.

CD. *Cahiers des Dix (Les)*. La Société des Dix, Charlesbourg. Québec: Librairie Garneau, Ltée.,1936.

Chagnolleau, Jean., *"Visages du Poitou"*, from the collection Horizons de France, 1965.

Cer, M.L. d'Armagnac del, comte de Puymègé; Les vieux noms de la France de l'Ouest et les familles d'origine francaise au dela des mers. Paris.

Chambalon, Louis., Records. Québec (1692-1702).

Charbonneau, André; Desloges, Yvon; Lafrance, Marc., Québec ville fortifiee du XVIIe siècle. Québec: Editions de Pelican, 1982.

Charbonneau, Hubert., Vie et mort de nos ancétres, étude demographic. Montréal: Les Presses de l'Université de Montréal, 1975.

Charbonneau, Hubert et Jacques Légare., Le repertoire des actes de bapteme, mariage, sepulture et des recensements du Québec ancien. 35 Volumes to date. Montréal: Les Presses de l'Université de Montréal, 1980-

PRDH. Charbonneau, Hubert., Programme de récherche en demographie historique de l'Universite de Montréal. Montréal: Les Presses de l'Université de Montréal, 1983.

Charlevoix, François-Xavier., Histoire generale de la Nouvelle-France. Paris: 1744.

Choquette, Robert., D'ou vienent nos noms et prénoms? Seleçion du Readers Digest. Montréal: l'Academie canadienne-française.

Choret, Jean-Baptiste., Records. Québec (1730-1755).

Chouinard, François-Xavier., La ville de Québec, histoire municipale: I Régime français. La Société historique de Québec, Cahier No.15. Québec: 1963.

CHR. Canadian Historical Review. Volume 1, Number 1, University of Toronto Press, 1920.

Closse, Raphaël-Lambert., Records. Montréal (1651-1656).

Cloutier, Prosper., Histoire de la Paroisse de Champlain. Trois-Rivières: Bien Public, 1915, 2 vols.

Coleman, Emma-Lewis., New England captives carried to Canada. 2 Volumes. Portland, ME: The Southworth Press, 1925.

Comparet, François., Records. Montréal (1736-1755).

Conan,   Laurie., *Silhouettes canadiennes*.

Coron,   François., Records. Montréal (1721-1732).

Costain, Thomas B., The White and the Gold: The French Regime in Canada. Doubleday & Co., New York, 1954.

Couillard-Després, Azaric., Histoire des seigneurs de la Rivière-du-Sud et leurs allies canadiens. Montréal: Sourds-Muets, 1918.

Couillard-Després, Azaric., Histoire de Sorel et Montréal. Montréal: Sourds-Muets, 1918.

Couillard-Desprées, Azeric., Louis Hébert: premier colon canadien et sa famille. Montréal: Sourds-Muets, 1918.

Courteau, Elmer., The Carignan Regiment. Published in English in the American-Canadian Genealogical Journal *Lost in Canada?*. Volume 8 #III, August, 1982. Joy Reisinger, Editor. Sparta, WI.

Courteau, Elmer., The King's Daughters. Sparta WI: Reisinger, Joy., privately printed, ca. 1980. Reprinted from a nine-part series published in *Lost in Canada?* from 2:2 1976 to 4:2 1978.

Croix, Jean de la., Gabriel Sagard.

Cusson, Jean., Records. Montréal & Trois-Rivières, (1669-1700).

D'Allaire, Micheline., L'Hôpital Géneral de Québec, 1692-1764. Montréal: Fidés, 1971.

Dartigue, Charles., Histoire de la Gascogne.

D'Auteuil, Lorenzo., Repertoire des Mariages de l'Isle-Verte, Paroisse St-Jean-Baptiste, 1766-1978 (1978).

DENFPF. Dauzat, Albert., <u>Dictionnaire Eytmologique des Noms de Famille et Prénoms de France.</u> Paris: Librairie Larousse, 1969, tome 3, p.20191.

David, Jacques., <u>Records.</u> Montréal (17719-1726).

Dawson, Nora., *La vie traditionelle a Saint-Pierre (Ile d'Orléans).* <u>Les Archives du Folklore 8</u>, Québec: Les Presses Universitaires Laval, 1960.

DBC. <u>Dictionnaire biographique du Canada (French) or Dictionary of Canadian Biography (English).</u> Montréal: Les Presses de l'Université Laval, 1969.

Déchene, Louise., <u>Habitants et Marchands de Montréal au XVII sieclé.</u> Paris & Montréal: Plon, 1974.

Defontaines, Pierre., <u>L'Homme et l'hiver au Canada.</u> Québec: Les Presses Universitaires Laval & Paris, Librairie Gallimard, 1957.

Dehornay-Laneuville, Jacques., <u>Records.</u> Québec (1701-1730).

Dejordy, George-Alfred., <u>Dictionnaire génélogique des familles du Richelieu et leur descendants franco-Americains, depuis l'Origine de la famille jusqu'a nos jours.</u> Saint-Hyacinthe: Impremerie La Tribune, 1909.

Delalande, J., <u>Le Conseil Souverain de la Nouvelle-France.</u> Québec: 1927.

Delisle, Luc., <u>La petite Histoire de Deschambeault 1640-1963.</u> Québec: 1963.

DeMerommont, Louis., <u>Records.</u> Trois-Rivières (1686-1689).

GFFDRR. Denissen, Christian., <u>Genealogy of the French Families of the Detroit River Region, 1701-1911.</u> Harold Frederick Powell, Ed., 2 Volumes. Detroit: Detroit Society for Genealogical Research, 1976.

Desaulniers, François Pierre Sévère Lesieur., Les Vieilles familles d'Yamachiche. Montréal: Beauchemin, 1898-1908, 4 vols. Reprint Montréal: Editions Elysée, 1980.

Deziel, Julien., Medaillons d'Ancétres. 2e serie. Montréal: Paulines, 1970-1973.

Dickinson, John-Alexander., Justice et Justiciable: La procedure civile a la Prévote de Québec. Cahier No.26. Québec: Les Presses de l'Université Laval, 1982.

DANFF   Dictionnaire et armorial des noms de famille de France. Nancy, 1974.

DDS Marteau de Langle de Cary & G. Taburet-Misofle Dictionnaire des saints. General Librarie Francaise. 1963.

Dionne, Narcisse-Eutrope., Galerie Historique. Québec: Laflamme et Proulx, 1910.

Dionne, Narcisse-Eutrope., Les Canadiens-français: origine des familles emigrées de France, d'Espagne, de Suisse, etc., pour venir se fixer au Canada, depuis la fondation de Québec jusqu'a ces derniers temps et signification de leur noms. Québec: Laflamme et Proulx, 1914.

Dollier de Casson, Histoire de Montréal. NYCD, O'Callaghan & Fernow

Douville, Raymond., Les prémiers seigneurs et colons de Sainte-Anne de la Pérade. Trois-Rivières: Bien Public, 1946.

Douville, Raymond., Chirugiens, barbiers-chirugiens et Charlatans de la region trifluvienne sous le regime français. Cahiers des Dix. Québec: 1950.

Douville, Raymond., Deux officiers indésirables des troupes de la marine, Cahiers des Dix XIX, Québec: 1954.

Douville, Raymond., Visages du vieux Trois-Riviéres. Cahiers No.18. Trois-Rivières: Edition du Bien Public, 1955.

Douville, Raymond; & Casanova, Jacques-Donat., La vie quotidienne en Nouvelle-France, le Canada de Champlain a Montcalm. Montréal: Librairie Hachette, 1964.

Douville, Raymond; & Casanova, Jacques-Donat., Daily Life in Early Canada. New York: MacMillan, 1967.

Douville, Raymond., La Seigneurie de Sainte-Marie. Québec: 1979.

DNCF Drouin, Gabriel., Dictionnaire national des canadiens français 1608-1760. 3 Volumes. Canada: The Institute Genealogical Drouin. 1975.

Dubreuil, Jean-Etienne., Records. Québec (1707-1739).

Dulaurent, Christophe-Hilaron., Records. Montréal/Québec (1722-1730).

Dumas, Silvio., La chapelle Champlain et Notre-Dame de Recouvrance. Cahier d'Histoire No.10. Québec: La Société Historique de Québec, 1958.

FR. Dumas, Silvio., Les filles du roi en Nouvelle-France. Québec: Société Historique Québec. Pub.24, 1972.

Dupont, Jean-Claude., Legendes de L'Amerique Francaise, Marquis Ltee., Montmagny, Qc., Canada, 1985.

Duprac, Jean-Robert., Records. Québec (1693-1723).

Duprac, Noël., Records. Québec (1723-1748).

Duquet, Pierre., Records. Québec (1663-1678).

Eccles, William J, Canada Under Louius XIV 1663-1701. Toronto: McClelland and Stewart., 1964.

Eccles, William J., Canadian Society under the French Regime. Montréal: Ernest Therrien et fils, 1968.

Eccles,   William J., The Canadian Frontier 1535-1760 (1969),
    Holt, Rinehart and Winston, Inc., 234 pages.

Eccles,   William J., *The Social, Economic and Political Sig-
    nificance of the Military Establishment in New-France.* Canadian
    Historical Review. Toronto: 1971.

Eccles,   William J., France in America. New York: Harper &
    Row, 1972.

Esmonin, Edmond., Etudes sur la France des XVIIe et XVIIe siécles.
    Paris: 1964.

Esnault, Gaston., Dictionnaire Historique des Argots Français
    (Larousse), 1965.

Enjalbert, Henri & Louis Papy., *"Visages de l'Aunis, de la Saintonge et
    de l'Angoumois"*, from the collection Horizons de France.

Faillon, Etienne-Michel., Histoire de la colonie française en Canada. 3
    Volumes. Montréal: Villemarie, 1865-1866.

Falardeau, Emile., Les Pionniers de Longueuil et leur origines 1666-
    1681. Montréal: G. Ducharme, 1937.

Falardeau, Emile., La Revue Poplaire. 1938.

Fauteux, Joseph-Noël., Essai sur l'industrie au Canada sous le Régime
    français. 2 Volumes. Québec: 1927

FCAGR. Auger, Roland J., *French Canadian and Acadian Genealogical
    Review.* Center Québecois des Récherches Généalogiques.
    Québec: 1968.

Ferland, Jean-Baptiste-Antoine., Cours d'Histoire du Canada, Vol. II,
    p.233f.

Ferland, Jean-Baptiste-Antoine., La France dans l'Amerique du Nord.
    Québec: 1965.

Ferland, Jean-Baptiste-Antoine., Histoire economique et sociale du
    Québec 1760-1850. Québec: 1966.

Fillion, Michel., Records. Québec (1660-1688).

Fleuricourt, Jean-Baptiste., Records. Montréal (1676-1702).

Foley, Jean-Paul., Batiscan s'erige premises paroissiales (1670-1708). Cahier published by the committee Bien Public. Trois-Rivières: 1981.

Forget, Ulysses., Les Franco-Americains et le Melting Pot et Onomastique Franco-Americain.

Forgues, Michel., Genealogies des familles de l'Ile d'Orléans. RAPQ. Québec: Public Archives,1905/6.

DBBNF. Fournier, Marcel., Dictionnaire Biographique des Bretons en Nouvelle-France 1600-1765. Québec: RANQ, 1981.

Frechette, E.-R., Edits, ordonnances royaux, declarations et arrets du Conseil d'etat du roi concernant le Canada. 3 Volumes. Québec: 1854-1856.

Fregault, Guy., Essai sur les finances canadiennes (1700-1750). Montréal: Fidés, 1958.

Fregault, Guy., La civilisation de la Nouvelle-France 1713-1744). Montréal: Fidés, 1969.

Frérot de la Chesnaye, Thomas., Records. Québec (1711-1743).

Gachet, René., Records. Québec (1711-1743).

Gagné, Lucien; & Asselin, Jean-Pierre., Sainte-Anne-de-Beaupré, Pilgrims Goal for Three Hundred Years, A brief history of the Shrine. Sainte-Anne-de-Beaupré: Redemptorist Press, 1971.

Gagnon, Phileas., Noms Propres au Canada-Français. Les Bulletin des Récherches Historiques. 1909.

Gallant, Patrice., Les Registres de la Gaspésie 1752-1850 (1961).

Gareau, G.-Robert., <u>Priemières concessions d'habitations 1673 Boucher-</u><u>ville</u> (1973).

Gariépy, Raymond., *Les terres de L'Ange-Gardien (Côte de Beaupré)*, <u>Société de généalogie de Quebéc. Contribution No 44,</u>, Quebec: 1985.

Gariépy, Raymond., *Le village de Château-Richer (1640-1870).* Cahier d'Histoire No.21.<u> La Société Historique de Québec</u>, Québec: 1969.

LSB&IO. Gariépy, Raymond., *Les Seigneurs de Beaupré et de L'Ile d'Orléans dans leurs debuts.* Cahiers de Histoire No.27. <u>Société Historique de Québec.</u> Québec: l'Imprimerie La Renaissance Inc., 1974.

Garneau, François-Xavier., <u>Histoire du Canada-française.</u> Québec: 1845.

Gatien, F.; Gosselin, D.; Fortier, J.-A., <u>Histoire de Cap-Santé.</u> Québec: Charrier & Dugal, Inc., 1956.

Gastineau (Gatineau) dit Duplessis, Nicolas., <u>Records.</u> Montréal & Trois-Rivières (1650-1653).

Gaudron de Chevremont, Charles-René., <u>Records.</u> Montréal (1732-1739).

Gaumond, Michel., *La Place Royale, ses maisons, ses habitants.* <u>Civilisation de Québec.</u> 1976.

Genaple, François., <u>Records.</u> Québec (1682-1709).

Geneste, ., <u>Records.</u> Québec (1750-1770).

Germain, Pierre., <u>Au Pays des Iles-de-la-Madeleine </u>(1976).

Georges Panneton & Antonio Magnan; <u>Le diocése de Trois-Rivières.</u> Le Bien Public, 1962.

Gingras, Henri., <u>Cap-Rouge 1541-1974.</u> La Société Historique de Cap-Rouge Inc., Éditions Etchemin, 1974.

Gingras, Raymond-Bourassa., Melanges généalogiques. *Cahier III, "Jumeaux Lussier franco-americainises.* Québec: 1980.

Gingras, Henri., Saint-Michel de Bellechasse 1678-1978. St-Romuald: Les Editions Etchemin, 1977.

Gingras, Raymond-Bourassa., Mélanges historique. *Cahier No.5.* Québec: 1975.

Gingras, Raymond-Bourassa., Mélanges Généalogiques. *Cahier X: Noms Québecois Americanises.* Québec: 1980.

Girouard, Desiré., La vieux Lachine et le Massacre du 5 Aout 1689. Montréal: Imp. Gebhardt-Berthiaume, 1889.

Glenisson, Caroline Montel., Un tour de France canadien ou Guide des Noms et des Lieux (1980).

Gloria, Jean., Records. Québec (1663-1664).

AG-Or. Godbout, Archange., Origine des Familles Canadiennes-Française. Lille: Desclée de Brouwer, 1925.

AG-TR. Godbout, Archange., Les Pionniers de la région trifluvienne (1634-1647). Trois-Rivières: Bien Public, 1934.

AG-59. Godbout, Archange., Les Passagers du Saint-André. La recrue de 1659. Montréal: SGCF Publication No.5., 1964.

AG-LaR. Godbout, Archange., Familles Venues de LaRochelle en Canada. RAPQ, 1970. Corrections and additions by Roland-J. Auger. This corrected version was retitled Emigration Rochelaise en Nouvelle-France. Montréal: Editions Elysée, 1980.

AGA-FNF. Godbout, Archange., Vieilles familles de France en Nouvelle-France. Québec: RANQ., vol 53, 1975, with additional notes by Roland-J. Auger, pp 156-158.

AGA. Godbout, Archange., Nos ancétres au XVIIe siécle, Québec: RAPQ, 1955-57.

Godet,   Rolland., <u>Records.</u> Québec (1652-1653).

Gosselin, Amedee-Edmond., <u>L'instruction au Canada sous le Régime Français 1635-1760</u>. Québec: LaFlamme & Proulx, 1911

Gosselin, Auguste H., <u>Vie de Mgr de Laval, premier eveque de Québec et apotré du Canada, 1622-1708.</u> Québec: Impr. Demers, 1890.

Gosselin, Auguste., <u>Henri de Bernières</u>. Québec: Impr. Demers, 1902.

Gosselin, David., <u>Dictionnaire Généalogique des familles de Charlesbourg depuis la fondation de la paroisse jusqu'a nos jours.</u> Québec: 1906.

Gosselin, David., <u>Figures d'Hier et d'Aujourd'hui a travers St-Laurent, Ile d'Orléans.</u> Québec: Franciscan missionaries, 3 vols, 1919.

Gourdeau de Beaulieu, Jacques., <u>Records.</u> Québec (1662-1663).

GGRF <u>Grand Guide des régions de France</u>. Encyclopedie Leland, tome 8, p.2483.

Gravier, Jacques., <u>Relation ou Journal du Voyage en 1700. New York:</u> 1859.

Grimble, Ian., <u>Scottish Clans and Tartans</u>. Harmony Books, New York 1973.

Guillet   de Chaumont., Nicolas-Augustin., <u>Records.</u> Montréal (1727-1752).

Guitet,   Jean., <u>Records.</u> Québec (1637-1638).

Guyart   de l'Incarnation, Marie., *Letters from the reverend mother, first superior of the Ursuline Convent of Quebec.* Edited by P.-F. Richardeau. Paris: 1876.

Hamelin, Eddie., <u>La paroisse de Champlain,</u> Trois-Rivières: Bien Public, 1933.

Hamelin, J., <u>Economie et société en Nouvelle-France.</u> Québec: Université Laval, 1960.

Hardy, Jean-Pierre & Ruddel, David-Thiery., <u>Les apprentis artisans a Québec 1660-1815.</u> Montréal: Les Presses de l'Université de Montréal, 1977.

Harris, R.-C., <u>The Seigneurial System in Early Canada.</u> Madison, WI., and Québec: 1966.

HCF. Sulte, Benjamin., <u>Histoire des canadiens français, 1608-1680.</u> Montréal: Wilson & Cie, 1882.

Henripin, Jacques., *La population canadienne au debut du XVIIIe siècle, Nuptialite-Fecondite-Mortalite infantile.* <u>Cahier No.22.</u> Paris: Presses Universitaries de France, 1954.

Henripin, Jacques., <u>Initiation a la Nouvelle-France, histoire et institutions.</u> Montréal: Holt, Rinehart and Winston, 1968.

Herlin, Claude., <u>Records.</u> Trois-Rivières (1659-1663).

Hiche, Henri., <u>Records.</u> Québec (1725-1736).

Hollier, Robert., <u>La France des canadiens; guide pratique du retour aux sources.</u> Montréal: Edition de l'Homme, 1962.

Horman, Doris., <u>La Guerre Iroquois.</u> Varennes: Ateliers des Sourds, 1972.

Hudon, Pierre-Henri., <u>Rivière Ouelle de la Bouteillèrie 1672-1972.</u> Montréal: Ateliers des Sourds, 1972.

Hugolin, O.F.M., <u>Le Pére Joseph Denis, Premier Récollet Canadien 1657-1736.</u> 2 Volumes. Québec: Impremerie Laflamme, 1926.

Huot, Pierre., <u>Records.</u> Québec (1730-1749).

Jacob, Etienne., <u>Records.</u> Québec (1680-1726).

Jacob, Joseph., <u>Records.</u> Québec (1725-1748).

Janneau, Etienne., <u>Records.</u> Québec 1691-1743)

DGFQ.   Jetté, René., <u>Dictionaire généalogique des familles du Québec, des origins a 1730.</u> Montréal: Les presses de l'Université de Montréal, 1983.

JJ.   *Journal des jésuites (Le)*. <u>Archives du Séminaire de Québec.</u> Montréal: Laverdiére et Casgrain, 1892.

Jodoin   Alex et J-.L Vincent., <u>Histoire de Longueuil et de famille de Longueuil.</u> Montréal: Privately printed, 1889.

Jouvre, Odoric-Marie., <u>Étude Historique et Critique sur les Actes du Frère Didace, Récollet.</u> Imprimerie de l'Evenement, Québec: 1911.

Jouvre, Odoric-Marie., <u>Les françiscans et la Canada: aux Trois-Rivières.</u> Paris: 1934.

JR.   <u>Relations des jésuites.</u> 6 Volumes. Montréal: Editions du Jour, 1972.

Juchereau & Duplessis., <u>Les Annales de l'Hôtel-Dieu de Québec.</u> 1939.

Julien-Labruyère, François., <u>Paysans charentais.</u> LaRochelle: Editions Rupella.

Kennet, Lee., <u>The French Armies in the Seven Years War.</u> Durham: 1967.

Labarée, Léonard W., <u>Royal Governments in America.</u> New York, 1930.

Laberge, Lionel., <u>L'habitant de la Côté de Beaupré.</u> Faculté des Sciences Sociale de l'Université Laval. Québec: 1948.

Laberge, Lionel., *Le fief de Charlesville*. Volume XII, <u>RUL.</u>

HFL.   Laberge, Lionel., <u>Histoire du fief de Lotinville (1652-1690).</u> l'Ange-Gardien: 1963.

Laberge, Lionel., <u>Rouen et le commerce du Canada 1650-1670.</u> l'Ange-Gardien: Editions Bois-Lotinville, 1972.

Labreque, Lucille., Inventaire de pieces detachées de cours de justice de la Nouvelle-France (1638-1760). Vols. 5-50. Québec: RANQ, 1971.

LaCetière, Florent de., Records. Québec (1702-1728).

Lachance, André., La Justice criminale du roi au canada au 18e siècle. Cahier No.22. Québec: Les Presses de l'Université Laval, 1970.

Lacoursière, Jacques & Claude Bouchard., Notre histoire Québec-Canada.

Lacoursière, Jacques., Histoire populaire du Québec - des origines a 1791. tome 1, Septentrion, 1995, p.409-412.

Lacroix, Yvon., Les origines de la Prairie (1667-1697). Montréal: Editions Bellarmin, 1981.

RANF.   Lafontaine, André., Recensement annotes de la Nouvelle-France 1681. Sherbrooke: Privately printed, 1984.

RAVQ.   Lafontaine, André., Recensements annotes de la ville de Québec 1716 & 1744. Sherbrooke: Privately printed, 1985.

RANF.   Lafontaine, André., Recensements annotes de la Nouvelle-France 1666 & 1667. Sherbrooke: Privately printed, 1986.

Lafontaine, André., Les Bailliages de Beaupré et de l'Ile d'Orléans, ANQ, 1987, Québec.

Lafontaine, André., Le Bailliage de Notre-Dame-des-Anges, ANQ, 1988, Québec.

Laforest, Thomas J., Our French Canadian Ancestors. The LISI Press, Palm Harbor, FL: Volumes I-XXX 1983-2000.

Lafosse, Antoine P. de., Records. Montréal (1717-1744).

Lajeunesse, Ernest J., The Windsor Border Region, Canada's Southernmost Frontier: A Collection of Documents. Toronto: University of Toronto Press, 1960.

Laliberte, Jean-Marie., Index des greffes des notaires décedes, 1645-1948). Compiled by Benoît Pontbriand. Québec: 1967.

Laliberte, François., Repertoire des Supultures a Sainte-Anne-de-Beaupré 1845-1979. Privately printed, 1981.

Lanctot, Gustave., Le Canada et la Revolution americaine. *Revue*, Canadian Historical Association, 1926.

Lanctot, Gustave., Les Troupes de la Nouvelle-France. *Revue*, Canadian Historical Association, 1926.

Lanctot, Gustave., A History of Canada, Volume III, (1965) Harvard University Press, Cambridge, MA.

Laneuville, Jacques D., Records. Québec (1701-1730).

Lang, Ernest., Dictionnaire Génélogique du Madawaska.

Langlois, Georges., Histoire de la population canadienne-française. Montréal: Editions Albert Levesque, 1934.

Langlois, Michel., Les Ancétres Beauportois (1634-1760). Published on the 350th anniversary of Beauport, 1984.

La Potherie, Histoire, I, *Chevalier de Troyes*, Journal (Caron).

La Roncière, Charles de., Une pope canadienne, Paris, 1930.

Larue, Guillaume de., (see also Rue) Records. Trois-Rivières (1664-1676).

Latousche, Jacques de., (see also Tousche) Records. Trois-Rivières (1664-1669).

Laurent du Portail, Louis., Records. Trois-Riviéres (1660-1663).

Le Blanc, Marcel., Esquisses villageoises (Saint-Gabriel de Rimouski). Édition du Centenaire, Rimouski 1974.

Le Blant, Robert., Histoire de la Nouvelle-France: les sources narratives du debut du XVIIIe siècle. Vol.1, Dax, s.d., 169-272

Le Clercq, Chrestien., Etabissement de la foy dans Nouvelle-France. English translation by J.G.Shea. New York: 1881.

DCB. Lefebvre, Jean-Jacques, Dictionnaire Biographique du Canada, Volume Premier. Les Presses de L'Université Laval, University of Toronto Press, 1967.

DGC. Le Jeune, Louis-Marie., Dictionnaire general de biographies, histoire, litterature, agriculture, commerce, industrie et des artes, sciences, moeurs et coutumes, institutions politique et religious du Canada. 2 Volumes. Ottawa: Universite d'Ottawa, 1931.

LeSage, Germain., L'Arrivée du Régiment de Carignan. Revue de l'Universite d'Ottawa, Vol. 35, Nr.1, 1965.

LeSage, Germain., Histoire de Louiseville 1665-1960. p.130.

LeTenneur, René., Les Normands et les origines du Canada-français. Preface by Jean Chapdelaine. Coutances: OCEP, 1973.

Lebel, Alphonse., Lebel 1665-1980. Cap Saint-Ignace, 1980.

Lebel, Gérard., Nos Ancétres: Biographies d'Ancétres. Ste-Anne-de-Beaupré: The Redemptorist Press, Volumes 1-23, 1977-1993.

Leblond de Brumath, André., Histoire Populaire de Montréal. 1926.

Leboeuf, J.-Arthur., Complement au dictionnaire généalogique Tanguay. 2 Volumes in 1. Montréal: SGCF, 1957 and 1977.

Leclerc, Laurent., Les Grondines trois cents ans d'histoire. Montmagny: Les Ateliers Marquis Ltées, 1980.

Lecomte, Jean., Records. Québec (1668).

Lecoutre, Claude., (see Lecoustre) Records. Québec (1647-48).

Lefebvre, Jean-Jacques, Dictionnaire Biographique du Canada, *Le Moyne de Longueuil et de Châteauguay, Charles*, Volume Premier, pp. 474-476.

Lefrancois, F.-Arthur., Histoire des Iles Etchemin. St-Romuald: Les Editions Etchemin, 1960.

Lefrancois, Jean-Jacques., Les 300 ans de L'Ange-Gardien 1664-1964. Québec: 1964.

Lemoine, Louis., *Longueuil en Nouvelle-France*. Société Histoire de Longueuil, Longueuil.

Lepage, Arthur., Normandie et Bretagne. 1939.

LePailleur, Michel., Records. Montréal (1733-1739).

LeProust, Jean., Records. Trois-Rivières (1746-1761).

LeRoy de La Potherie, Claude-Charles., Histoire de l'Amérique septentrionale. Paris: 1922.

Lesieur de la Pierre, Charles., Records. Trois Rivières (1689-1696).

Lespinasse, Jean de., Records. Québec (1637).

Letourneau, Hubert & Labreque, Lucille., Inventaire de pieces detachées de la Prévôte de Québec (1668-1759). Québec: RANQ, 1971.

Letourneau, Raymond., Sainte-Famille, l'Ainée de l'Ile d'Orléans, (1984).

Letourneau, Raymond., Un Visage de l'Ile d'Orléans, Saint-Jean. 1979.

Litalien, Rolland., Le prêtre québécois à la fin XIXe siècle - style of life and spirituality according to Msgr L.-Z. Moreau. Fides.

Loiseau, Antoine., Records. Montréal (1730-1760).

Louet, Jean-Claude., Records. Québec (1717-1737).

Louisiana, *La Voix des Prairies*, Evangeline Genealogical and Historical Society.

Malchelosse, Gérard., Mélanges historiques. 21 Volumes. Montréal: G. Ducharme, 1918-1934.

RC. Malchelosse, Gérard., *Le Régiment de Carignan,* Mélange historique. Volume 8. Montréal: G. Ducharme, 1922.

Malchelosse, Gérard., Les Forts du Richelieu (1947).

Maluoin, René., *La Seigneurie Notre-Dame des Anges.* Société Historique de Québec, Québec: 1955.

Malouin, René., Charlesbourg 1660-1949 (1972), La Liberté Inc., Québec.

Marc-Antoine, O.F.M., St-Michel de la Durantaye (1929).

Marchal, Léon., Ville-Marie 1642-1665 (1942).

Marcil, Eileen., *Les Tonneliers du Québec.* Cahier No.32. Musée National de l'Homme, 1983.

Marie-Antoine, Sister, OFM., Saint-Michel de la Durantaye 1678-1929, (1929).

Marshall, Joyce., Word from New France: The Selected letters of Marie de l'Incarnation. Toronto: University Press, 1967.

Martin, Albertus., Bishop of Nicolet. Les Emigrants Bourguignons au Canada sous le Régime français (1973), *Annales de Bourgogne*, Volume 45, 40 pages.

Martin, Claude., Letters de la Venerable Mére Marie de l'Incarnation, premiere superieure des Ursulines de la Nouvelle-France. Paris: 1681.

Massicotte, E.-Z., *Les colons de Montréal de 1642 a 1667.* Volume VII. MSRC, 1913.

Massicotte, E.-Z., *La Population de Montréal en 1673*. Canadian Antiquarian and Numismatic Journal. 1914.

Massicotte, E.-Z., *L'ameublement a Montréal aux XVIIe et XVIIIe siecle*. BRH. 1915.

Massicotte, E.-Z., Faits Curieux de l'Histoire de Montréal. 1924.

Massicotte, E.-Z., Inventaire des Contrats de mariage Conserves aux Archives Judiciares de Montréal. 12 Volumes. Québec: ANPQ, 1924.

Massicotte, E.-Z., *La coutellerie de table et de traite sous le régime français*. BRH. 1935.

Massicotte, E.-Z., Histoire de Sainte-Geneviève-de-Batiscan, Trois-Rivières: Bien Public, 1936.

Massicotte, E.-Z., *Tissue d'autrefois*. BRH. 1936.

Massicotte, E.-Z., *Le costume civil masculin a Montréal au XVIIe siècle*. Volume 1. MSRC. 1939.

Massignon, Geneviève., Les Parlers Français en Acadie (sans date).

Maugue, Claude., Records. Montréal (1674-1696)

Mederic, Paul., *Les Seigneurs du Gouffre*. Cahier d'histoire régionale, Serie A. Québec: 1973.

Mederic, Paul., *Les Messieurs du Séminaire*. Cahiers d'histoire régionale, serie A, No.2. Québec: Baie Saint-Paul, 1975.

Menard, Pierre., Records. Montréal (1673-1693).

Merommont, Louis de., (see also Demerommont) Records. Trois-Riviéres (1686-1689).

Metru, Nicolas., Records. Québec (1678-1700).

Michaud, René., L'Isle-Verte vue du Large. 1970.

Michner, James A., <u>Centennial</u> (1974), Random House, Inc., New York and Toronto, 909 pages.

Michon, Abel., <u>Records.</u> Québec (1706-1747).

Mitchell, J., <u>The Contest in America between Great Britain and France.</u> London: 1757.

Mitchell, Elisabeth., <u>Messire Pierre Boucher, seigneur de Boucherville 1622-1717.</u> Montréal: Librairie Beauchemin Ltée, 1967.

Mondoux, Soeur., <u>l'Hôtel-Dieu, premier hôpital de Montréal 1642-1717.</u> Montréal: Therien Frères Ltée, 1942.

Monro, William B., <u>Adventures of New France.</u> Yale University Press, 1918.

TRV. Montagne, Madame Pierre., <u>Tourouvre et les Juchereau: Un Chapitre de l'Emigration Percheronne au Canada.</u> Québec: Société Canadienne de Généalogie, 1965.

Montagne, Pierre., <u>Le Perche des Canadiens.</u> Cahiers percherons, Special number published in 1974.

Moreau, Michel., <u>Records.</u> Montréal (1681-1698).

Morice, A.-G., <u>Dictionnaire historique des Canadiens et des Métis français de l'Ouest.</u> (1908).

Morisset, Gerard., *Québec et son evolution.* Cahiers d'Histoire No.4. <u>Société Royale du Canada.</u> Québec: Société Historique de Québec, Université Laval, 1952.

Morisette, Rémi., <u>Les Vielles Familles de Neuville</u> (1984).

Mouchy, Nicolas., <u>Records.</u> Québec & Montréal (1664-1667).

MSGCF. Memoires de la Société Généalogique canadienne-française. <u>Société Généalogique canadienne-française.</u> Montréal:1944.

Munro, William B., <u>Adventures of New France</u> (1918), Yale University Press, New Haven, CT.

Myrand, Ernest., ed., <u>1690, Sir William Phipps devant Québec: histoire d'un siege</u>, Québec, 1893.

Nadeau, Eugène., <u>Mére Léone.</u> Montréal: Fidés, 1950.

Nish, Cameron., <u>Les Bourgeois-Gentilshomme de la Nouvelle-France 1729-1748.</u> Montréal: Fidés, 1968.

Noppen, Luc & John R. Porter., <u>Les églises de Charlesbourg et l'architecture religeuse du Québec</u> (1972), Ministry of Cultural Affairs, Québec.

Noppen, Luc., <u>Les églises du Québec de 1600 à 1850</u> (1977). Fides: Montréal

Normandin, Daniel., <u>Records.</u> Trois-Riviéres (1686-1729).

NR.   *Nos Racines: L'Histoire Vivante des Quebécois.* St-Laurent: Les Editions Transmo Inc., 1979.

O'Reilly, Helene., <u>Monseigneur de Saint-Vallier et l'Hôpital géneral de Québec.</u> Québec: C. Darveau, 1882.

Olivier-Lacamp, Gael & Légare, Jacques., *Quelques caracteristiques des ménages de la ville de Québec entre 1666 et 1716.* <u>Histoire Sociale,</u> Volume 12. 1979.

Oudain, René., <u>Records.</u> Montréal (1674).

Ouellet, Gérard., <u>Ma Paroisse Saint-Jean Port-Joly.</u> Lévis: 1946.

Ouellet, Gérard., <u>Histoire de Sainte-Anne de la Pocatière 1672-1972.</u> Lévis: Impremerie Fortin Ltée, 1973.

Ouemet, Germain., <u>Étude parue dans le Houymet</u>, Vol.1, Numero 1.

Oury, Dom Guy., <u>Correspondance de Marie de l'Incarnation</u>, Abbaye Saint-Pierre de Solesme, 1971.

PAC. Public Archives of Canada, Manuscript Division. General Inventory of Manuscripts. 7 Volumes. Ottawa: Information Canada 1971-1977.

Panet,   Records, Québec, 1785.

Paradis, Andrée., L'Avénement d'un costume canadienne. *Revue Cap-aux-Diamants,* summer, 1988.

Paradis, Louis L., Les Annales de Lotbinière 1672-1933. Québec: Les Ateliers de l'Action catholic, 1933.

Paradis, Alexandre., Kamouraska (1674-1948). Québec: 1984.

Parent,   Anne-Marie.,   Notre Pierre et nos autres Aieux. Privately printed, 1968.

Parent, Marie-Jeanne Lortie Parent et Jean-Pierre., Deux Coqs de saint-Pierre m'ont raconté (1979).

Parent, Roger D., Clément Lérige, Sieur de la Plante, et sa descendance; généalogie d'une famille canadienne. Montréal: 1942.

Park, Zenon., Yesterday Hier (1983).

Payeur, J.-H., La destinée dans l'Histoire (1987).

Pelletier, Edmond., Album Historique et Paroissial de Notre-Dame du Portage, 1723-1940. Québec: Impr. Paroissiale, 1942.

Pérrot,   Nicolas., Memoire sur les moers, coustumes et religion des sauvages de lAmerique septentrionale. Edited by Jules Tailhan. Paris and Leipzig: 1864.

Petit,   Pierre., Records. Trois-Riviéres. (1721-1735).

Peuvret de Mesnu, Jean-Baptiste., Records. Québec (1653-1659).

Pillard, Louis., Records. Trois-Rivières.

Pinguet, Jacques., Records. Québec (1726-1748).

Piraube, Martial., Records. Québec (1639-1645).

Plinguet, Vincent & Laporte, S., Histoire de l'Ile Dupas et de l'Ile Saint-Ignace. Joliette: S. Laporte, 1974.

Pollet, Arnould-Balthazar., Records. Trois-Riviéres (1730-1754).

Pontbriand, Benoît., Mariages de Saint-Antoine-de-Tilly (1702-1900), comte de Lotbiniére. Publication No.16. Québec: Publications généalogique, 1962.

Pontbriand, Benoît., Mariages de Sainte-Croix, comte de Lotbinière 1725-1965. Publication No. 26. Québec: Sillery, 1965.

Pothier, (Pottier) Jean-Baptiste., Records. Montréal & Trois-Riviéres (1686-1711).

Poulin, Pierre., Records. Trois-Riviéres (1711-1728).

Poulin, Joseph-Claude., Les Métiers a Québec d'apres le recensements de 1716 et 1744. Québec: Les Presses de l'Université Laval, 1965.

Pouliot, Joseph-Camille., L'Ile d'Orléans. Québec: 1927.

Presse, Hyacinthe-Olivier. Records. Trois-Riviéres (1737).

Preston & Lamontagne, Royal Fort Frontenac.

Prevost, Robert., La Presse, Montréal, 1993.

Proulx, Armand., Répertoire des Mariages de Saint-Louis de Kamouraska (1709-1967).

Provost, Honorius., La Canoterie. Le Canada Française #28. 1941.

Provost, Honorius., La Censive Notre-Dame de Québec, Québec: Publications des archives du Séminaire de Québec, 1954.

Provost, Honorius., Le Séminaire de Québec: documents et biographies. Québec: Publication des archives du Séminaire de Québec, 1964.

Puymége, Maurice Leo d'Armagnac del Cer, comte de., <u>Les vieux noms de la France de l'Ouest et les families d'origine française au delà des mers</u>. Paris.

Puyperoux de Lafosse, Antoine., <u>Records.</u> Montréal (1717-1744).

Québec, District Judiciaire de Montréal. *Contrats de Mariage, 1650-1839*. Public Archives of Canada.

Rageot, Gilles., <u>Records.</u> Québec (1666-1692).

Rageot, Charles., <u>Records.</u> Québec (1695-1702).

Rageot, François., <u>Records.</u> Québec (1711-1753).

Ragueneau, Paul., <u>La vie de Mére Catherine de Saint-Augustin.</u> Paris: 1671.

Rameau, Edme., <u>La France au Colonies</u>, 1859.

Raimbault, Pierre., <u>Records.</u> Montréal (1679-1727).

Raimbault, Joseph-Charles., <u>Records.</u> Montréal (1727-1737).

RANQ.	<u>Inventaire des Greffes des Notaires du Régime Français.</u> 27 Volumes. Québec: Roch Lefebvre, 1942-1976.

RANQ.	<u>Rapport des Archives Nationales du Québec.</u> For an Index, see Québec: <u>Ministère des Affaires Culturelles.</u> *Table des Materieres des Rapport des Archives du Québec.* Tomes 1 to 42. (1920-1964). Formerly known as RAPQ and RAQ. Québec: Roch Lefebvre, 1965.

RAPQ.	<u>Inventaire des Ordonnances des Intendants de la Nouvelle-France.</u> 4 Volumes. Québec: National Archives, 1919.

RAPQ.	<u>Ordonnances, Commissions, etc., des Gouverneurs et Intendants de la Nouvelle-France, 1639-1706.</u> Québec: National Archives, 1926.

JDCSNF RAPQ. Jugements et Deliberations du Conseil Souverain (ou Superior) de la Nouvelle-France (1663-1716). Québec: National Archives, 1927.

RAPQ.   Inventaire des Concessions en Fief et Seigneurie. Québec: National Archives, 1928.

RAPQ.   Bibliographie des monographies et histoires de paroisses. Québec: National Archives, 1937.

RAPQ.   Inventaires des Insinuations de la Prévôte de Québec. 3 Volumes. Québec: National Archives,1939.

RAPQ.   Bibliographie de généalogies et histoires de familles. Québec: National Archives, 1940.

RAPQ.   Godbout, Archange., Nos Ancétres au XVIIe siècle. 6 Volumes. Québec: National Archives, 1951.

RAPQ.   Tables des materes des Rapports des Archives du Québec. 42 Volumes. Québec: Queen's Printer, 1965.

RAPQ.   Etat sommaire des Archives nationales du Québec à Montréal. Québec: National Archives, 1975.

Remy,   René.,   Records. Montréal (1669-1675).

Renaud, P.-E., Les origines economiques du Canada. Québec: Enoult, 1928.

RHAF.   *Revue d'Histoire de l'Amérique Française*. L'Institute d'Histoire de l'Amérique Française. Montréal, 1947.

Richard, Louis., *Les Masse*. Le Trifleuvien. 10 April, 1906.

Richard, Joseph-Arthur., Histoire de Cap Saint-Ignace 1672-1970. Montmagny: Les Editions Marquis, 1971.

Rigaud, Elie-François., Records. Trois-Rivières (1762).

Rivet, Pierre., Records. Québec (1707-1719).

Roger,   Guillaume., Records. Québec (1653-1657).

Roquebrune, Robert de., *de Etudes Onomastics: Origine de noms canadiens*. Bulletin Recherche Historique.

Roquebrune, Robert de., *de L'Origine des Noms canadiens*. Le Canada.

Roquebrune, Robert de., Les Canadiens d'Autrefois. 2 Volumes. Montréal: Fidés, 1970.

Ross, Eric., Beyond the River and the Bay. University of Toronto Press.

Rouer, Louis., Records. Québec (1653-1656).

Rouillard, Eugène., *Respect aux Noms Primitifs*. Bulletin de la Société de Geographie de Québec.

Rouillard, Joseph., Records. Trois-Riviéres (1742).

Rouleau, Marc., Le Terrier de Neuville 1680-1980 (1984).

Rousseau, François., *Hôpital et société en Nouvelle-France: l'Hôtel-Dieu de Québec a la fin du XVIIe siècle*. Revue d'histoire de l'Amérique française. Volume 31,#1, June 1977.

Rousseau, Jacques, & Bethune, Guy., Voyage de Pehr Kalm au Canada en 1749. Montréal: Editions Pierre Tisseyre, 1977.

Roy, Camille., Histoire de la litterature canadienne. Québec: Typ. Laflamme et Proulx, 1930.

Roy, Christian., Histoire de l'Assomption 1967. (1967).

Roy dit Châtellerault de Villeray, Michel., Records. Trois-Rivières (1668-1709).

Roy, J.-Edmond., *Les archives du Canada a venir en 1879*. Mémoires de la Société canadienne-française. Montréal.

Roy, J.-Edmond., Guillaume Couture Primier Colon de la Pointe Levy. Lévis: Mercier & Cie, 1884.

Roy, J.-Edmond., <u>Notice historique sur la Famille de René de la Voye</u>. (1899).

Roy, J.-Edmond., <u>Histoire de la seigneurie de Lauzon.</u> 5 Volumes. Lévis: 1897-1904.

Roy, J.-Edmond., <u>Histoire du notariat au Canada, depuis la fondation de la colonie jusqu'a nos jours.</u> 2 Volumes. Lévis: 1899-1900.

Roy, Léon., <u>Les premiers colons de la rive du du Saint-Laurent.</u>

Roy, Léon., <u>Les Terres de la Grande-Anse, des Aulnaies et du Port-Joly.</u> Lévis:Fortin et Fils, 1951.

LTIO. Roy, Léon., <u>Les Terres de l'Ile de Orléans: les terres de St-François, les terres de St-Laurent.</u> Montréal: Editions Bergeron, 1978.

Roy, Marie-Antoinc., <u>Saint-Michel de la Durantaye 1678-1929.</u> Québec: Charrier & Dugal Ltée, 1929.

Roy, Marie-Antoine., <u>Les Lettres, les Sciences, les Artes au Canada sous le régime français.</u> Paris: Jouvre et Cie, 1930.

Roy, Pierre-Georges., *Le duel sous le régime français* <u>BRH</u>, XIII, (1907), 131f.

Roy, Pierre-Georges., <u>Inventaire d'une collection de pieces judiciares, notariales, etc.</u> 2 Volumes. Beauceville: 1917.

IOINF. Roy, Pierre-Georges., <u>Inventaire des Ordonnances des Intendants de la Nouvelle-France.</u> 1919.

Roy, Pierre-Georges., <u>Le Sieur de Vincennes, fondateur de l'Indiana et sa famille.</u> Québec: Charrier & Dougal Ltée, 1919.

Roy, Pierre-Georges., <u>Inventaire des Insinuations du Conseil Souverain de la Nouvelle-France.</u> 1921.

Roy, Pierre-Georges., <u>La vieux Québec.</u> 2 Volumes. Lévis: 1923-1931.

Roy, Pierre-Georges., Papier-Terrier de la Companie des Indes occidentales conserve aux Archives Judiciaries de Québec (1667-1668). Beauceville: L'Eclaireur, 1931.

Roy, Pierre-Georges., Inventaire des proces-verbaux des grandes voyers. 6 Volumes. Beauceville: 1923-1932.

Roy, Pierre-Georges., Vieux Manoirs, Vieilles Maisons. 1927.

Roy, Pierre-Georges., Inventaire des concessions en fief et seigneurie, fois et hommages.

Roy, Pierre-Georges., L'Ile d'Orléans. Québec: L.A. Proulx, 1928.

Roy, Pierre-Georges., La ville de Québec sous le régime français. 2 Volumes. Québec: Imprimeur du Roi, 1930.

Roy, Pierre-Georges., Inventaire des jugements et deliberations du Conseil superior de la Nouvelle-France de 1717 a 1760. 7 Volumes. Beauceville: 1932-1935.

Roy, Pierre-Georges., Les Juges de la Province de Québec. 1933.

Roy, Pierre-Georges., Inventaire des Contrats de Mariage du régime Français Conserves aux Archives Judiciaires de Québec. 6 Volumes. Québec: 1937.

Roy, Pierre-Georges., Jugements et deliberations du Conseil Souverain de la Nouvelle-France (1663-1716). 6 Volumes. Québec: Index published by Roy in 1940.

Roy, Pierre-Georges., Inventaire des testaments, donations et inventaires du régime français. 3 Volumes. Québec, 1941.

Roy, Pierre-Georges., Inventaire des greffes des notaires du régime français. 23 Volumes. Québec: 1941.

Roy, Pierre-Georges., Atravers l'Histoire de Beaumont. 1943.

Roy, Pierre-Georges., Toutes Pétites Choses du Régime Français. 1944.

RC.   Roy, Regis & Gérard Malchelosse., <u>Le Régiment de Carignan: son organization et son expedition au Canada (1665-1668).</u> Georges Ducharme, Montréal: (1925).

Rue,   Guillaume de la., <u>Records,</u> Trois-Riviéres (1664-76).

RSHS.   *Saguenayensia*: <u>Revue de la Société historique du Saguenay.</u> Volume 1, no 1, Jan/Feb 1959- . Chicoutimi, Québec.

Sagard, Gabriel., <u>Histoire du Canada</u>, pages 429-430.

Saint-Père, Jean de., <u>Records.</u> Montréal (1648-1657).

Saintonge, Jacques., <u>Nos Ancétres.</u> Volumes 4-5-6-7. Ste-Anne-de-Beaupré: Redemptorist Press, 1983.

Saintonge, Jacques., *Nos familles et leur Origines.* <u>Le Nouvelliste de Trois-Rivières.</u>

Salone, Emile., <u>La colonisation de la Nouvelle-France.</u> Paris: Librairie orientale et américaine, 1900.

Salviel, Elie de., <u>366 anniversaires Canadiens.</u> 1943.

Scott, H.-A., <u>Une paroisse historique de la Nouvelle-France. Notre-Dame de Sainte-Foy.</u> Québec: JAX Laflamme, 1902.

Seguin, Robert-Lionel., <u>L'equipment de la ferme canadienne aux XVIIe et XVIIIe siècles.</u> Montréal: Librairie Ducharme Ltée, 1959.

Seguin, Robert-Lionel., <u>La civilization traditionnelle de l'habitant aux XVIIe et XVIIIe siècles.</u> Montréal: Les editions Lemeac, 1973.

Seguin, Robert-Lionel., <u>Les divertissements en Nouvelle-France.</u> Musée national bulletin #227, #6 de la serie folklore. Ottawa: 1968.

RLS.   Seguin, Robert-Lionel., <u>La vie libertine en Nouvelle-France au XVIIe siècle.</u> 2 Volumes. Montréal: Lemeac, 1972.

Seguin, Robert-Lionel., <u>L'Injure en Nouvelle-France.</u> Montréal: 1976.

Senet, Nicolas., Records. Montréal (1704-1731).

SGQ. *L'Ancêtre*. Société de généalogie de Québec. Ste-Foy: 1961.

SGCE *L'Entraide* Société de Genealogie des Cantons de l'Est, Sherbrooke, Québec.

SHA. *Cahiers de la Société Historique Acadien.* Société Historique Acadien. Moncton: 1961.

Shortt, Adam., Canadian Currency, Exchange and Finance during the French Régime. 2 Volumes. Ottawa: F.A. Auckland, 1925.

Simard, André., Les Eveques et les Prétes seculiers au Diocese de Chicoutimi. 1969.

Simonnet, François., Records. Trois-Rivières (1741)

Sirois, N.-J., Monographie de St-Ignace du Cap St-Ignace depuis 1692 a 1903. Lévis: 1903.

SRC. *L'expedition du Marquis de Denonville.* Société Royale du Canada. Section I, Ottawa: 1899.

Stacey, P.C., Introduction à l'etude de l'histoire militaire a l'intention des étudiants canadiens, Ottawa, Imprimeur de la Reine.

Stanley, George F.G., Nos Soldats. (1980).

Stuart, Donna Valley., *French Names in Detroit.* The Detroit Society for Genealogical Research. Detroit: 1973.

LMH. Sulte, Benjamin., *Trois-Riviéres d'autrefois.* Les Mélanges Historiques. Montréal: 1932.

Sulte, Benjamin., *Histoire de Saint-François-du-Lac.*

Sulte, Benjamin., *Canadian Militia Under the French Regime.* Les Mélange Historiques. Volume 1. Edited by Gérard Malchelosse, Montréal: G. Ducharme, 1918.

Sulte, Benjamin., *La Rivière du Loup.* <u>Les Mélange Historiques.</u> Volume 8. Montréal: G.Ducharme, 1922.

RC. Sulte, Benjamin., *Le Régiment de Carignan.* <u>Les Mélanges Historiques.</u> Annotated and published by Gérard Malchelosse. Reprinted in the Proceedings of the Royal Society of Canada, vol xvi, May, 1922.

HCF. Sulte, Benjamin., <u>Histoire des canadiens français, 1608-1680.</u> Montréal: Wilson & Cie, 8 vols in 4, 1882.

Sulte, Benjamin & Gérard Malchelosse., <u>Le Fort de Chambly</u> (1922).

Sulte, Benjamin., <u>Les forges Saint-Maurice.</u> Ducharme, 1920.

Tailhandier, Marien., <u>Records,</u> Montréal (1688-1731).

Talbot, Eloi-Gérard., <u>Inventaire des Contrats de mariage au greffe de Charlevoix.</u> Société historique du Saguenay. Publication No.8. Saguenay: 1943.

Talbot, Eloi-Gérard., <u>Recueil de généalogies des comtes de Beauce-Dorchester-Frontenac (1625-1946).</u> 11 Volumes. Beauceville: College du Sacre-Coeur, 1948-55.

GFOCMIB. Talbot, Eloi-Gérard., <u>Généalogie des Familles Originaires des Comtes de Montmagny, L'Islet et Bellechasse.</u> 16 Volumes. Château-Richer: Talbot, privately printed, 1976.

Talbot, Eloi-Gerard., <u>Généalogie pour les comtes de Charlevoix et de Saguenay.</u> Publications la Sociéte historique du Saguenay #5. La Malbaie: 1979.

DGFC. Tanguay, Cyprien., <u>Dictionnaire genealogique des familles Canadiennes.</u> 7 Volumes. Montreal: Reprint Editions Elysee, 1975.

ATR. Tanguay, Cyprien., <u>A travers les Registres.</u> Montreal: 1886.

RGCC. Tanguay, Cyprien., <u>Repertoire General du Clerge Canadien.</u> 1893.

Terrien, Leo., <u>Archives de la Haute-Normandie.</u> 1986.

Tessier, Albert., <u>Les Forges du Saint-Maurice 1794</u>. Editions Boreal Express, 21 pages; Trois-Rivières (1935).

Tetreau, Jean-Baptiste., <u>Records.</u> Montréal (1712-1728).

Tetu, Henri., <u>Histoire du Palais Episcopal de Québec.</u> Québec: Pruneau et Kirouac, 1896.

Thwaites, Reuben Gold., <u>Father Marquette</u>. D.Appleton and Company, New York, 1902.

Thwaites, Reuben Gold., <u>The Jesuit Relations and Allied Documents (1610-1791).</u> New York: Pageant Book Company, 1959.

Tousche, Jacques de la., <u>(see also Latousche) Records.</u> Trois-Rivières (1664-1668).

Tremblay, Nerée., <u>Saint-Pierre et Saint-Paul de la Baie Saint-Paul.</u> 1956.

Tremblay, Paul-Mederic., <u>La Tremblay Millenaire.</u> 1975.

Tremblay, Paul-Mederic., <u>Messieurs du Séminaire.</u> 1976.

Tremblay, Paul-Mederic., <u>Le Perche des Aieux.</u> 1979.

Tronquet, Guillaume., <u>Records.</u> Québec (1643-1648).

Trotain, Francois., <u>Records.</u> Trois-Rivières (1687-1732).

Trudel, Jean., <u>Sculpture traditionelle du Québec.</u> Québec: 1967

CI. Trudel, Marcel., <u>Catalogue des Immigrants 1632-1662</u> (1983).

Trudel, Marcel., *Le Régime seigneurial.* Brochure No.6. <u>Société Historique du Canada.</u> Ottawa: 1956.

Trudel, Marcel., *L'Eglise canadienne sous le Régime militaire 1759-1764.* 2 Volumes, RHAF-VIII:25-71. Québec: Les Presses Universitaires Laval, 1957.

Trudel, Marcel., L'Esclavage au Canada français: histoire et condition de l'esclavage. Québec: Les Presses Universataires Laval, 1960.

T27. Trudel, Marcel., Le Comptoir, 1604-1627. This is the second Volume of "l'Histoire de la Nouvelle-France." Montréal: Fidés, 1966.

Trudel, Marcel., Initiation a la Nouvelle-France, histoire et institutions. Montréal/Toronto: Holt, Rinehart, Winston, Ltd., 1968.

Trudel, Marcel., An Atlas of New France. Second Edition, Québec: Les Presses de l'Université Laval, 1973.

LTSL. Trudel, Marcel., Le Terrier du Saint-Laurent en 1663. Ottawa: 1973.

T63. Trudel, Marcel., La population du Canada en 1663. Montréal: Fidés, 1973.

Trudel, Marcel., Montréal, la formation d'une société 1642-1663. Montréal: Fidés, 1976.

Trudelle, Charles., Paroissee de Charlesbourg (1887), 314 pages.

Turcotte, L.-P., l'Ile d'Orléans. 1867.

Upshall, Michael et al., The Hutchinson Paperback Dictionary of Biography. Arrow Books, london 1990.

Vachon, Paul., Records. Québec (1658-1693).

Vachon, André., *Inventaire Critique des Notaries Royaux des Gouvernments de Québec, Montréal et Trois-Rivières.* Revue d'Histoire de l'Amérique Française. In 8 parts, 1955 to 1957.

Vachon, André., Histoire du Notariat Canadien. 1962.

Vachon,   André., *La restauration de la tour de babel ou La vie a Québec au milieu du XVIIe siècle.* RHAF-XXIV, 1970.

Vachon, André., Les Documents de notre Histoire. *L'Enracinement, Le canada de 1700 a 1760* (1985).

Vaillancourt,   Emile., La Conquete du Canada par les Normands: Biographie de la Prémiere Generation Normande du Canada. Montréal: G. Ducharme, 1933.

Vallée, Arthur., Michel Sarazin 1659-1735. Québec, 1927, p.188.

Varennes, Kathleen Mennie de., Annotated Bibliography of genealogical Works in Canada. Canada: Fitzhenry and Whiteside, 1986.

Veron de Grandmesnil, Etienne., Records. Trois-Riviéres (1705-1720).

Verreau, Barthelemi., Records. Québec (1710-1718).

Veyret, Pierre., La population du Canada. Paris: 1953.

Villata, Bruno., Le Régiment de Carignan, etait-il vraiment française?. *SGCF*, Montréal: 1922.

Were-Wolves and Will-O-the-Wisps, French Tales of Mackinac Retold. Mackinac Island State Park Commission publication, 1974.

Wilhelmy, Jean-Pierre., Les Mercenaires Allemands au Québec, (1984), 331 pages.

Yon,   Armand., *Etudes et bibliographie...la dolce vita en Nouvelle-France a la veille de la guerre (1740-1758).* Cahiers des Dix. Volume XXXVII, Québec: 1960.

Zoltany, Yves F., Philippe de Riguad de Vaudreuil, Governor of New France, 1703-1725. McClelland and Stewart Ltd., 1974.

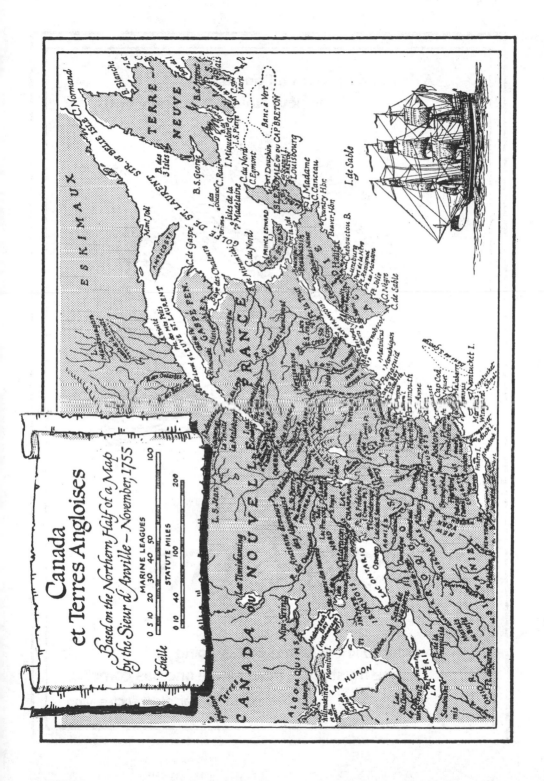

Canada
et Terres Angloises

*Based on the Northern Half of a Map
by the Sieur d'Anville — November 1755*

Echelle

MARINE LEAGUES
0 5 10   20   30   40   50   100

STATUTE MILES
0 10   40   100   200

«A défaut de savoir où l'on va,
on peut savoir d'où l'on vient!»

GÉNÉALOGIE

ANCETRE

"In order to know where one is going
...one must know from where one has come"

— translated from an old French saying